It was the best of times…

Notes on a busy life

Colin Fitzgerald

It was the best of times...
Notes on a busy life

First published in Australia by Black Tie Productions Pty Ltd 2020
enquiries@blacktieproductions.com.au

Copyright © Colin Fitzgerald 2020

 A catalogue record for this book is available from the National Library of Australia

All Rights Reserved
ISBN: 978-0-6487612-0-4 (pbk)
ISBN: 978-0-6487612-1-1 (ebk)

Editing, typesetting and design by Publicious Book Publishing
Published in collaboration with Publicious Book Publishing
www.publicious.com.au

Cover design by Nine Lives Studio
9Livesstudio@iinet.net.au

No part of this book may be reproduced in any form, by photocopying or by any electronic or mechanical means, including information storage or retrieval systems, without permission in writing from both the copyright owner and the publisher of this book.

For my three wonderful daughters, Rachel, Claire and Louise; seven terrific grandchildren, Emme, Hayley, Millie, Grace, Patrick, LJ, and Walker; and as yet unborn and unknown, great-grandchildren!

Contents

Acknowledgements .... *i*
Foreword .... *iii*

Chapter 1	Wet Pants and Christmas Carols	1
Chapter 2	Firewood and Photography	13
Chapter 3	Wages and Wasps	31
Chapter 4	Bedsit and Bridegroom	41
Chapter 5	A Barman and Two Babies	57
Chapter 6	Undertakings and Undertakers	67
Chapter 7	New Job and Old Friends	81
Chapter 8	Renovation and Relocation	95
Chapter 9	Another Baby another Job	107
Chapter 10	Sales and Betrayal	121
Chapter 11	Debacles in Deptford	135
Chapter 12	Blackfriars to Broadway	147
Chapter 13	Marrakech to Manhattan	161
Chapter 14	A Wedding and a War	177
Chapter 15	A Bad Debt and a Good Deal?	195
Chapter 16	The Saddest Loss	217
Chapter 17	Country Life and City Strife	229
Chapter 18	New Arrivals and a Departure	241
Chapter 19	Lonely Garret and Lonely Hearts	249
Chapter 20	Affliction and Affections	259
Chapter 21	Temporary Insanity	267
Chapter 22	True Romance	277
Chapter 23	A Trousseau in Tucson	285

Postscript *299*

Acknowledgements

I am extremely grateful to the Australian author, Louise Cusack, for her appraisals and re-assessments. Her suggestions and overall advice were invaluable. I owe a huge thank you to my editor, Lesley Wyldbore (Publicious). Her meticulous scrutiny and fine-tuning of my manuscript enhanced it immensely. My appreciation also to Andy McDermott of Publicious Book Publishing, for his professional guidance throughout the book publishing process.

My good friend, Ian Watkins, always showed enormous patience as he cheerfully instructed me through the complexities of the powerful Microsoft WORD programme. But mainly I owe a massive debt of gratitude to my amazing wife, Viola. Her continual encouragement as I scribbled away, ever gave me the heart to persevere to the finish of this work.

Foreword

I've lost count of how many times I've heard someone say, "You should write a book". Well, no one has ever said that to me! But personal reflections of seventy-five years of a busy life are bound to contain many titbits of humour, sadness, pride and anguish, particularly if it contains three marriages, many relationships, several businesses and two murderers!

My life throughout the austerity of the 1950s, the sex-obsessed swinging 60s, the big hair and glorious glam rock 70s and the cocaine fuelled 1980s is awash with tales of excesses *and* deprivation. From bicycles and baked beans to a Rolls Royce and caviar. From maisonette to mansion and back again. From pokey rooms to penthouse. From happy marriages to ruinous divorces. So many stories to relate. It is said that opportunity knocks but once, fortunately, it has knocked many times at my door, and I always rushed to let it in, although there were times when I wished I hadn't!

It might be considered conceited to write one's own biography, particularly if you don't happen to be a famous film star, sportsman or politician, but if, like me, my descendants have an interest in their ancestry, then I believe it to be worthwhile. Sadly, I know nothing at all about my great-grandparents, and very little about my grandparents. Of all these forebears I was only acquainted with my paternal grandmother, and she died when I was eleven years old so I hardly knew her at all. I do know that she suffered some horrific events in her life which I will touch upon later.

My maternal grandfather fought at and survived the Battle of the Mons, the first military battle of the First World War, with nearly

7,000 men either killed or wounded. He survived, and his heroic actions were rewarded with something that impacted profoundly on my mother, which has been passed on to me, and certainly passed on to my daughters. Sadly, he later brought shame and disgrace to his family and possibly triggered the premature death of his wife.

My own father, an unassuming painter and decorator served for twelve years in the Royal Navy, surviving three wartime sinkings and even participated in the historic Bismarck chase. So there are many stories to tell, not least my own adventures in business in London and New York. Who would have thought that this boy from Gloucester would one day have to deal with Manhattan's mafia?

Chapter 1

Wet Pants and Christmas Carols

Those born in 1944, as I was, were called "war babies", but World War II ended in 1945 so I have absolutely no memory of it. Gloucester, my place of birth, escaped fairly lightly from the destructions of war. German bombs did hit a few areas as the city was very industrial being home to the Gloucestershire Aircraft Company Limited,[1] where during the height of the war, fighter aircraft were rolling out every twenty minutes!

My very earliest memory is being held in my mum's arms at Gloucester railway station waiting for my dad to come home on leave from the Royal Navy. It was dark, very noisy and smoky. This enormous old steam engine ground into the station with men in uniforms waving through every window. I distinctly remember wondering how they were all going to get out of the windows! Of course, in these old railway carriages the windows were doors which all opened, and suddenly I was being carried home to 51 Lysons Avenue high on my dad's shoulders, with me wearing his naval petty officer's peaked cap.

Throughout this narrative there will be many times when I will digress as and when a sudden memory or incident prompts my memory. So my first digression concerns Gloucester railway station. I should really say Gloucester railway stations – plural – as when I was growing up in Gloucester there were two! There was the Great Western Railway station, the GWR, where the present-day central

---

1. Later renamed the Gloster Aircraft Company.

station is, and the London, Midland and Scottish Railway station, the LMS – I'm only mentioning this partly because it's a minor footnote in Gloucester's history, but also it leads to a funny story a bit later on.

The LMS station, known as Gloucester Eastgate, used to be where the enormous ASDA superstore now stands on Bruton Way. Its trains ran between Birmingham and Bristol, and it was linked by a 300-yard overhead pedestrian bridge to the Central Station. As a 16-year-old apprentice camera operator, I used to catch the 6 a.m. milk train from the Eastgate station once a week to get to Bristol Technical College on my day release studies for a City and Guilds certificate.[2] The old carriages had no heating and the torturous journey took almost two hours to travel the thirty odd miles as the milk train stopped at about twenty tiny village stations before it reached Bristol Temple Meads station. Then, two separate bus rides and I was a frozen mess by the time I reached the college. I didn't finish the course!

Now back to the two stations. After their shifts finished, the railwaymen – drivers, stokers and guards – would all drink at The Windmill pub which was just down the road from the Horton Road railway crossing – the pub was demolished in the 1980s to make way for the Metz Way flyover. The bar was originally one long room partitioned into two by a small off-sales vestibule. The GWR railwaymen always used the left-hand bar, and the LMS railwaymen always used the right-hand bar. Both bars had their own shove-ha'penny slates[3] and dart boards, but mostly the men would sit playing cribbage, a card game.

Either from camaraderie with their workmates, or more probably from allegiance to their respective rail companies, neither side would ever drink in the other's bar. Long after the railway companies were

---

2. The City & Guilds of London Institute is an educational organisation in the UK founded in 1878.

3. Shove-ha'penny is a bar-room game played on a small rectangular tabletop board, usually made of stone or slate. Using the ball of the thumb, pre-decimal half-penny coins are shoved from the edge of the board. The object is to get three coins inside parallel, horizontal lines etched into the slate. The winner is the first person to fill all nine 'beds' of lines.

nationalized and merged this tradition continued. A railwayman from one side was never seen in the other's bar; it would be considered worse than disloyal, a betrayal, an act of treachery. Then the unthinkable happened; a new landlord arrived.

Either unaware or uncaring about this time-honoured custom, he removed the dividing off-sales vestibule creating one long bar, "the longest in Gloucester", he boasted at the time. The non-railway patrons found this very amusing, my dad included, as he was a regular drinker there. The railwaymen didn't find it so funny. It caused some principled arguments leading to temporary boycotts and scenes which came close to brawling. Then someone came up with a simple solution and drew a thick chalk line through the centre of the bar.

They maintained the division and the chalk line for years, possibly until the pub was finally demolished. Even though many had long retired from the railways they all still chose to drink at their respective ends of the bar!

****

Anyway, back to 51 Lysons Avenue, the house in which I was born. I think we lived there until I was six or seven years old. Dad didn't leave the navy until 1948 so for four years it was just Mum, me and my older sister – by four years – Molly. My younger brother Pat was also born there in 1948, obviously, like me, the result of one of Dad's rare trips home on leave!

Mum had left home in Birmingham when she was about fifteen. Her mum had died at a very early age from cancer, and her dad had remarried a woman who was the cleaner where he worked and who had six children from a previous marriage! Apparently, Mum couldn't get on with her new stepmother so up and left. After walking the streets for several hours, she stepped into a pub for the first time in her life. There she was lucky enough to meet an elderly couple.

Presumably they were sitting having a quiet drink, minding their own business when in came a distraught little waif who poured her heart out to them. This lovely couple not only took pity on her but took her under their wing and gave her bed and board in their home. She got a job as a seamstress in a local clothing factory and lived happily with them for the next couple of years.

When she was seventeen, for whatever reason she decided to move to Gloucester. She took up lodgings in my grandmother's house in Newark Road. Gran had two sons, Bob and Pat, and three daughters Kitty, Ethel and Molly, so it must have been a bit crowded! Gran had a pretty tragic life. Her firstborn, a boy – William I think – as a toddler just learning to walk fell into her open fireplace while her back was turned in the kitchen and was burned to death! I can't imagine how horrific that must have been.

Her eldest son, Bob, was killed in the war. And her eldest daughter, Kitty, spent most of her adult life in Broadmoor, a prison for the mentally deranged after murdering her husband with an axe! Even Aunty Ethel was a bit doolally,[4] and she couldn't control her saliva. As a child I remember avoiding standing in front of her when she was eating, or risk getting sprayed with food and spittle. I used to joke that you needed an umbrella and plastic mac when you were talking to Aunty Ethel! I think that Dad and Aunty Molly were the only normal ones.

Incidentally, it was Aunty Ethel who told me, when I was only about eight years old, that my sister Molly "isn't yer real sister"! It didn't make a scrap of difference to me, I'd always thought of Molly as my sister, and after seventy-five years, still do. Mind you, Mum wasn't too pleased when I quizzed her on this, that I'd learned it from "bloody Ethel"!

The story of Mum and the two brothers is quite amazing. Mum told me that when she moved into lodgings with them it was Pat, my dad, who she first fell for. But Pat was a bit of a lad. He was only interested in getting out and about with his mates, "off bending his elbow" as his teetotal father often used to complain. Whereas his older brother, Bob, was more serious and home loving, and had

---

4. Mildly eccentric or crazy.

fallen deeply in love with Mum, so she took the safe option, even though she always carried a torch for Pat.

Both brothers joined the Royal Navy, Pat in 1936 three years before the beginning of the Second World War. He told me the story that after he'd finished his apprenticeship as a painter and decorator, he bumped into a friend with whom he'd been apprenticed. The friend was wearing a dashing naval officer's uniform. When Dad enquired as to how he had managed to acquire such a smart outfit, his friend told him that if you had served an indentured apprenticeship in any trade, then you could enlist as a petty officer in the Royal Navy.

Dad told me that he was immediately taken with the idea and added that he could easily see how wearing this uniform could increase his attractiveness to young available women, which I suspect was unnecessary as photographs from that period show that he was already a handsome young man. Nevertheless, he unhesitatingly signed on for twelve years' service and went on to become a war hero, surviving three sinkings and gaining a chest full of medals.

Meanwhile Mum had married Bob who also enlisted in the Royal Navy as soon as war was declared. He was commissioned as a gunner and posted onto merchant ships as their only protection from enemy aircraft. In the middle of the night of the 4th April 1942, while steaming off the coast of Australia, no doubt on a darkened blacked-out merchant vessel, he tripped and tragically fell to his death in the deep hold of the ship.

He was buried at sea but has a memorial plaque in the naval dockyard at Plymouth in Devon and on the Gloucester War Memorial on the corner of Park Street and Trier Way. He also has a memorial plaque in the naval dockyard at Newcastle, New South Wales, which has a certain irony as the last ship that Dad served on was the battle cruiser HMS *Newcastle!*

Mum told me that during the war bad news was delivered by telegram by young men on red motorbikes. I vaguely remember these as they continued to deliver telegrams as a quick means of communication long after the war ended. This being way before the telex machine and long before households had telephones, let alone email.

She said that when one of these "dreaded" red motorbikes appeared on the street, all the neighbouring women would gather at the unfortunate recipient's house to console the bereaved mother or wife, or sometimes both. The telegrams invariably began with "His Majesty, King George VI, regrets to inform...". Early in April 1942, one of these telegrams arrived at *her* door.

It's hard to imagine the grief of a young mother with a two-year-old daughter learning of her husband's sudden death on the other side of the world from a two-line telegram. It got worse. She told me that Bob used to write home to her almost every day. The post took six weeks to reach her. So for the ensuing six weeks she would be receiving letters from him telling her how much he loved her, and how he couldn't wait to be back home with her and his little daughter.

After several weeks of these she couldn't bring herself to read them. She lay in bed in the mornings dreading the plop on the linoleum covered hallway floor of another letter through the front door letterbox.

Things did get a lot happier for the young mum, as Bob's brother, Pat, would visit her when he was home on leave. Obviously wanting to console in their shared bereavement and seeing his little niece would have been his primary motivation, but I think also it would have given Mum the opportunity to express to Pat her hidden secret feelings for him which, wonderfully, were reciprocated.

Whether it was because it was wartime and life was so unpredictable and precarious, or whether Dad had always harboured a love for Mum, who knows, I think it was the latter, but they married, had two sons, and lived very happily together for the next fifteen years or so.

I do know the depth of Mum's feelings for Dad at that time. As an inquisitive ten-year-old I was rummaging through boxes of stuff under the stairs and came across an old biscuit tin full of letters tied up in pink ribbon, some were unopened. There was also a small diary dating from the 1940s. Page after page, after what must have been one of Dad's visits, was written, "If only I could tell him, if only he knew how much I love him". I confessed to Mum that I'd read this diary, and reminded her of what I'd read, some ten years later, when she was leaving Dad.

I mention that I was an inquisitive child, although this cannot be accredited to my education, indeed more likely the opposite as I hated school. From infants, through junior and then secondary school, I couldn't wait until my fifteenth birthday when I could kiss it all goodbye. There were several factors that influenced my attitude to school. I think one of the first happened in my earliest year at infant school.

There was assembly in the main hall for all three classes, with probably around a hundred children there. We were all sitting cross-legged on the floor in three long rows either side of the hall. After a while we were asked to stand up. I didn't and remained sitting down. I'd wet myself and was sitting in a little puddle of pee and didn't want anyone to see what I'd done. I remember the head teacher coming over and telling me to stand up. Then seeing what I'd done she called over another teacher to help me.

Looking back, if that teacher had had any compassion, she would have helped me to my feet, put a comforting arm around me, reassured me that it wasn't a problem and accidents can happen to anyone and quietly, without fuss, helped me out of the hall and into some dry shorts. Instead, with a look and a grunt of disgust she hoisted me up by my ankle and wrist, holding me at arms' length from her body and carried me dangling upside down, totally humiliated, through the entire length of the hall to the shrill merriment of the whole school.

She then left me alone and miserable sitting on a pile of newspapers in the corner of the empty classroom. Not the best start to one's school days. And it got worse – no, I didn't shit myself – in my final year at infants when I was old enough to walk to school on my own, Mum would wave goodbye until she'd seen me turn the corner of the street and then I would go and hide. Often the milkman would find me cowering behind a hedge and bring me back to an angry mum. She'd then have to drag me, stamping and screaming to the classroom, where I would sit shamefaced and tearstained until the end of day bell would ring, releasing me from my misery.

Mentioning being shamefaced and tearstained has reminded me of an incident that happened around this time. It was something that made such a deep impression on me that it's lasted throughout my life. I could only have been about four or five years old and was playing in the garden with the boy who lived next door. We had set up a 'shop' and had covered a tabletop with items from our houses: cereal boxes, tins of beans, jars of jam, etc. and were happily playing at shopkeepers.

I suddenly remembered that Mum had an old purse which I thought she no longer used. I found it in the kitchen cabinet and was intending to pretend to be a customer. I walked up to our table set with produce and opened my purse. To my amazement instead of it being empty as I'd expected, there was a half crown coin inside. A half crown was two shillings and sixpence, a lot of money then, nearer £6.00 in today's money. Thinking that Mum couldn't want the money as it was in an old unused purse, I shot off to buy myself a cake from the local corner shop.

Arriving at the shop I asked the lady behind the counter for a cake, at the same time reaching up over the counter and handing her my half-crown coin – I was so small I could barely see over the counter. She turned around and reached up to a high shelf and brought down a large boxed sponge cake, obviously thinking that my mum had sent me to buy a family-sized cake. "No, no" I said, "I just want a bun". Returning the cake to the shelf she then handed me a sticky jam doughnut and a large handful of change. I sauntered back home clutching the change and munching on my very satisfying jam doughnut.

As soon as I entered the house, I knew something was seriously wrong! Standing in the kitchen with arms folded were my mum and my friend from next door's mum, both wearing formidable frowns on their faces. Behind them was my friend, trying unsuccessfully to hide the smirk on his face.

Even though I had convinced myself that I was innocent of any misdemeanour as the half crown was unwanted, my face probably told a different story, especially as it was covered in incriminating sugar from the jam doughnut. Mum accused me of stealing from her, and in spite of my protests I was dealt a thorough spanking on my bum and sent straight to bed.

I have never forgotten my feeling of shame, but I'm grateful for the lesson, as throughout my life I have been meticulous in ensuring that I have never taken anything that I knew didn't belong to me.

Remembering the milkman reminded me that he made his deliveries from his milk cart, pulled by a horse. In fact, in the 1950s most deliveries arrived at your house from a horse-drawn vehicle. The milkman, coalman, grocer, even the corporation dust carts removing rubbish were pulled by horses, but they used the huge Shire horses with the massive hooves, hence the name carthorses I suppose.

The street next to ours was one which all the horses used as their personal urinal, great stains on the tarmac up and down the street. It really stank in the summer. They'd drop their big jobbies anywhere. We had a neighbour who grew roses. As soon as a horse had done its business he would rush out with a bucket and scoop it up, still steaming, for his garden.

Sometimes a delivery man would let me sit up on the footrest behind the horse's arse. When the horse raised its tail, you had to quickly move your head to one side, or you'd cop the full force of one of its farts. It was like sitting in the middle of a field of mouldy hay!

One day Mum was returning home from an evening out with a girlfriend at the cinema. Walking alone up our darkened street she thought it was safe to let rip a blast of wind that she'd been sitting on all night. It startled her to hear an even louder reply to it from across the street. It was the greengrocer's horse acknowledging her from his stable. Dad used to say that he'd always bet on Mum against a team of able seamen in a farting competition.

And back to school. Another reason for me to hate those schooldays were the many times we moved house, consequently with different schools each time. New teachers, new faces in the classrooms; it was horrible being the new boy at such a tender age.

The motivation for Mum and Dad moving so often isn't hard to fathom. Prior to the 1970s, house prices were pretty static. You had to own your house for at least three years just to recover your removal expenses, solicitor's and estate agent's costs. This was long before houses became commodities and house prices the preoccupying conversation of aspiring young couples. To better your situation and sell your house at a profit, certainly within a five-year period, you had to improve it. So that's what Dad, being a decorator and a fairly accomplished builder, with Mum the young aspirant, did.

I would imagine that they would have wanted to move on from the house at 51 Lysons Avenue anyway, as it was originally the home chosen by Mum and her late husband, Bob, Dad's elder brother. They would have wanted to have a home they'd chosen for themselves, so Dad was always busy renovating after he'd finished his day's work. Evenings and weekends, he'd be replacing old lath and plaster ceilings, installing a bathroom, repainting and generally modernizing.

The move in 1950 from the terraced house in Lysons Avenue to a semi-detached in Hartington Road was only a few streets away. Dad did the moving himself, piling our furniture onto his tradesman's hand cart and pushing and dragging it round to our new home, with me tripping and skipping alongside him. I don't remember how many times he made the journey but it must have been quite a few.

We only stayed in Hartington Road for a couple of years. Just long enough for Dad to convert a back bedroom into a bathroom and repaint and wallpaper the entire house. There were a good bunch of kids living in the street. We spent most of our time playing hide and seek, tag and, of course, 'cowboys and Indians'.

One family must have been quite well off as they owned a car, the only one in the street. They were also the first family I knew to install a fridge. The owners were Mr and Mrs Jewell – an appropriate name come to think of it. Mrs Jewell would make orange squash lollipops in her fridge and sell to them to us kids for a penny each. On hot summer days there was often a queue of us at her back door.

It's worth noting that in the early 1950s, Britain was still enduring appalling austerity following World War II. Only two per cent of households owned a fridge. Things that we take for granted nowadays like chilled milk, butter and cheese, not to mention ice-cubes and crisp vegetables, were unavailable to ninety-eight per cent of families.

Mum stored our meat on a stone shelf in the kitchen larder. The meat was more usually rabbit which was our regular Sunday roast dinner. As children we loved watching Mum preparing the meal. We would implore her to "make the rabbit dance"! She would lift the skinned creature by its front paws, then jiggle it around the roasting tray, before laying it down among the potatoes and sliding it into the stove.

Food rationing had been imposed during the Second World War, and it continued until 1954. I can clearly recall when doing my Saturday morning errands having to take our ration books with me to the local grocery shop. Long before teabags were introduced from America, we bought our tea in loose packets. Each person was allowed only 2 oz, – about 50 g – per week! I would hand over the ration book, and the grocer would carefully tear out the appropriate number of stamps. Fruit was nearly impossible to find. I never saw bananas or sweets – called lollies in Australia – until I was about nine years old.

One day my sister Molly ran excitedly into the house after returning from town. She'd seen Cadbury's chocolate Crunchie bars displayed in one of the shop windows. She emptied her money box, which I remember was in the shape of a red Post Office mailbox. This was no easy task. You had to slide a kitchen knife into the narrow 'letterbox', then carefully catch the pennies that were inside onto it and gently ease them out through the tiny slit. Having retrieved her few pennies, she ran the whole two miles back into town.

She arrived home about an hour later in tears. The Crunchie bars she'd seen in the window were just cardboard replicas. Sweets were virtually impossible to find until rationing of confectionery ended in 1953. The only food item that wasn't rationed was rabbits and pigeon, hence our Sunday roast. It is interesting to note that rationing improved the health of the British people. In fact, infant mortality declined and life expectancy increased due to a varied diet with enough vitamins. Also, obesity was extremely rare, and morbid obesity unheard of.

My other memory of Hartington Road is where I had my first exciting taste of a money making enterprise. I had learned to play the recorder, well, I managed to struggle through about six tunes, mostly Christmas carols. So from the end of November until Christmas Eve I'd stride off into the dark and play outside people's front doors.

I had a set routine. I'd give them a verse of *Good King Wenceslas*, then a polite knock on their door. Before they could answer I'd start *The First Noel*; more often than not they'd open and interrupt my first notes with a few pennies. If that didn't work, I'd finish the verse and knock again, a bit louder and begin *Oh Come All Ye Faithful*. This generally did the trick. Rarely did I have to get to *While Shepherds...* What joy to return home, a frozen mite, and count out all my pennies, thre'penny bits and the occasional sixpence!

Chapter 2

Firewood and Photography

In the spring of 1953, we moved to Goodyere Street, definitely another step up as this house – Nr. 16 – had a name, Rydal Mount. Although it was back to a terraced property, it had two large attics and a conservatory. It was not really a conservatory in the true sense of the word, more just a sloping framed glass roof at the rear of the house between ours and our neighbour next door. With the extra rooms Mum took in lodgers or paying guests as she would have preferred to call them.

The move meant another change of school for me, this time from Carlton Road to Widden Street, a slightly lower standard of education as I was to find out later.

The big event in the summer that year was the coronation of Queen Elizabeth II. Mum and Dad had managed to buy a television set for the occasion. It had a tiny, black and white 9-inch screen which only offered a very fuzzy image, but it sat proudly in the living room while our lodgers and neighbours crowded around to watch the ceremony as it was beamed live into our home.

Television, in its infancy in the 1950s, was a world of difference to the entertainment that we watch today. The highlight for young children was *Watch with Mother*, a series that included such innocent delights as the *Flower Pot Men* and *Andy Pandy*. Of all the escapades of these simple marionette puppets, my favourite was *Muffin the Mule*. Muffin clip-clopped around on top of a baby grand piano, dancing to tunes being played and sung by the beautiful Annette Mills, older sister to the famous actor, Sir John Mills.

An evening television drama that captivated the nation at the time was a six-part science fiction series, *The Quatermass Experiment.* The narrative revolved around astronauts who had returned to earth with their spaceship infiltrated by a being from outer space. This organism escaped, grew to a monstrous size and lodged itself on an entire wall inside Westminster Abbey. From here it was intending to spore and take over the world! The sight of this writhing mutant creature terrified me as a credulous nine-year-old.

The show was broadcast live, and I learned much later that the footage of the monster inside the abbey was actually a large photographic blow-up of a section of the abbey, with the producer and his wife standing behind it wearing gloves festooned with bits of vegetation, which they poked through holes in the photograph and wiggled around! A far cry from Ridley Scott's movie, *Alien.*

As Gloucester was in a valley, the reception was particularly poor. It wasn't until the 1970s when the company British Relay strung cable across the front of houses that reception was improved.

One of our lodgers, Barry, who was only seventeen years old but seemed like a grown-up man to this nine-year-old, had spent the whole of coronation day in the kitchen crying over a 'Dear John' letter that he'd received from his girlfriend. Barry often babysat for us kids when Dad and Mum went out on a Saturday night. He would treat us to bottles of lemonade, presumably to keep us quiet and well behaved.

Goodyere Street was where I got my second inspiration for a business. There was an open fireplace in the living room, the only source of heating in the house apart from the stove in the kitchen. There was no central heating in these houses at that time. On cold winter mornings I can clearly remember scratching the frozen condensation from the *inside* of my bedroom window to be able to look outside to see how bad the weather was.

Anyway, we bought our fuel from the log man. He would deliver sacks of wood, not logs exactly, but sawn-off sections of timber joists and rafters that we called chumps. He charged six shillings for a sackful. Dad would take one of these chumps and chop it up for kindling to get a fire started. I'd saved up the six shillings needed and bought my own sackful.

Every spare moment I was out in the 'conservatory' chopping firewood and tying them into small bundles, enough to light a fire, ready for sale at thre'pence a bundle. I'd made a small trolley from old pram wheels and a flat piece of wood onto which I could load my bundles. I would pull it around the neighbourhood selling them door to door. Though extremely labour intensive the markup was excellent as I could get between thirty and forty bundles from each sack.

My big moment came when I approached the local corner shop and they placed an order for twelve bundles. Hey, I'd hit the big time! I kept all my profits in an empty sweet jar, which still bore the label Golden Humbugs. I don't suppose that I was grossing more than six shillings a week but counting it out when the jar was full there was enough to buy a new school blazer, £2.19s.11p. – wasn't I the proud nine-year-old!

After two years in this house we moved again, this time for different reasons. From around the mid-1950s large numbers of immigrants were arriving in England, mainly from the West Indies. Many were settling in Gloucester, particularly in the area around where we were living.

It's difficult to imagine now at this time of writing, 2019, but at that time if a black family moved into your street, the value of your property decreased. And if they moved next door to you, no white family would consider buying your house, a shocking indictment on the prevailing attitudes of the time.

A lady six doors from us sold to a black family, so Mum and Dad quickly sold and we moved to the other side of town, to 22 Granville Street. Sixty years on it's easy to be critical and uncomprehending of that racist behaviour. I confess I'm not certain what I might have done if I'd been in their shoes at the time. I like to think that I would have stayed and helped make the new arrivals more welcome, but I don't know, although I did get my chance a bit later in life.

On to Granville Street. We moved into this street that was full of kids around my age; I'd missed this back in Goodyere Street. The downside was another change of schools, though not quite as drastic a change, as I went back to Carlton Road School and joined the class that I'd left two years before.

Unfortunately, as I mentioned earlier, the standard of education at my previous Widden Street School wasn't as high as at Carlton Road. After only a week and just beginning to enjoy the company of my old classroom pals, the headmaster arrived and asked me to collect my books and things from my desk and follow him. He guided me across the hall to another classroom. I'd been demoted to the B stream; another teacher, another classroom of new faces, a new boy all over again!

I have mostly happy memories of growing up in Granville Street. Although it was considered a better neighbourhood, the house itself was quite dilapidated. With rising damp, no bathroom, and only an outside toilet, Dad had a lot on his plate to make it liveable. My memories of that outside lavatory are not so happy. Its whitewashed brick walls supported an open-raftered ceiling revealing the cobweb covered roof slates above. The high wall-mounted, rusting flush box had a long chain which required two or three heavy yanks to release the water to flush the bowl.

Long before our bums were pampered with a choice of soft, scented, absorbent toilet paper, there was only one brand, Izal. Later there appeared another, Bronco, advertised "for the bigger wipe". Both were like wiping your arse with glossy tracing paper!

Dad created a ground-floor bathroom by knocking through the kitchen wall and converting a lean-to coal shed. Prior to this, bath nights were a bit chaotic. We had an old galvanized tin bathtub which hung on a nail outside the back door. On Saturday evenings it was dragged into the kitchen, and all four rings on the gas stove were used to heat up saucepans of water.

Dad had first dip, then Mum, then my sister Molly. By the time it was my turn the water level, which by then, hardly covered the bottom of the tub, was not only barely warm, it was also an unappealing grey colour, covered in a thick layer of soap scum! To get around the lack of depth, I used to prop up one end of the tub with three thick volumes of our *Odhams Encyclopedia of Knowledge*. I dread to think what it was like by the time it was my younger brother, Pat's turn!

It was in the last year of junior school in my new classroom that I met and formed a friendship with a boy who lived a couple of streets away, Martin Cambridge. We'd meet up on the way to school stopping off at the local corner shop bakery where we'd each buy a dripping cake.

I think these must have been a local delicacy as I've never seen them anywhere since. They were presented in a large flat baking tray from where they were cut into dozens of 3-inch squares which were sold for thre'pence each. They were a sort of multilayered sticky slab, filled with raisins and sugar, often with a very treacly base. We always tried to get a corner one as they were the stickiest! It was while munching on these on our way to school that we hatched a plan.

Neither of us liked school lunches. Our mums would give us the five shillings to give to our teacher on a Monday morning which would pay for our lunches for the week. We decided to say that we didn't need school lunches that week as we would be going home at lunch time to eat. This would allow us to spend the money throughout the week on more enticing nourishment like sticky buns, doughnuts and sweets.

As our teacher approached Martin for his lunch money I wondered if he'd have the nerve to go through with our mini insurrection. He did! Martin was seated a few desks in front of mine, and as our teacher approached me, Martin turned and gave me an encouraging wink. The teacher held out his hand for my lunch money. When I told him that I was also going home for lunch he gave me a piercing stare which I countered with my choicest innocent aspect!

Our teacher's name was Mr Baker which, looking back, was quite appropriate considering where Martin and I would be spending our lunchtimes until the school year ended. Years later I heard that Martin had become a slaughterman in a local abattoir, then joined the police force and ended as a high-ranking officer; there must be a connection there somewhere.

****

The main event in that final year of junior school was sitting the eleven plus examination. It was a shocking ordeal for an eleven-year-old child, as those who passed were rewarded with a place at a grammar school and generally scored a new bicycle as well, whereas those who failed were sent to a secondary modern school and got nothing.

Secondary modern schools, which were replaced in the 1970s by 'comprehensive' schools, weren't equipped academically to advance their pupils to a university education. It was generally recognized that they were overwhelmingly dominated by children of poor and working-class parents, while grammar schools were dominated by children of wealthy, middle-class parents. My parents were neither wealthy nor middle-class, but I managed to pass and was awarded a place at The Crypt Grammar School. I don't think it was because I was particularly bright, more likely because Gloucester had a surfeit of grammar schools. Only one kid failed in our class, imagine how he felt.

The Crypt Grammar School was founded in 1539 and was one of the oldest grammar schools in the country. The four years that I spent at The Crypt were the least happy of all my schooldays; I hated just about every day there. Bullying was pervasive from the staff and the prefects. It was education by fear and humiliation, instead of encouragement and praise. Even the prefects were allowed to beat you, generally using one of their gym shoes.

The first term we were evaluated then streamed. I found myself in the bottom stream, the C stream. Even at that age I recognised that I was in the company of deadbeats and losers, so I was determined to get myself out of it. At the end of my second year I was bottom of the class for term work, but top of the class in end-of-year exams. I suppose I could pull a rabbit out of the hat when it was needed. I was then promoted to the B stream. New faces, new boy. Again.

Maybe due to a miserable time at school and my general antipathy to it all I sought out more pleasurable distractions outside of school. Looking back most of my hobbies and pastimes were tinged with a pecuniary slant. A fairly profitable venture at the time was breeding white mice. I'd commandeered the garage at home, Dad not owning a car then, and filled it ceiling to floor with mouse cages. I kept two local pet shops supplied with young mice at sixpence each, which they were selling for one and thre'pence! Mice breed amazingly fast so I was quickly running out of space in the garage. Soon my bedroom was stinking of sawdust and mouse excrement as I converted my chest of drawers into a mouse high-rise. I realize now what indulgent parents I had.

Another interest of mine at the time, although not one to earn any money, was chemistry. I'd been given a chemistry set for Christmas and was quite taken with the idea of making large crystals. The instruction booklet inside the chemistry set demonstrated how easy it was to dissolve copper sulphate crystals in water making a saturated solution, then pick out a small growing crystal, tie a piece of cotton around it, suspend it in the solution and watch it grow!

I had all of Mum's saucepans warming over the gas hob dissolving copper sulphate crystals, with no success at all. I only mention this as another example of my wonderfully indulgent parents. I don't ever recall being admonished, despite turning most of Mum's cutlery, pots and pans a deep copper sulphate blue.

It must have been around this time that I was experimenting making gunpowder and fireworks. I learned that by mixing a combination of potassium nitrate, sulphur and carbon you should get an explosive result. After adding some iron filings, I did manage to achieve some minor twinkling effects, but sadly the words "squib" and "damp" spring to mind. I wouldn't recommend this pursuit today as you would probably be arrested as an ISIS terrorist!

It Was The Best Of Times...

****

While on the subject of chemistry, one of the very rare lessons at school that could remotely be considered as fun was conducted by a young chemistry teacher, Mr Byatt. We were being taught how hydrogen and oxygen could be produced in a Kipp's apparatus in our chemistry laboratory. He then took it upon himself to collect the two gasses combined in a beaker and thrust it over a lighted Bunsen burner. To all our delight there was a loud bang as the gasses exploded.

Getting quite excited by this he repeated the experiment, but with a larger beaker. This time there was a massive bang accompanied by a large orange flash across the room to ecstatic cheering and applause from the entire class. Not content with this, he took an even bigger beaker, warned us all to duck under the lab benches, and then produced a room shuddering, thunderous boom, this time singeing his eyebrows and all the hairs on his arm. I think he might have continued if it wasn't for the appearance of "Pisser" Ewan, the headmaster, frowning through the glass panel of the lab door.

For a while, Bill Byatt was my hero and epitomized what a good teacher should be. Looking back, he probably wasn't much older than I at the time but watching him drive his white open-topped sports car at speed down the school's driveway filled me with hero worship.

A more peaceful recreation of mine at the time was fishing. I'd made my own rod from a 9-foot length of bamboo, even browning it in patterns over the gas hob, and purchasing and fitting metal ferrules so that it could be dismantled into three sections. I bought a cheap reel and guides, and all the remaining tackle, floats, hooks, weights, etc. So after digging up a few worms from the garden, I was off for the day.

We were lucky enough to live close to the Gloucester and Sharpness Canal, which bypasses the River Severn that flows from its source in Shropshire and through Gloucester, before emptying into the Bristol Channel. So along with a few gravel pits, there was a huge variety of fishing spots from which to choose.

The River Severn is one of the very few rivers in the world to boast a tidal wave, called a bore. It occurs throughout the year but is at its most impressive during the spring tides. I have witnessed it many times when fishing the Severn, reaching between two to six feet in height, though much higher ones have been recorded. These days it's popular to surf the wave.

When I was growing up the spring bore brought with it millions of baby eels called elvers. Though numbers have subsequently diminished over many years, I've since read that they are now returning in large quantities and are even appearing on restaurant menus. As a little boy there was nothing more exciting than accompanying the elver fishermen, particularly at night. Their large nets were made of silk or nylon stretched over a frame shaped like a wheelbarrow with a long pole attached. As they reckoned the night tides were more fruitful, they would stake their spot on the riverbank, light a small fire and wait for the shouts of "Tide-O" coming from downstream, as amazingly the bore travelled upstream against the current.

You could hear the wave approaching from quite a distance. It sounded like a slow-moving, roaring and hissing steam train. As soon as the main wave had passed, the fishermen would wade into the water's edge, plunging their large nets into the dark, surging river. On good nights they hauled in enough to fill a small tin bath, which they sold later around the streets of Gloucester; generally a small basin full sold for a few shillings, enough for their beer money for the weekend.

When Mum heard the shout of "elvers" coming from the street, she'd dash out of the house with a basin to purchase our dinner. While alive and wriggling, these baby eels, barely three inches long, were transparent with their gut showing as a thin black thread through their bodies, and a red blood spot under their two black dots of eyes. It sounds quite barbaric now to think we heated up a frying pan with a knob of lard or bacon fat, then dropped them alive and wriggling into the hot pan, then quickly put a lid on to stop them from leaping out! I assume they didn't like it much.

After a couple of minutes, they turned completely white and opaque, not unlike small strands of spaghetti, but with their two tiny black dots of eyes still showing. An annual local delicacy, and absolutely lip-smackingly delicious!

****

One of my exploits at that time was as a junior magician, holding shows for the local kids in our garage; I'd long since given up on the mouse enterprise ever since arriving home from school to find the garage doors prised slightly ajar. Inside were our two cats, Smokey and Joey, licking their paws and wearing guilty expressions between their whiskers, so the garage was freed up again!

The magical productions were quite short-lived and not financially rewarding, charging only two old pennies for admission, plus I wasn't a particularly accomplished conjurer. The shows were probably almost as dire as my model theatre presentations. I'll never know how Mum, Dad, my sister Molly and my brother Pat could sit patiently in our front room in the dark watching, again and again, an over-dramatized puppet theatre production of a Shakespeare play, generally *The Tempest*, as I loved creating the thunderstorm.

It was predominately the set design and the stage lighting that really fascinated me. I'd bought a transformer for 17s.6p. from a local electrical store. This enabled me to light rows of battens at 2.5 volts per bulb, plus a floodlight at 3.5 volts which was great for lightning effects; the thunder came from my larynx! I was useless at the actual puppets. I gave up on overhead marionettes as being too difficult to manipulate, so settled for slide-in characters from stage left and stage right, with me doing the voices for the entire cast; I rarely managed to get past opening night!

Fuelling the post-war economy, a financial device was gaining in popularity. Hire Purchase, or its moniker 'the never-never', allowed customers to purchase expensive items which they would otherwise have been unable to afford. These days it has been superseded by the ubiquitous credit card.

Mum and Dad took advantage of this method of payment and 'purchased' a new form of home entertainment, the radiogram. This was a large wooden cabinet which housed a radio, plus the new-fangled, auto-change record player. This elegant piece of furniture, with its big 10-inch speaker, replaced our old wind-up player, and was given pride of place in the living room. As children we weren't allowed to touch it at first, in case we left fingermarks on it! Our old collection of fragile, Bakelite 78 rpm records, which included Dad's favourites, Mario Lanza, Caruso and *The Donkey Serenade*, were supplanted with new vinyl 45 rpms – known as singles – and 33 rpm long-playing discs – called LPs.

In the evenings on the radio, we listened enthralled to the futuristic, science fiction series *Journey into Space*, with the adventures of its leading characters, 'Jet' Morgan, 'Doc' Matthews, Mitch and Lemmy. Sunday mornings we woke up to the *Billy Cotton Band Show*, followed by *Forces Favourites*. These were followed after lunch by my favourites, *Educating Archie*, and the American family sitcom, *Life with the Lyons*.

We could also receive the commercial station, Radio Luxembourg, beamed from its powerful transmitter in the centre of Europe. Its nightly entertainment included the popular quiz shows *Take Your Pick* and *Double Your Money*, with their ebullient hosts, Michael Miles and Hughie Green. Both these shows enjoyed high audience ratings when they were transferred to commercial television in the 1960s.

****

It was around my eleventh birthday that my granny, Dad's mum, died. I hadn't been able to get to see her so much living in Granville Street, unlike our previous house which was just around the corner from where she lived in Widden Street. I wish I'd got to know her better. As I mentioned in the foreword, my main reason for writing all this is to give my descendants some inkling of *their* forebears, and the circumstances in which they lived.

Granny's house wasn't the regular two-up, two-down terraced house in which most of us working-class families lived. Hers was actually a two-up and *one* down, as the two bedrooms were on top of each other, creating a third storey. There was just one small living room approached directly off the street, and a tiny scullery leading off it. She had a thick, ceiling to floor, reddish brown curtain across the inside of her front door to stop the freezing winter draughts from blowing into her living area. A tiny open fireplace, with a large metal hob to one side of it for boiling a kettle, was the only heating in the house.

Gran's occasional visits to our house in Granville Street were announced with a tap on the door from her walking stick accompanied by a frail "it's only me". Her fingers were swollen and bent with arthritis, "Me screws are getting rusty", was her only complaint from her condition. I know nothing about granny's husband. I think his name was William, where my middle name comes from, but I've no idea what his trade was, or even if he had a trade at all. Maybe I could discover more by researching through the genealogy websites that are currently available, but then maybe I'll leave that up to my family.

I do know more about my maternal grandfather from the stories that my mother told me and what I've gleaned from his military records. His name was Daniel Farley and he must have been an interesting character. After a poor education he left school and became a labourer. On the 9th October 1902, when he was barely eighteen years old, he enlisted for three years with the army, joining the Duke of York's Lancers of the Line, a cavalry regiment.

After completing his three years he re-enlisted for a further ten years, this time signing on as a gunner. On the 4th August 1914 Britain declared war on Germany. The following day Daniel was posted with the British Expeditionary Force to France to the notorious Western Front. Less than three weeks later he was fighting in the first major battle of the war, the Battle of Mons.

Firewood and Photography

Despite being outnumbered by a total of three to one by the German guns, men and cavalry divisions, the British fought courageously inflicting thousands of casualties on the enemy. The battle raged for two days until the sudden retreat of the French Fifth Army, fighting on the right flank, forced the British to withdraw having suffered nearly 2,000 dead or wounded.

There followed a 2-week retreat to the outskirts of Paris, where the British regrouped and were joined by six French field armies together with whom they mounted a victorious counterattack, the Battle of the Marne. The British and the French lost over 80,000 men killed in this action! It's impossible to imagine the horrors that these men experienced. For Daniel, it continued for another twelve months until his posting in France ended and, on his demobilization, he could return home.

Mum said she was told that he returned home to Birmingham to a hero's welcome. In gratitude for his service to his king and country, his local authority at Aston rewarded him, a humble, unskilled labourer, the permanent position of janitor/caretaker of the local library.

The library was housed in a massively imposing red-brick Victorian piece of architecture which is still standing today. I know this as I took Mum to find it a year or so before she died. She pointed out the basement apartment that went with her dad's job, where she was born, and where she lived until leaving home when she was fifteen. She told me that it was growing up in this library that gave her a cherished passion for books and reading. I certainly inherited that passion and have passed it on to my daughters.

Daniel became a popular local figure, a pillar of the community, so much so that he was entrusted to run and manage the local pub's Christmas Club fund. This was a facility that a lot of pubs would organize for the benefit of their patrons, whereby a small amount of money was collected from them each week, then generally invested in a savings account with a local bank earning extra interest. It was a happy situation as, just before Christmas the monies, complete with the extra interest would be paid out to all the investors enabling them to enjoy a financially worry-free Christmas; and "good old Dan" as he was always affectionately known, was the respected treasurer.

Mum told me that just before Christmas a policeman came knocking on their door; Dan had disappeared with the Christmas Club funds! She couldn't remember if there had ever been a prosecution, but there was certainly a scandal, and she never forgave him. She not only felt the shame and disgrace, but also blamed him for her mother's early death. Shortly after this unfortunate episode her mother was diagnosed with an aggressive cancer and died soon after at the early age of forty-five. Her father was soon remarried to his cleaning lady, a woman who brought her six children with her precipitating my mum's early departure from her home. It's hard to believe that a man, with all the plaudits and recognition that he'd earned, would sacrifice it all for some petty larceny – the mind boggles!

****

For my fourteenth birthday, Mum and Dad gave me a camera. It was an inexpensive Coronet Viscount and I was thrilled. At 4 p.m. when school finished there was a camera club meeting in the physics lab, so I joined. I knew nothing at all about photography, so was really only expecting to learn something about shutter speeds and aperture settings on my new camera.

There were only about four or five of us at the meeting, and the agenda for that evening was developing prints in the darkroom. We all crowded into the little darkroom with the teacher, Mr Thacker, demonstrating by the soft glow of a yellow safelight, how a print was produced. After placing the negative in an enlarger's neg' carrier he then exposed it to a sheet of photographic bromide paper and then immersed the paper in the developer chemical.

Well, the moment I watched that image slowly appearing on the blank sheet of bromide paper, being swirled around in the tray of developer I was enthralled and totally captivated! I decided there and then that this was what I wanted to do when I left school. I just knew that I had to get a job in photography. After nine years, with five changes of school, I had finally discovered something that really interested me. From then on, my hard-earned morning and evening paper round wages were not going to be wasted on magic tricks or electrical dimmers for my model theatres, it was all going to be invested in darkroom equipment.

My first purchase was a developing tank; a small black plastic device for developing black and white film negatives. This I could do at home having blacked out the window and converted our bathroom into a darkroom; yet another example of Mum and Dad's tolerance, as not only could they not use the bathroom in the evenings when I was working in it, it also had the only toilet in the house!

I couldn't afford a proper enlarger, so I made one from a converted mouse cage. I did, however, buy a quality lens for it, spending ten shillings and sixpence in Walwins, the chemist shop on Southgate Street. Like most chemist shops in those days, they had a small photographic department. I think Boots – the national UK pharmacy chain – is the only one to continue this tradition.

My mouse cage enlarger allowed me to project images onto the bathroom wall where I'd pinned the photographic bromide paper. I'd set up my developing dishes, the developer and the fixer, on a piece of hardboard resting on the bath, using the sink for washing the prints afterwards. I'd spend every evening and weekends in the bathroom; no one could ever get in to use it!

At this time there were only the four of us living in the house as Molly had left home and was living in a bedsit on Barnwood Road. She'd gone through a rebellious teenage girl period, always clashing with Mum and Dad until finally she decided to move out. I went and visited her one evening and thought her new billet was quite nice. Being the mischievous little sod that I was I decided to hang some guilt on Mum and Dad. I told them that Molly was living in terrible conditions, with just old newspapers covering the bare floorboards, hardly a stick of furniture and no food! Maybe I was attempting to transfer my own guilt.

Much as I loved my sister, I must have made her life miserable with my constant teasing. Beneath all my tormenting I had enormous respect for her. She was always writing plays, poems and letters. As a young teenager she wrote dozens of fan letters to rising actors; Peter Cushing, Sterling Hayden and Patrick Troughton, to name a few. They all used to reply in handwritten letters until they became famous when they could afford to employ secretaries.

One of the letters that she received from Peter Cushing he'd written from Spain where he was filming *The Black Prince* with Alan Ladd. She even wrote to Doctor Albert Schweitzer, the philanthropic missionary in Africa, requesting his permission to have a play that she'd written about his life performed. He naturally declined!

Some years later I 'borrowed' these letters – there were quite a pile of them – to show some friends at work and lost them! I don't know how she ever forgave me! Not only did Molly give me my interest in poetry and Shakespeare, one of her boyfriends, who said he'd played for Lancashire, coached me on my batting skills and furthered my everlasting passion for cricket.

When Molly got married, she trusted my new interest in photography, and allowed me to be her wedding photographer. Unfortunately, I had recently changed cameras and unknown to me there was a problem with the lens. Out of dozens of photographs that I'd taken, only a couple were actually in focus; I don't know how she forgave me for that either!

Looking back, I can remember the late 1950s as a period of great change and anticipation. Rock 'n' Roll was just beginning to be aired on the radio, albeit only broadcast from the European station, Radio Luxembourg, with its very crackly reception. Bill Haley and his Comets had been around for a couple of years, but it wasn't until Elvis and his first hit, *Heartbreak Hotel* in 1956, stormed the charts that things really got exciting. We waited impatiently for his next releases, each one bringing with it a sense of reformation and rebellion. *Blue Suede Shoes* and then *Hound Dog* seemed the embodiment of teenage insurgence; well it did to this 14-year-old!

Then Britain got its own Elvis when Cliff Richard was launched with *Move It* in 1958. Again, we eagerly awaited follow up releases.

It's difficult to imagine the euphoria during this transition of music and culture. Having for years been fed a diet of soft ballads by artists such as Alma Cogan, Vera Lynn and David Whitfield, the new beat and sounds were quite dramatic, particularly to a boy poised on the threshold of adulthood. With my newfound photography hobby which I was already turning into a small money-making venture taking portrait shots of Mum's friend's children, and my school years about to come to an end, I felt I was on the doorstep of a whole new beginning. Little did I realize that working life, especially my first year, would be so arduous and oppressive and not at all how I'd envisaged it would be.

Chapter 3

Wages and Wasps

The school year ended in July 1959 and I had turned fifteen in May that year. I had hardly attended school in those final few weeks, I just couldn't be bothered with it. I'd had a 'chat' with the careers master and was not impressed at all. It appeared that the main goal was to achieve a minimum of five 'O' levels in the GCE examinations[5] in the forthcoming year. This would almost guarantee you a place as a clerical officer in the Civil Service, very exciting!

Or, having gained five 'O' levels you could advance to the sixth form and sit 'A' level exams. Achieving a minimum of two of these could get you into university or at least a position as an executive officer in the Civil Service, even less exciting to me! I couldn't wait to get out. I spent most of my time either skiving off with a classmate, Roger Gough, who always had a plentiful supply of cigarettes, or revisiting all the photographic shops in town to see if they had any vacancies.

I was so desperate to start working that I even applied to join the police force as a cadet. I had visions of becoming a police photographer, attending crime scenes and solving every cold case criminal mystery. I went for an interview at the local police station, which conveniently was on the corner of our street.

The station sergeant had to take my chest measurement and height. This huge and very stern police sergeant wrapped a

---

5. General Certificate of Education, now the General Certificate of Secondary Education (GCSE).

tape measure around my chest and noted, not too impressively, "28 inches". He then ordered me to expand my chest. I wasn't too sure what he meant and must have looked a little puzzled. "Puff yer chest out lad!" he barked. I did my best but I don't think the tape moved more than half an inch, maybe it even shrank. He then took my height measurement, "Five feet, two and a half inches".

The "We regret" letter that I received from the force stated that the minimum height requirement for a cadet was 5 feet, 4 inches. They spared me any mention of my chest measurement! I always thought that it was quite amazing that in the following two years I grew to six feet tall. It's no wonder that my long trousers I so proudly wore, were always flapping above my ankles.

It was at this time that Mum and Dad's marriage was breaking down. Now that Pat and I were growing up, Mum had gone back to work. She was doing clerical work for the Civil Service and later in the accounts department of British Telecom. She worked in an office full of younger women who all seemed to revel in relating their real or more likely imagined sexploits!

I'm obviously not qualified to say whether this influenced Mum, but she certainly changed persona around this time. I could hardly say anything at home without some spicy response charged with innuendo; "Ooh, as the actress said to the bishop," was a favourite riposte. I found this mildly embarrassing, but nowhere near as bad as how she began to treat Dad. She was always putting him down, criticizing everything he said as "a typical builders remark". I felt so sorry for him, often standing up to Mum on his behalf.

Things got a lot worse when Mum started 'seeing' a friend of Dad's. Every Tuesday, Thursday and Saturday night Mum would get dolled up and strut up the street to her assignation, generally being met on the corner by him driving his shiny, black Ford V8 Pilot; Mum was always impressed with cars. I was not so impressed having to watch Mum walk past us lads hanging out under a streetlamp, and have to receive the taunts from my mates, "Off to see her fancy man, eh?" was the usual one. I don't know how Dad managed to cope with it. The fact was in the end that he couldn't. A physical fight with her lover hadn't put an end to it, so finally he exploded in a violent attack on Mum. A shocking incident which I find too painful to elaborate on.

They continued to live together on and off for another five years. Mum told me years later that she wanted to stay at home until Pat reached fifteen, after which she felt she could leave permanently. I always thought they would both have been happier if they had separated immediately, I certainly would have been. I would rather have lived with one happy parent than two who were constantly bickering. Twenty years or so later they did make several attempts at reconciliation but I think both had grown too far apart for it to work.

In that summer of 1959, I finally found a photographer in town who said he'd take me on as an assistant. However, the vacancy was not going to be ready for a couple of months. In the interim Dad got me a job with his employer, a small building firm based in Cheltenham, owned by a bustling, rotund, rosy-cheeked Mr Griffiths.

When Dad presented me to my potential future employer, he looked me up and down and asked, "What can the lad do?" Dad gave an enthusiastic response on my behalf, telling Mr Griffiths that I was a great help to him with renovation work round the home. "He can do sanding and undercoat priming; he'll be very useful," he almost gushed. So I was taken on as a general labourer and gofer.

We were working on a big semi-detached house on Barnwood Road, repainting the exterior. I was put to work sanding a very rusty set of front railings. The main difficulty I experienced as I embarked on my working life was having to stand on my feet all day. This took a lot of getting used to, having spent most of my school days sitting on my arse. I don't suppose I was the first lad to experience this discomfort.

Apart from the excruciatingly boring jobs that I was given to do I was immediately struck by Dad's different demeanour at work compared to home. Away from Mum's constant sniping at him he actually seemed a happy person, laughing and joking with his workmates, always with a smile on his face – it was wonderful to witness.

It was only a small group of men working on the site. The one I remember most was a young guy who rode a very powerful motorbike, a Triumph Bonneville. He took me for a spin on his pillion one day. This was long before the compulsory wearing of helmets became law, so reaching a speed of nearly 100 mph along Estcourt Road was breathtakingly exhilarating, although I wouldn't recommend it nowadays.

Aside from the menial work that I was entrusted to do I did enjoy the company of the work gang. I loved the jovial banter that was constantly bandied about, the gentle Mickey-taking and the shared laughter, although I wasn't too sad to leave when the vacancy at the photographers became ready, I'd had enough of sanding railings and window frames.

It was early in November that I began working for Richard Hall Photography. The single-storey shop fronted on to Clarence Street, roughly where Primark is now. There were darkrooms at the rear of the shop, a studio for portraiture and a finishing room for retouching, trimming and glazing. There was an overgrown garden at the back with several small sheds and an outside toilet, the only one in the building. There were no doors between the darkrooms, nor to the outside yard, just a series of light traps, which meant in the winter the rooms were freezing cold as there was no heating either.

Richard Hall, the eponymous owner of the business, was quite short. He was not a lot taller than I was, and I was only knee high to a midget at that time. He was probably in his late sixties, although his attire would have placed him a lot older. From his laced-up ankle high boots, to his pin-striped three-piece suits, complete with a white, winged collar shirt, all topped off with a shock of long, curly, collar length white hair – which might have made Albert Einstein envious – he could have quite easily stepped out of the pages of a Dickens novel, but with an outlook less Micawber and more Ebenezer Scrooge.

His wife, who he only ever referred to as "Mrs Hall" or more frequently, "Madam", worked in the studio. If you've ever seen those very old coloured photographic portraits, that's what she did, sitting all day at her easel and paint box, giving monochromatic babies blue eyes, golden locks and pink matinee coats, or blue if they were boys.

She once told me that she and Mr Hall had no children, and their home had no television or even electricity. They spent their evenings with her sitting quietly listening, while Mr Hall read aloud to her by the light of a gas lamp. She never told me what he read to her; I doubt that it was Lady Chatterley's Lover!

Interestingly, it was during that year, 1960, that Penguin Books, published DH Lawrence's notorious novel. Subsequently they were prosecuted under the archaic 'Obscene Publications Act' which fortunately had recently been updated to allow publishers to escape conviction if they could show that a work had 'literary merit'. The trial, which was held at the Old Bailey in London, was a watershed and a major public event.

The prosecution was ridiculed as being out of touch when the chief prosecutor, Mervyn Griffiths-Jones, asked the jury if it were the kind of book "you would wish your wife or servants to read"! The defence called an array of famous novelists and literary critics as witnesses attesting to the book's literary merit and after six days the jury returned their verdict of not guilty. The result not only heralded the liberalisation of publishing but was also considered to be the beginning of the 'permissive society'.

Back to Richard Hall's, I can remember three other members of the staff; Mrs Grimes – now there's a Dickensian name – who performed general cleaning duties and sometimes served in the shop; and a young attractive girl who did the trimming of the prints and the glazing. I never did find out her name as we were all discouraged from talking to each other in the workplace.

The third member was Miss Dyer with whom I worked most closely. Miss Dyer was a tall willowy lady, probably in her forties. She wore a severe, grey, pudding basin haircut which framed a friendly face. I liked Miss Dyer; she was very helpful to me, explaining my duties with patience and enthusiasm, unlike Mr Hall. I always felt sorry for her as she seemed to have a very spartan existence living with, and caring for, her two much older sisters, who apparently were both very unwell. At that time, she would have been regarded as an 'old maid', very politically incorrect these days. She did tell me a heart-warming story about a popular comedian of the time.

Jimmy Clitheroe was a northerner from Lancashire. He was a tiny man who never grew more than four feet three inches. He always played the part of a little boy. He had a very successful radio show, *The Clitheroe Kid*, which ran for years. Apparently, he was appearing in pantomime at a local theatre, but one of Miss Dyer's sisters, who was a huge fan of his, was too ill and bedridden to get to see him. So Miss Dyer went to the theatre and waited patiently at the stage door for him to appear.

When he did, she told him about her sister and asked if there was any chance that he might visit her. This celebrated comedian turned up at her house the next day in his Rolls Royce, with flowers and chocolates, and sat by her bedside for quite a while. She told me that his Rolls Royce had been specially adapted with extensions on the foot pedals so his tiny legs could reach them, and he sat on a pile of cushions to be able to see over the bonnet! A sad footnote to the story was that he'd never married and had lived all his life with his elderly mother. On the day of her funeral he took his own life with an overdose of sleeping tablets; he was only fifty-one years old.

Miss Dyer made a big impression on me. At Christmas she gave me a book, *The Adventures of Tom Sawyer*; I hadn't got her anything.

To begin with I found my work quite interesting, although it's fascinating looking back sixty years to see the revolutionary inventions that have transformed photography. It wasn't until 1975, sixteen years after I was working for Richard Hall, that a 25-year-old electronics engineer from New York, Steven Sasson, built the first digital camera. He was working for Eastman Kodak who decided not to pursue the invention as it conflicted with their film production which, at the time, was ninety per cent of their business. Digital cameras weren't in mass production until the mid-90s, and it wasn't until 2002 that they were incorporated into mobile phones. In 1959 amateur photography was predominately restricted to black and white small prints, produced from negatives that had been shot onto short rolls of film. Like long-playing vinyl records, it's delightful to see that these reminders of the past are apparently making a comeback.

My day began with me cycling around Gloucester collecting all the roll films from various chemist shops and corner stores, and even the department store, Bon Marché, later to become Debenhams.

Back in the darkroom I would unroll all the films and attach them to a hanger, clip a weight onto their ends, then lower them all into the developing trough. This was a big earthenware pot about a foot square and three feet deep; deep enough to accommodate 35 mm films which were beginning to gain in popularity. After enough time in the developer I would lift them all out and lower them into the fixer pot. All of this was obviously performed in complete darkness.

The main problem that I had to contend with was a wasp nest in the darkroom. I could hear them all buzzing around me but wasn't able to see them. As they found easy access up my legs, because my trousers were always up above my ankles, I took to keeping my cycle clips on to prevent their entry. You can't imagine how disconcerting it was to feel them crawling around your inner thighs, waiting for the sting to happen. At least the cycle clips put an end to those attacks. Unfortunately, as I had to work with my sleeves rolled up, it didn't prevent these unwelcome pests from stinging my exposed forearms. Eventually Mr Hall got pest exterminators in and had the nest removed.

There was one other discomfort that I had to endure during the winter months. The darkroom I worked in led directly to the back yard. There was no outside door, just a walk-through light trap. The water tank for washing the films was positioned next to the exterior opening; consequently, it was always freezing over with a thick layer of ice on the surface.

It wasn't too pleasant plunging my arms up to my elbows fishing out the films, having first had to break through the ice, and all this for two pounds a week, less five shillings and five pence for my National Insurance contribution. At this time, I had mates of my age doing apprenticeships in the building trade earning twice what I was getting.

I persevered with my duties but was becoming more disillusioned as each month went by. I would have preferred to have been learning studio work, and maybe assisting at wedding photography, but obviously I was more useful doing the more menial tasks. Either a recognized indenture wasn't available for commercial photography, or more likely Mr Hall couldn't be bothered with the paperwork, I felt I was just drifting and not getting set on a proper career path.

My frustration wasn't helped by Dad's constant insistence that I should get indentures. I thought I was being smart by responding that I didn't need false teeth – I guess I was just being a smart arse! Making matters worse, Mr Hall called me into his office one day to give me some 'instruction'. He began by telling me that every camera must have a lens. I was about to question this by saying, "What about a pin hole camera?" I'd made a few of these back in my school camera club days. It was just as well I didn't as he then said, "If you'd said a pin hole camera doesn't, I'd wrap your knuckles, as a pin hole is the lens!" I learned to keep my mouth shut in the future.

In retrospect, Dad was hugely supportive and sympathized with my disenchantment. He was working with a building gang repainting the interior of a local printing company, Priestley Studios. He had seen that they had a large photographic department in the company and told me that I should apply to them for any vacancies.

I was very sceptical and didn't think that Dad really knew what he was looking at, so I didn't do anything about it. Dad recognized my cynicism and, unbeknown to me, wrote to the company on my behalf. He told them that his son had worked in photography for eight months but was looking for an apprenticeship, and were there any vacancies?

As luck would have it, they were about to advertise for an apprentice but were expecting to employ an art college graduate. They replied to Dad offering me an interview. I was still quite pessimistic about my chances, but Dad was very enthusiastic, even insisting he take me to Bon Marché to buy a new sports coat for the interview. I went for the interview and was shown around the department. It all looked so modern and exciting, with a large gallery camera, a huge enlarger and fabulously equipped darkrooms. I was told that the wages would be a percentage of the print union's journeyman rate, which was currently fourteen guineas a week. This would mean that if I got the job, I'd be doubling my present wage!

My interviewer, Peter Kell, was the manager of the department, and it all seemed so friendly. Everyone was on Christian name terms, something that was completely new to me. To my total surprise I was offered the job there and then based on my eight months experience at Richard Hall's. I was told that I would have to serve a three-month probationary period after which I would be signed up for a five-year apprenticeship. This included a day release to attend the Bristol College of Printing to gain a City and Guilds certificate. I was over the moon!

Later, when I was handing in my notice to Mr Hall, he told me that I was being stupid, that he'd had great plans for me. He went on to inform me that when I reached twenty-one, he was going to pay me £10 a week! This illustrated to me just how out of touch he was with current salaries. I could barely keep the smile off my face!

Chapter 4

Bedsit and Bridegroom

It was late June 1960 when I began working at Priestley Studios. The company was one of the larger employers in the city. Its printing works stood on the corner of Commercial Road and Ladybellegate Street. (I visited it in 2015 and sadly discovered that it had been razed to the ground and was now a car park.) The company was owned by a bald, bespectacled, portly gentleman, Charles Priestley, who bore a remarkable resemblance to an illustrious band leader of the day, Billy Cotton. He drove a stately S Class Bentley motor car. His rare visits to the darkrooms were received with reverential kowtowing by my boss Peter.

The business was very successful, producing posters, show cards and point-of-sale displays for some impressive clients including Cadbury's chocolates, Clarks' shoes and Wall's ice cream. To me it was all so exciting and very different to what I'd been doing up until then. In the darkrooms, or Graphic Arts department as it was known, we were pioneering fine-line, four-colour halftone work for the silk screen process. It all sounds so terribly old-fashioned now, with everything being digital these days, but back then we were even using photographic glass plates. We soon switched to film and were regularly producing high resolution colour images for the point-of-sale market.

I loved the work and was so happy with my new job; I had some terrific workmates. The photo stencil department was run by Neil Daft – (yeah, what a surname!); he was only nineteen but seemed so much older and more grown up than me at only sixteen, and he had a girlfriend!

Like me, he also had a love of books, and introduced me to Ian Fleming novels. We would wait expectantly for the next James Bond adventure to be published, and then exchange reflections on it. He always had a more mature opinion than I.

My immediate boss, Peter Kell, was a very jovial chap, with a great sense of humour. He often had me in fits of laughter. He was also an excellent tradesman, with a wide knowledge of the graphic arts industry. I was very fortunate to be apprenticed to such a journeyman, who was also our trade union father-of-the-chapel, so ensured we all received our fair wages and working conditions.

We worked a 48-hour week when I began working for Priestley's including four hours on Saturday morning. This was better than Richard Hall's when I worked all day on Saturdays. Soon the Saturday morning was dropped, and not long after the hours were reduced to a 40-hour week.

As Priestley's was only a mile away from Granville Street, I had the time to cycle home and back at lunchtime. The downside of this journey was that I had to pass the Moreland's match factory on Bristol Road – these days the site of the Moreland's Trading Estate, a reminder of Gloucester's great industrial heritage. Before it closed in 1976, Moreland's was a thriving business producing their famous boxes of England's Glory matchsticks.

The company had been founded in 1867 by one Samuel J Moreland, and during the 1960s employed dozens of young women factory workers, known affectionately as Sammy's Angels! These girls, wearing their corporate pale green smocks, would form a long line sitting on the pavement outside the factory every day enjoying their lunchbreak.

They took great delight in jeering and wolf-whistling at passing male cyclists. Being a young, blushing victim of their taunts, I have forever had sympathy for young girls receiving the same treatment when passing male-dominated building sites!

When I'd completed my three months' probationary period Peter arranged for my indentures to be signed. It was quite an occasion; Dad was invited to attend the official signing, which was to be held in the chairman, Mr Priestley's, office.

That day I was busy in the darkroom mixing chemicals, wearing not only my white smock, but also a heavy, protective, long rubber apron which almost reached down to my feet. The intercom buzzed in the darkroom, and a green light was flashing above it; the light indicating that a call was coming from the chairman's office. Peter answered it and I heard Mr Priestley's voice, "Send Fitzgerald down please, Peter". I asked Peter if I should take off my apron and smock to look a bit smarter. He suggested I leave them on to look busy.

I went down to the ground floor to the row of administrative offices; I'd never visited this part of the building before. Mr Priestley's office was at the far end of a long corridor. There was a red light beaming above the door. I approached with not a little anxiety and knocked tamely on the door. "Come." I pushed open the door and immediately saw Dad. He was sitting behind an enormous table, next to him on his right sat Mr Priestley, and on Mr Priestley's right was his secretary, Miss Jarman. On Dad's left was the company secretary, Mr Martin, and on his left was Mr Wallace Mitchell, the trade union branch secretary from Bristol. They all looked up to greet me.

I'd never been in the office before, it was very imposing. What I didn't know was that there was an immediate step down inside the doorway. As I entered, I not only stumbled and dropped down to my knees, but my knees got trapped behind the heavy rubber apron that I was wearing. As I attempted to stand up quickly, I just projected myself forward and ended doing a crab-like crawl across the carpet.

Red-faced and acutely embarrassed I couldn't bring myself to look at Dad or the others. I was so flustered I didn't even sign my name correctly on the indentures, putting two 'g's' instead of one 'z' and one 'g', and not crossing the 't'. I still have the beautiful copperplate hand-laid deed bearing my rattled signature as testimony.

It Was The Best Of Times...

Even though I had left school some two years previously, I still maintained a close friendship with an old school pal, David Whitmore. He lived a few streets away in Frampton Road. We had both been big Cliff Richard fans, although by now my musical tastes were moving more towards traditional jazz and classical music introduced and encouraged by my new friends at work. Dave worked as a shop assistant in Currys Electrical store which was on Eastgate Street at that time.

One day he told me that the shop had taken on a new assistant working in the basement department selling toys, baby's prams and general nursery items. He said she had just returned from Australia, was fifteen years old and didn't have a boyfriend. I was seventeen years old and had never had a girlfriend. Mum always teased me when I was critical of the girls in the audience on the TV show *Top of the Pops*. She often said, "I wonder what the girl that you bring home will be like?"

The next Saturday on the pretence of visiting Dave at the shop, I stole a sneak peek at this new girl whose name was Janet. I snuck to the top of the basement stairs and peered down. There was Janet, a slim, attractive girl, wearing a beehive hairstyle, – this *was* 1961! She was standing in the middle of about twenty, 6-inch tall, clockwork penguins, which she'd wound up and had waddling and flapping all around her feet, I was immediately smitten!

I don't know if Dave had put a word in for me or not, but a few days later I plucked up the courage to ask her for a date. After some coaching from Pete and Neil at work, with advice on how I should conduct myself while asking for a date, which included suggestions that I shouldn't smoke or chew gum, and even that I should wear gloves, then as she approached, take the right-hand glove off to be able to shake her hand! I'm not sure if the last suggestion was serious or not but it didn't matter as I didn't possess a pair of gloves.

Anyway, a few days later when I had summoned up the nerve, I was waiting apprehensively outside Currys for Janet to finish work. When she approached, I blurted out my request, and to my absolute delight she accepted my invitation.

I think our first date was to the cinema. It may have been to see Elvis Presley in *G.I. Blues*, I do remember walking out halfway through the film as it was so dire; and then we would have walked round to Lyons Corner House, which was just inside Northgate Street, to have a cup of tea.

Jan told me that she lived with her mum, and the two of them had just returned from Australia. The family had emigrated about three years earlier, but it hadn't worked out for them. At that time the Australian government subsidized the fare to Australia for migrants. It only cost £10 to emigrate, in fact I remember Mum and Dad had considered emigrating under this scheme, but for one reason or another they didn't pursue it.

The downside to this scheme was that if a migrant wished to return to England within a certain period of time, they not had only to pay their own fare back but also repay the balance of the original outbound fare, which was quite a considerable sum. The migrants were known in Australia as "ten-pound Poms" which was considered a stigma at the time, but nowadays, along with descendants of deported convicts, worn as a badge of pride.

Jan told me that her grandparents had paid for her mum and herself to return and that hopefully the rest of her family would be returning sometime soon. Initially Jan and I went out together for about three months. It was during this period together that she turned sixteen. Her birthday coincided with Neil Sedaka's top twenty hit *Happy Birthday Sweet Sixteen*, tra-la-la-la-la-la-la-happy-birthday-sweet-sixteen... etc. It became our favourite song for a while, until the first time we saw him on television. We were so disappointed to discover that his voice belied his looks. Instead of our expected Elvis look-a-like he appeared as a chubby, moon-faced, bouncy little chap.

I can't remember why we broke up at that time, it was probably a teenage spat of one sort or another, but whatever caused it, we remained apart for nearly a year.

It was during this time that I started saving hard to buy a Lambretta motor scooter. I was fed up with taking the train every week to Bristol to the technical college – I mentioned in chapter one about the freezing conditions on the early milk train. To help with the purchase I sold off virtually everything I owned which wasn't very much, only amounting to my bicycle and my stamp collection. I kept my camera as I was still making a bit of money doing the occasional portrait for friends.

I also got an evening job as a barman at the local pub, The Avenue Hotel, on the corner of Tuffley Avenue and Bristol Road. It was amazing that they employed me as I was only seventeen, still a year younger than the legal age to drink alcohol, let alone sell it!

My very first customer had me completely confused. He arrived at the little off-sales hatch at the end of the bar and said he'd come for a paint bottle. I looked all along the shelves but couldn't see any paint bottles. I went out and found the landlord, Stan, to help me. I told him there was a man who'd come to pick up a paint bottle. Stan was equally confused so followed me back to the off sales. As soon as he saw the gentleman he laughed and told me that the customer was Irish and was asking for a *pint* bottle!

I worked for Stan and Peggy for a few months, long enough to save enough money for a deposit on a second-hand, but beautiful, cream and turquoise 150 cc Lambretta. I bought it from a dealership on the High Street in Cheltenham, Williams and Co. Unfortunately, I'd never ridden a motor scooter before so I had no idea how the gears, clutch or anything worked. Looking back, it was criminally reckless of them to sell it to me without any lessons or training on it. Instead, they put it on a trailer and drove it to the Shurdington Road. Having told me I'd be alright as there was only one roundabout to negotiate to get back to Gloucester, they left me to it.

Not knowing that I had to change down gears to get up a hill, the poor machine spluttered to a halt on the first incline. Luckily a passer-by got me going again and I managed to get right to the turn into Granville Street before I crashed; I didn't know how to use the brakes to slow down! Fortunately, the only damage was a broken windshield and a severely lacerated pride as the spill was witnessed by a lot of my mates and neighbours in the street.

It turned out that the scooter was fabulous for buzzing around town, but quite a challenge for the journey to Bristol each week. Travelling at only 30 mph along the old A38 it took at least an hour and a half, and on icy cold winter mornings, with no windshield or gloves, I was beginning to miss the comparative warmth of the freezing milk train.

As the weather turned warmer, I ventured further afield on my scooter. Mum still had relatives in Birmingham that she kept in touch with, so I decided to visit them. Before the M5 motorway was built, the route from Gloucester to Birmingham was along the A38 trunk road. It was a pleasant country ride that only took a couple of hours.

What surprised me most on arriving in Birmingham was the totally different accent that was spoken. Gloucester folk's accent was often likened to farmers or even pirates! Very guttural with lots of "errs" and "arrhs". In the space of fifty miles or so, it changed to a higher register, almost a completely different language. Instead of, say, the weather being "great" or "nice isn't it", it became "groit" or "noyce eentit".

It caused me to ponder where exactly this major change could occur. I pictured a short row of terraced houses, somewhere halfway between Gloucester and Birmingham, where the occupants of the northern half all spoke with this higher register, all "groits" and "loiks" and "noyce eentits"; meanwhile their immediate neighbours in the southern half of the row were all "arrhs" and "errs"!

Maybe it was narrowed down to just a pair of detached houses where next-door neighbours conversed with each other in completely different dialects. I recognized the huge difference between Lancashire and Yorkshire accents, but at least there's the Pennine Hills to separate them. Where, I wondered, was the language boundary between Gloucester and Birmingham?

It Was The Best Of Times...

****

During this period when Jan and I had split up I started to hang out with a friend who lived opposite us in Granville Street, Graham Mitchell. Graham was about three years older than me and appeared quite the man about town. He always wore incredibly smart suits and had a great job as a sales representative, initially for a company that made chicken incubators. He drove a smart Vauxhall Victor company car and spent his working days travelling the country visiting clients.

He took me with him on several occasions, driving out to west Wales and the north of England. I was in awe of him and decided that when my apprenticeship was finished, I would get a job in sales, travelling around the country like he did. Graham got married very young to a glamorous French girl, Claudette, who taught French at Denmark Road girl's high school. They introduced me to many of their friends, and I always tagged along to their parties and trips to pubs and clubs.

One of their friends, McDougal (Mac), was also a salesman; he worked for Bowyers sausages. He was a huge, 'hail fellow well met' sort of guy who finally made enough money from sales to buy The Little Thatch restaurant at Hardwick. These guys inspired me and made me determined to one day become a salesman.

Eventually Jan and I got back together again and became 'an item'. In the summer of 1963 we were invited, along with Jan's mum Gladys, to stay with Jan's brother Derek, in London for a short holiday. Derek was married to a very attractive girl, Sheila, who seemed quite exotic to us as not only had she been married before, but also had a young daughter, Jane, from her first marriage.

I'd met Derek a couple of times when he'd visited Gloucester and liked him a lot. He was about five years older than me and was a teacher at a secondary school. They lived in a first-floor flat in Lewisham in south-east London. To us they seemed so sophisticated and knowledgeable. Jan's mum took the coach for the journey while we decided to go on my scooter.

It was our first trip to London; in fact, it was the furthest I'd ever ventured away from Gloucester. Now I look back in horror at undertaking such a journey for the two of us on a tiny 150 cc Lambretta. However, we made it without any unpleasant events, unlike the return journey home.

After nineteen years living in parochial Gloucester, I found London sensational. I couldn't get over the scale; the sheer size of the buildings – Centre Point at the end of Oxford Street had just been completed – the number of people, the variety of entertainment, the noise, the smell, I fell in love with it! By comparison Gloucester seemed so tiny, so boring, and so dull. I decided that when my apprenticeship was finished it would be London where I'd be looking for work.

Jan and I made the most of our holiday there. Travelling around on my scooter we crammed in so much. At that time the latest spectacle at the cinema was 'Cinerama'. The technique employed three projectors projecting the film onto a semi-circle of three screens, which gave the audience the impression of being right there in the centre of the action. It was a forerunner of today's vastly superior IMAX.

The films were being shown at the Casino Cinema on Old Compton Street; the cinema has now been converted back to a theatre, the Prince Edward, where *Miss Saigon* performed for many years. I don't think that these days I could sit through five hours of *How the West was Won* and *The Wonderful World of the Brothers Grimm*, but at the time it was all so magical.

Another treat was my first visit to a major theatre. The musical, *Oliver*, which had been playing for a couple of years was still the big hit of the West End. It gave me an everlasting love for musicals; I'm almost embarrassed to admit that I've seen *Miss Saigon* seventeen times.

That short holiday planted the seed for the future. I somehow had to get into sales and move to London. I had no idea how many milestones would need to be overcome, and how that plan would so often be thwarted on the journey. The first setback occurred sooner than I expected when my Lambretta broke down on the way home. This was long before the M40 was built, it was dark and we were in the middle of nowhere. I think we were somewhere between Beaconsfield and Witney.

I pushed the machine for a mile or two until we came to a small hotel set back from the road. The manager kindly let me leave it in his garage to pick up later, and Jan and I set off to hitchhike our way back. We finally arrived home about eight hours late. Jan's mum was furious and obviously sick with worry. It wasn't the only time I was to cause her an upset!

****

I had become increasingly unhappy at home. I was not only having to witness the slow sorrowful breakdown of Mum and Dad's marriage, but at eighteen years old I felt the need to break out on my own. I found a small bed-sitting room on the top floor of a three-storey house on Westgate Terrace, off Lower Westgate Street, just across the River Severn.

The two pounds fifteen shillings rent took quite a chunk out of my eight pounds a week wage; after taxes, national insurance and repayments on my scooter it didn't leave much to live on, but at least I felt some independence and away from the strife at home. The room I rented was quite large, covering the top floor of the house, and it had a shower cubicle just outside the room on the top floor landing. This wasn't as good a feature as I first thought as often when using it, I'd receive a nasty electric shock!

A guy who rented the ground-floor flat had told me that he was in electronics so I asked him to investigate this electrical fault for me. He discovered that a heater in my room was wired incorrectly, with a live wire connected to the earth system which connected directly to the water pipe in my shower.

Later when I tackled the landlord about this he apologised and said that he'd wired the house himself but he was colour blind so often mixed up the wires. I was very cautious switching on the power after that. As the guy downstairs worked in the electronics industry, I asked for his help assembling a kit amplifier I'd bought recently. We stayed up all night building it and finally around 4 a.m. it was finished.

We switched off our soldering irons and turned it on. Seconds after the little red power light came on there was an almighty BOOM and the whole thing exploded into a cloud of smoke! It turned out to be a faulty capacitor, whatever that is, and not the wiring in the house, so the manufacturers replaced it with one that was already built and working.

The biggest problem living in my bedsit was the smell! Just across the river on Westgate Street was the notorious Westgate Tallow Works. The factory was engaged in the production of candles and glue all made by crushing old beef and mutton bones. The lower end of Westgate Street was infamous for the stench that this factory produced. Thankfully it was closed in the late 60s.

Unfortunately, during the hot summer of 1963 with a southeasterly breeze blowing, the smell carried right to my front windows forcing me to keep them permanently closed. This, combined with my state of near penury, persuaded me to swallow my pride and move back to Granville Street. It wasn't a bad decision. On previous visits home there were always delicious smells coming from the kitchen. Mum would invariably ask me if I'd like something to eat. Despite being ravenously hungry I could never accept, pretending that I was full to bursting from my over filled pantry, which of course was always empty.

In the early autumn of that year Jan presented me with two pieces of interesting news. She was very excited to learn that her grandparents had paid the fares for her two older brothers, Mick and Graham, to return to England, and would be arriving home in about four weeks. She wasn't too excited about the other more concerning news that she had missed her monthly period.

An old wives' tale current at the time was that a period could be induced by drinking a concoction of gin and cod liver oil; we decided to experiment with it. Dad was working away from home, so on an evening when Mum was going out, I arranged for Jan to come over to imbibe this cocktail. I'd bought a quarter bottle of gin from an off-licence and a bottle of cod liver oil from the chemist shop and mixed a hearty glassful for Jan to drink.

The two liquids had to be thoroughly shaken and drunk quickly before they separated again. After a couple of large glasses Jan started to feel woozy, so I suggested she lay down on my bed. She promptly passed out! I couldn't rouse her, and then Mum returned home! "What have you done to this girl?" Mum was not too happy. I tried to explain that we'd had just a couple of innocent gins and they must have gone to Jan's head.

After a short while Jan started to come around accompanied by some violent vomiting. Mum insisted that Jan should stay the night with her, as she was in no state to ride home pillion on my scooter. I then had to ride to Jan's mum to tell her what was happening. After telling Gladys that Jan had become unwell and that Mum was looking after her for the night, Gladys took the news very well and even ventured the cause as "It's probably her time of the month". *If only she knew* I thought to myself!

When Jan's next period didn't occur, she went to her doctor for a pregnancy test. He told her to return in a week's time for the result. On the evening of Friday the 22nd of November 1963, I was sat with Jan in the large waiting area of her doctor's surgery. The room was full of the predictable quota of pale, pensive faces and a background chorus of sniffles and coughing when Doctor Cormack burst from his surgery. He was a short tubby man and he stood breathless in the centre of the room. "I've just heard on the radio that President Kennedy has been shot!" he announced to everyone.

Before this unimaginable news had had time to sink in, he beckoned to Jan and me to follow him into his room, "And your girlfriend's pregnant!" he added to us. At the time I wasn't too sure which piece of news shook me the most? There was Kennedy, this young, fresh Democrat, who'd stood up to the Russians over the

Cuban missile crisis, even seeking advice from our ageing Prime Minister MacMillan, shot, gone! And here was my seventeen-year-old girlfriend expecting our baby, and myself, a third-year apprentice earning only £8 a week! How the world changes in a flash!

They say that bad things always happen fast, but it wasn't all bad. I'd always thought that one day Jan and I would marry; we just had to do it sooner than I'd expected. Looking back, it's difficult to imagine the prevailing attitude to pregnant brides. It was regarded as a disgrace almost, certainly a stigma that you didn't want broadcast, very different to today's outlook, so we had to act fast.

As Jan was under the marriage consent age of eighteen, we needed the written permission of both her parents. Her mum was no problem, but her dad was living in Australia; we sent him a telegram straight away. Jan's two brothers, Mick and Graham, had just returned from Australia, and I'd been a bit nervous as to how they would accept me, particularly as I'd unintentionally but prematurely obliged them to become uncles.

I needn't have worried as they were both very supportive and positive. They'd both led quite a sheltered life under their father's dominance. Although slightly older than me they were both quite callow and naïve, but also generous and hardworking guys. Their main concern was how to buy a decent suit each for the wedding!

I was also apprehensive about telling Mum and Dad. I chose a night when Mum was going out and then suggested to Dad that we go down to The Avenue pub for a beer. After about five pints I still hadn't plucked up the courage to tell him. We tottered home and finally over a nightcap of a tot of whisky, I blurted it out. We were both a bit tiddly and got the giggles.

By the time Mum came home we were hysterical with laughter. Mum, unfortunately, didn't see the funny side but was more practical, suggesting that Jan and I came to live in the house in Granville Street until we found a place of our own. Dad's final observation at the end of the evening was to say, "Well, you won't be breeding any giants!" as Jan was quite petite.

We'd had a telegram back from Jan's dad giving his consent, so the wedding date was set for Thursday 5th December, less than two weeks since we'd had Jan's pregnancy confirmed. I had to ask the firm's works manager, Alan Cunnington, for two days holiday from work. When I told him why I needed it he looked at me and said, "Put your foot in it have you lad?" I didn't want to be smart and say that it wasn't my foot that had got me into trouble, I just nodded and tried to look sorry for myself. "Don't worry," he said "I did the same myself when I was your age, you'll be fine," and with a fatherly pat on my shoulder he agreed to the short holiday time off, which was brilliant as we'd been in touch with Derek and Sheila, who'd invited us to their flat in London for our honeymoon.

The wedding ceremony at the local registry office went off very smoothly, apart from Jan's mum proposing that she and Jan would walk from their flat in Alfred Street, almost two miles away, to the registry office, as *she* had on her own wedding day! I insisted on arranging a limousine to pick them up. Jan looked lovely in a black and white check suit topped off with a white pillbox hat.

After the ceremony, our small wedding group walked over to The Wellington Hotel, now The Station Hotel, on Bruton Way. It was still early – around 11 a.m. – and the pub had just opened. I remember it smelled awful of disinfectant as the cleaners had just finished. We all had a quick drink then Jan and I caught the train to London. Mick had written 'Just Married' in lipstick on our carriage window so we had the carriage to ourselves the whole journey.

Lewisham does not sound overly glamorous for a honeymoon destination, especially sleeping on a put-you-up in your brother-in-law's living room, but Derek and Sheila made us very welcome and we had a fabulous time. In four days, we managed to see and do so much. As well as another visit to the theatre, this time to see the musical *Pickwick* with Harry Secombe blasting out his showstopping *If I Ruled the World*, we also got to the Astoria cinema to see, in jaw-dropping Panavision 70 mm, *West Side Story*. An amazing experience with the entire audience bawling their eyes out at the end, including me!

We also met up with my workmate Neil and his girlfriend for an evening. They were regular visitors to London and took us to a couple of interesting pubs, one of which, Dirty Dicks on Bishopsgate, is still there. Nowadays it's a smart tourist eatery, but when we were there it was still maintaining its Dickensian heritage. It had a dirt floor, hundreds of cobwebs dangling from the low rafters above your head and inches of thick dust everywhere; a bit like home really – only joking!. The other was The Blue Boar on Leicester Square, now a touristy gift shop. There they had a huge wheel of cheese on a tree stump, with a dagger next to it for you to help yourself. These vignettes reinforced our love of London and my determination to one day move there. We took the train back to Gloucester on the Sunday evening; Dad was there at the station to meet us and drive us back to Granville Street to start our married life together.

Chapter 5

A Barman and Two Babies

The first three months of our married life we spent living in Mum and Dad's house at 22 Granville Street. As I've written about in chapter four, if a girl got pregnant before she was married it was regarded as a social disgrace, a stigma, and a minor scandal that generated a disproportionate amount of local gossip. To that end Jan and I hid her confinement for as long as we could. At the company Christmas party that year Jan wore a tight corset under a slim fitting dress to keep the gossipmongers guessing. We even won the Twist dance competition together, although I can take little of the credit, being gifted with the proverbial two left feet, whereas Jan was a naturally talented dancer.

A young married couple living with parents is not an ideal arrangement. Overall, we all made the best of it, but Jan and I were daily scanning the local classifieds, searching for an affordable place of our own. On a combined income of not much more than ten pounds a week, this was not an easy task. Buying a property was out of the question, apart from not having saved enough for a deposit, at that time you couldn't own property until you had reached the age of twenty-one; I was nineteen, and Jan only seventeen. As we were soon to become a family this created an added difficulty as most flats on the market operated a 'no children' policy.

Eventually, after several tearful disappointments we got lucky. A friend of Mum's daughter, Tanya, was moving out of a small flat in

Pembroke Street and suggested we go around and view it before it was advertised.

The neighbourhood appealed to me for several reasons: it was very familiar to me as it was just two streets away from Goodyere Street where I had spent a few years of my childhood; I had happy memories of selling my firewood bundles to the houses in these streets; I had attended the local Widden Street School as a junior, and my gran had lived nearby.

It also attracted me as it had changed quite dramatically since we'd moved away and was now regarded as a 'black' area, a ghetto almost. This may seem a strange appeal but it was prompted by certain current events. For some time I'd had seconded to me at work a young guy, the son of an owner of a printing company in South Africa who was a friend of our company chairman, Charles Priestley.

Bob Sinclair had been assigned to me as we were the same age. He was working with us to gain experience before rejoining his father's firm in Cape Town. Bob and I got on very well, I liked him a lot; we socialised together all the time. Our only difference of opinion was on apartheid. Bob was a white Afrikaner with a fervent racist conviction. He argued that apartheid was the only answer to the racial situation. I couldn't accept this.

Neither could I accept what was happening at that time in America. Very recently in the southern state of Alabama, George Wallace had been elected governor on a segregation ticket, provoking riots and deaths throughout the state when he barred black students from enrolling in university. When I remonstrated this with Bob, his response in his thick, guttural Afrikaner accent was an astounding, "en iducated bleck is a dangerous bleck"! I could not accept this thinking. Only months before I had been captivated by Dr Martin Luther King's *I Have a Dream* speech, and I wanted my children to grow up in a mixed environment without preconceived notions of racial differences. So it was with this attitude that I jumped at the chance of a flat in Pembroke Street.

The interview for the flat was quite bizarre. The house was owned by an old lady, Mrs Baker, who lived with her son, Paul. They were one of the few remaining white families in the street. Mrs Baker was very old, probably in her eighties; her son Paul was in his early thirties but looked a lot older, in fact he could have easily doubled for the comedic actor, Charles Hawtrey, famous for his roles in the earlier *Carry On* films.

When we arrived to view the flat Paul invited us into their small front sitting room, where we met the elderly Mrs Baker who was sitting crouched in front of a small twin bar electric fire. After our introductions he showed us up to the flat on the first floor. It consisted of just two unfurnished rooms. The small front living room also doubled as a kitchen; there was no sink, just a Baby Belling twin hob stove. The other room off the landing was the bedroom. Beyond this there was a bathroom which we were all to share. Paul's bedroom was one of the attics on the second floor above us, and Mrs Baker slept in the middle room on the ground floor next to their sitting room.

They had a small breakfast room on the ground floor with a tiny scullery next to it. It was all rather impoverished and depressing, but the main appeal was that Paul and his mum had no objection to a baby in the house, besides which Paul seemed a very nice bloke. However, just as we were leaving and saying goodbye to Mrs Baker, she looked up and told us that Tanya, the outgoing tenant, had cooked extra food to give her and Paul a meal every day, and she hoped we could continue with that service! This was a bit of a blow as Jan and I weren't sure if we could afford to feed ourselves let alone two more mouths. I also doubted the Baby Belling's capabilities not to mention ours. In spite of this we decided to take the flat, particularly as the rent was only £2 a week.

It was the spring of 1964 when we moved in. Jan was beginning to 'show' but continued to work. She had changed jobs and was now working as a sales assistant for a wholesale tobacconist, Charles Dickens Ltd, which was on Eastgate Street near The Cross. She was earning slightly more than she had been at Currys but our joint income still wasn't enough to live on, let alone save enough for a deposit on a home of our own. We budgeted very carefully; we even had a shopping list of our week's groceries pinned on the back of a cupboard door, with the total not allowed to exceed three pounds!

My Lambretta had long since given up the ghost with a busted gearbox and lay rusting at the back of Mum and Dad's house. I was using my sister, Molly's old Hercules bicycle to get to work and back. Paul was very understanding and sympathetic towards us. When we moved in, he reassured us that we needn't provide meals for him or his mother and was quite apologetic about her expectations. He became a very good friend and we regarded him as part of our family.

The neighbourhood proved just as colourful as I had anticipated. The flat was in a row of terraced houses; our next-door neighbours on one side were a Jamaican couple, Scotty and Vi. On the other side were a Polish family, Felix and Margaret. A large house opposite was home to a series of itinerant boarders, mainly from Africa and the West Indies. Up and down the street was an assortment of families predominately from the Caribbean.

These early arrivals of the largely West Indian diaspora were very different to the second and third generation, more anglicized citizens that we see today. They were extravagantly colourful, often sporting loud Hawaiian shirts, wide baggy trousers and wide-brimmed fedora hats; so gregarious that they would stop their car in the middle of heavy traffic to shout a greeting to you. It was not unusual to see two friends holding a jovially raucous conversation from either side of the street to each other. It was just as well that Jan and I didn't mind the singer Jim Reeves, as each Sunday morning he was blaring from the open window across the street from our living room, although I'll be more than happy if I never hear *I Love You Because* again!

This was all so refreshingly different to the reserve of my compatriots. I was very happy in this environment, unlike some of my fellow countrymen who felt resentment and regarded the influx as an intrusion.

It did become more difficult later with the arrival of immigrants from Pakistan and Bangladesh as we didn't share the common denominator of our cultural attraction to pubs and alcohol. I did make good friends with a young accountant from Pakistan, Ayub, who lived around the corner. After an evening together in our flat, I found him outside retching secretly behind our hedge. He was embarrassed and apologetic; he said it wasn't the beers I'd given him; it was the pork sandwiches I'd thoughtlessly been serving him. Even though it was strictly against his religion, he'd been too polite to decline them.

To supplement our meagre income, I took an evening barman's job at a local pub, The Mason's Arms. It wasn't ideal finishing work at 5 p.m. dashing home and grabbing a quick bite then off to work again until gone 11 p.m. but at least it enabled us to save a small amount each week. We had a savings account at Lloyds Bank on Eastgate Street. Jan and I often met up at lunchtime; we'd sit in Lyons Corner House on Northgate Street, making a cup of tea and a slice of cake last long enough to fill the lunch break.

On one occasion neither of us had any cash at all. We checked our Lloyds savings bank book which was holding forty pounds and one shilling. A cup of tea at Lyons was sixpence. We didn't want to break into the lovely forty pounds we'd managed to save, so I persuaded Jan to ask the teller if we could withdraw just the one shilling! I was too embarrassed to ask the teller myself so I hid lamely behind one of the impressive pillars that the building boasted. After a moment Jan returned clutching the one shilling coin to enable us to buy the two cups of tea. I asked her if they had minded her withdrawing just one shilling. Jan said that the teller had rebuked her saying that the bank normally liked to receive seven days' notice for large transactions! Wonderful that some people keep their sense of humour.

It was now getting close to the baby's arrival. In preparation for the birth Jan had been attending relaxation classes with Scotty's wife Vi from next door. Vi was pregnant with their first child and hers was due at the same time as ours; I thought it was wonderful that our kids would grow up together. We'd made a space for a carrycot by the side of our bed and Jan had her small suitcase packed and ready to go. When the baby still hadn't arrived ten days after the due date, I'd virtually given up and almost forgotten about it. So at 3 a.m. on 14th June when Jan woke me to say she was getting uncomfortable pains I think I suggested she try to go back to sleep.

When it became apparent that this finally might be the moment, I raced upstairs to the attic to wake Paul as he'd offered to drive us to the hospital. He shot up and bundled Jan and me into his old Wolseley car. By now Jan's pains were becoming much more forceful and frequent. She was writhing in severe discomfort.

Before the modern high-rise building that now stands on Great Western Road, the Great Western Hospital was a series of sprawling, single-storey, wooden and brick huts. We were met at the door of the maternity wing by a nursing sister who led Jan inside. The sister turned to me and told me to go home and telephone later in the morning; husbands, in those days weren't allowed anywhere near the actual birth. I must admit that I was quite relieved as I was exceedingly apprehensive around hospitals, a faint-heartedness I carry to this day. I awoke later that morning and ran around to the public telephone box that stood on Park Road next to Gloucester Park. I was told that all went well and that I had a beautiful baby daughter – prior to the invention of ultrasound scanning, the gender of your unborn was unknown until birth. I was also told that I could visit that evening.

The large maternity ward held around twenty beds which were all curtained off for privacy during visiting hour; a nurse pointed out where Jan was. She was sore but in good spirits and I was surprised that there was no baby around. The babies were all together in their cots in a crèche next to the ward and I was told I could visit our baby later when I was called!

Halfway through visiting hour a bell rang and a nurse announced in a sonorous tone "Fathers, it's baby time!" I peeked out through the curtaining to see about a dozen men bashfully stepping through their curtained areas and sheepishly making their way towards the crèche; I joined them. We all shuffled into the small nursery searching for a cot with our name tag on it.

And so it was, around 6.30 on that balmy summer evening I got my first glimpse of my daughter. Several of the babies were protesting tearfully, but this proud father's was sleeping peacefully. Jan and my thoughts were now focused on deciding upon a name.

Earlier in the year we'd settled on the name Juliet if the baby was a girl, but recently the British pop group The Four Pennies had released a single entitled *Juliet* which had reached number one in the charts a few weeks earlier. As we didn't want it thought that we'd been influenced by this song we had to decide on another name. Neither of us was religious, but despite its biblical connection we both loved the name Rachel, quite uncommon at the time. So it was Jan and Rachel that Paul and I drove back from the hospital some ten days later.

I was still only in the fourth year of my apprenticeship taking home about £8 a week. I was grabbing every overtime opportunity and still working most evenings as a barman at The Mason's Arms. Jan had stopped working to have the baby so we were always skint.

Again, my thoughts turned to joining the police force. I was now eligible to enlist as a constable as I'd reached six feet in height. I was extremely tempted as the starting pay was fourteen pounds a week with a guaranteed pension of two-thirds of your salary after thirty years' service. I calculated that I could retire at forty-nine with a nice income for the rest of my life.

Dad was aghast that I would consider breaking my apprenticeship. He implored me to finish and have my indentures to fall back on. At work, my journeyman, Pete, told me that I would be his "biggest disappointment to date" if I quit before gaining my indentures. It was a difficult time. I was forever borrowing money from my workmates to see us through the week. I was eventually persuaded to stay and see my apprenticeship through until the end. It was a hard decision but I enjoyed my work and thought I could see a future with it. I took an extra barman job, working weekends at the Parkend Hotel on Parkend Road and we muddled along.

My brother Pat had left school and taken a job as a farmhand on a 1,000 acre farmstead at Sandhurst on the outskirts of Gloucester. He kept us amused with stories of his work there. One of his many tales concerned the toilet arrangements on a farm; of course, there were none! So one of his first experiences was learning to squat down behind a hedgerow. Unfortunately, he was wearing a one piece set of overalls, so he had to unbutton the complete front of the garment and pull it right down behind him around his ankles. Having finished his business he hauled up his overalls back up over his shoulders, only to discover to his dismay and disgust, that his 'droppings' had all fallen into the collar of his apparel and were now all bespattered on the back of his neck!

There's an interesting epilogue to the farm at Sandhurst. Six years later in the General Election of 1970, Jack Diamond, a treasury cabinet minister was ousted from his safe labour seat of Gloucester after twenty years' service. The Conservative candidate, Sally Oppenheim, won the seat by appealing to the housewives of Gloucester. She campaigned on a bicycle, cycling round the street with a basket of provisions attached to the handlebars, calling out the high cost of groceries under a Labour government.

She was married to a London businessman, Henry Oppenheim. They bought the 1,000-acre farm at Sandhurst – where Pat had worked – because as Mrs Oppenheim explained, her "husband has always wanted to go into farming". Within months they'd successfully applied for planning permission to eradicate the farm and build hundreds of houses on it. Few people in Gloucester would have known that the Oppenheims were domiciled in The Bishop's Avenue in North London, also known as Billionaires Row, the richest street in the world. I did ponder at the time that working-class wives generally performed more menial roles, whereas rich men's wives could become members of parliament. Thank goodness things since then have moved in the right direction, particularly for women.

Our life over the next six months fell into a regular, steady pattern, and we adapted nicely to our new addition. Jan proved to be a very capable mum, and even though I remember the first four weeks as being quite testing, with four-hourly feeds and endless nappies we soon arrived at the more rewarding age of returned smiles, happy gurgling and grateful nights' sleep.

By Christmas that year we discovered that Jan may be pregnant again. This was confirmed early in the new year with our second baby's arrival due in August. When I happily informed my mum of our good news, she accused me of "breeding like a rabbit"! This wasn't quite the response I'd expected but she soon welcomed the news and was almost as excited as we were. We had been gifted an old wooden cot which I'd repainted and was now Rachel's bed, squeezed next to ours in our small bedroom. Her little carrycot could now be used for the new baby, and further squeezed on the other side of our bed.

Our second baby arrived with an even quicker birth than Rachel's. From memory Jan was in labour for only four hours until little Claire arrived. Again, thankfully, I was not permitted at the birth. Paul, our landlord, babysat 14-month-old Rachel while I had my first visit to our second child. She was so tiny, weighing in at less than six pounds. So now I had two gorgeous baby daughters and we were a family of four.

When I returned home from my hospital visit Paul handed me Rachel saying, "I think she's done something"! I took Rachel realizing she needed her nappy changing. I'm ashamed to confess that I'd never changed a nappy before as Jan had always taken control of that chore. This was long before the advent of disposable nappies. A nappy seemed almost as big as a bath towel, but a lot more complicated, especially to a beginner. Baby Rachel was lucky her tummy wasn't skewered by the alarmingly large nappy pin used to fasten the ends together.

It was around this time that old Mrs Baker died. She'd been unwell and in a part-time care home for some while. Paul very generously offered us her old bedroom for us to use as a nursery bedroom, we jumped at this as he wasn't charging any extra rent for the room. I set about redecorating it. After I'd scraped all the old wallpaper off and repainted the woodwork, I was tempted to write some cheeky graffiti on the bare wall with my white paintbrush, prior to hanging new wallpaper. I thought it would be amusing to Jan and Paul and some future decorator. So in large type I painted "HELP, WE ARE THE LAST WHITE PEOPLE IN THE STREET!"

Just as I was standing back admiring my work, our front door opened and Scotty, our Jamaican next-door neighbour walked in. Before I could stop him, he'd stepped into the room to see how the decorating was going. I was so embarrassed at this silly prank and immediately regretted the mischief. Fortunately, Scotty had a great sense of humour; he saw the funny side and roared with laughter. I do remember making that wall the first to cover with the new wallpaper.

Chapter 6

Undertakings and Undertakers

As well as the new baby's nursery giving us a bit more space in our bedroom, Paul also let me have the use of the small rear attic that was next to his bedroom. I was soon putting it to good industrious use.

One of the old designers at work had come across an original catalogue of the Great Exhibition of 1851. The exhibition had been housed inside a colossal glass structure built specifically for it in the middle of Hyde Park. It was over 500 metres long and over a hundred wide. It had been organized by Queen Victoria's husband, Prince Albert, and showcased all that was modern at the time as a celebration of the industrial revolution. The building itself was an architectural marvel and was nicknamed the Crystal Palace.

The exhibition ran for six months; when it finished the entire building was relocated to an area near Sydenham in south London, and the suburb was renamed Crystal Palace, sadly the building burned down in 1936. Inside this heavily illustrated catalogue were four engravings that caught my eye. They were line drawings of early Victorian Landau and Brougham carriages, like those the queen uses on state occasions. I thought how impressive these would look if they were silk screen printed in a white raised gloss ink on a textured, linen, black background card, with a white frame around them. Sold as a set of four, they would make a wonderful wall decoration.

I copied them on the big gallery camera at work, and using my new attic workshop, made photo stencils and assembled the silk screen frames from which to print them. A printer friend at work, Kenny Manning, agreed to print a sample set for me in his loft at home. I bought the framing material, thin strips of wood, from a timber merchant and set to, mitring the corners, gluing the frames together and painting them white.

Within a few weeks I had a complete set of sample pictures. I took them to the department store, Bon Marché and met one of the store's buyers. He liked them and thought they would sell well, especially for the Christmas gift market. He said he could take up to a hundred sets. I was chuffed, not least as I was selling them for a pound a picture, four pounds a set, a total order worth £400 – a fortune!

Going into mass production presented problems that I hadn't anticipated. The frames alone took weeks to assemble with all the mitring, gluing and nailing, and then they still had to be painted. Kenny was happy to print the order if I could help him.

Night after night we clambered up into his loft, bent over crammed against the roof rafters, our eyes streaming from the acrid cellulose ink that we were using in such a confined space with no ventilation. Attaching the frames to the prints and the backing board proved equally arduous and even more time consuming. Eventually, after several months work, the job was completed and I headed off to the Bon Marché to discuss delivery.

I hadn't discussed delivery packaging with the buyer but was confident that we could resolve that issue once I'd confirmed completion of the job. I arrived at the store and sought out the buyer. He greeted me with a puzzled expression on his face which was a bit disconcerting. I reintroduced myself, reminding him of my wall prints product.

"You're too late," he said, "We're a week before Christmas, the market's over, merchandising is dead now."

I was aware that the job had taken far longer to accomplish than I'd first anticipated, but I'd completely lost sight of the importance of the retail deadline. I was shattered, distraught, totally gutted. What could I do? I thanked him and left. Somehow, I had to find the money to pay the joinery and Kenny, and work out what the hell I was going to do with 400, white-framed, carriage wall prints?

That Christmas, every relative, friend, and even casual acquaintances received a set in their Christmas stocking, which managed to offload a few. In the evenings after work I roamed the streets of the neighbourhood with the remaining, peddling them door to door. I managed to sell enough to square my debts, the balance remained, for a long time stacked up in the attic workshop.

Despite this setback I was determined to go after money-making opportunities. I had got to know a local personality, Chas Phipps. Chas had started his working life as a schoolteacher in the Forest of Dean. He was also an accomplished entertainer appearing in local clubs, performing, of all things, as a ventriloquist act! He eventually established his own club, The Dolphin Club on Worcester Street – nowadays an Indian restaurant stands on the site.

The venue was quite exceptional for its day. It was not only a boutique theatre restaurant, but also had several floors of gaming, including roulette, blackjack, and a salon privé for poker. Not least among the attractions were the many variety cabaret acts that performed there, including Les Dawson, Bob Monkhouse and Val Doonican; quite impressive for Gloucester at that time.

In his leisure time Chas was a champion water skier. He was the first person to water ski the Severn Bore, and even held the world distance record when he skied the River Severn from Lydney to Gloucester, some forty miles!

Chas approached me for help with all the printing and promotional requirements for his new Dolphin nightclub. He needed menus, posters and stationery, etc. To produce all this Ken and I needed proper premises as his loft would no longer suffice. We managed to rent a small lock-up shop front in Alvin Street. It was owned by a lovely Italian man, Mr Boselli, who had an ice cream manufacturing business in Gloucester. He kept a room at the back of the shop for storing all his ice cream ingredients, sugar, eggs, flavouring, etc. and we had the use of the shop area at the front of the building.

The large windows at the front of the shop were whitewashed over so no one could see inside, but the premises were overlooked by the eleven-storey Clapham Court tower block opposite. Both Ken and I were anxious not to be seen going in and out of the building as we were still employed by Priestley Studios. Every weekday evening, after clocking off from work at Priestley's we would cycle round to Alvin Street and furtively let ourselves in, making sure we kept our backs to the tower block opposite. Safely inside we could start our night's work.

I had rigged up a vacuum table to make the photo stencils of the images required, and Ken was set up with all the silk screen printing paraphernalia. Most of our work was for Chas and his Dolphin Club, predominately posters, signage and general advertising material.

We were still using fast drying cellulose inks for most of the work, but the downside of this was the noxious fumes they gave off during the printing. By the end of an evening, in the confined space that Ken and I were working in, with no ventilation, our eyes were streaming so badly we could hardly see each other!

To add to our woes, after a couple of months toiling in this poisonous environment, Chas hadn't paid us for any of the work that we'd delivered. Every time I tried to get what was owed by visiting his nightclub, I was told he was either not there or too busy to see me. Things were getting quite desperate as we had no money to pay Mr Boselli the rent that we owed so I decided to pay Chas a visit at his home.

It was pouring with rain, coming down like stair rods on the Saturday morning I cycled the several miles out to his house. He lived in a beautiful, detached 1930s property on tree-lined Wellsprings Road, Longlevens. By the time I arrived there I was pretty well soaked but I was cheered to see his large Mercedes saloon car parked in the driveway, and better still, Chas was sitting behind the wheel. I jumped off my bike, ran up to the car and tapped on the windscreen. The driver's door's electric window slid smoothly down, "Hi Chas, have you got a cheque please, I'm desperate and I need to pay…"

"Sorry Colin, really busy right now, gotta dash…"

With that, the window slid back up and Chas took off. Adding insult to injury I hadn't realized that I was standing in quite a deep puddle, and now I could feel the water soaking through to my socks – I always had holes in my shoes, generally covered over with homemade cardboard insoles – and as the rear wheels of the Mercedes drove over the puddle a huge gush of muddy water splashed up dousing me.

If this wasn't enough, his car was towing a trailer carrying his waterskiing, luxury, motorboat. Before I had time to jump back, the wheels of the trailer also hit the puddle to give me a second drenching. I clearly remember standing in that driveway, soaking wet, watching the Mercedes driving off, feeling very sorry for myself and wondering how on earth I was going to pay the rent on our premises particularly as I'd recently received a request to contact our landlord urgently!

Gerardo Boselli was a lovely man. Like the Tartaglia family before him, he had also migrated from Italy to Gloucester where he strove to establish his ice cream business. Long before the bells and sirens of Mr Whippy and Mr Softy, these ice cream vendors would drive around the streets of Gloucester shouting out their wares for sale.

It wasn't unknown for Mr Boselli to drive his van right into a school playground to allow the schoolchildren leaving for the day access to his vehicle away from the potential danger of busy road traffic. He was always generous with his portions and would often offer a wafer or broken cornet to a child with no money. How he would react to a tenant who couldn't pay his overdue rent, I was about to find out.

The rain had stopped and I had dried out by the time I walked round to his house later that day. He lived not far away in a grand four-storey, bay-windowed, brick, semi-detached house facing the park on Weston Road. He greeted me with his customary big smile and invited me into his front sitting room.

The decor was amazing. It was a high ceiling room typical of the period, but with an extremely unusual, if not outlandish feature. Occupying one complete corner of the room was an enormous Cotswold stone structure. Stretching from the ceiling to the floor it was a backdrop to a cascading waterfall! It was hideous and Mr Boselli was obviously very proud of it. It was a tad overstated for my taste.

"Nowa," he said in his heavy Italian accent, "youa boysa, giva me a biga problem."

I was about to offer my apologies and explain the difficulties I was having getting paid from our biggest client, when he went on, "My ice a creama, issa tasta funny! Eesa no gooda!"

I was obviously looking quite perplexed.

"Eesa your inka, issa make a sugar bada."

I now realized what he was referring to. The overpowering smell of the cellulose inks we were using was permeating through into his back storage room and polluting the sacks of sugar stored there.

"Isa so sorry boysa, but youse has to stopa worka."

It was amazing how good-natured and apologetic he was being about it all. He even waived the outstanding rent, which was incredible considering we could have ruined his business by poisoning his ice cream!

Incidentally, the money that I was trying to extract from Chas was around £75 – doesn't sound much now but it equates to approximately £1,000 in today's money – and I never got a penny. I think The Dolphin Club eventually went bust, but Chas went on to become quite the impresario bringing bigger named stars to various venues in Gloucester.

The Boselli Ice Cream Company ceased trading back in 1989 and sadly Mr Boselli died in November 2008. These days all that remains of his company is a large painted advertisement on the end terraced house at 58 Priory Road where it all began. It can still be seen as you drive west along St Oswald's Road, a fading memory of a business and a lovely man who I'll never forget.

****

Baby Rachel had taken her first, wobbly unaided steps at the early age of ten months. As a proud dad I naturally assumed that she was advanced for her age. So when her baby sister Claire arrived, Rachel seemed, to me anyway, to be even more grown up. As a two-year-old toddler she appeared quite independent. I was babysitting Claire on a Saturday morning while Jan had gone shopping, taking Rachel with her.

I was busy painting the front door, when Rachel arrived home on her own telling me that she had "lost mummy". I wasn't particularly concerned, more impressed that she had managed to find her way back alone. It didn't occur to me that Jan would be going frantic. I went back to my painting, when half an hour later, an ashen-faced Jan arrived totally distraught, crying that she'd lost Rachel. It had happened in a split second when she had turned her back to pay for some groceries and Rachel had wandered off. I felt guilty for not realizing how terrified Jan would be, but this was nowhere near the blind panic that I would be experiencing a few months later when I nearly blew the house up!

Meanwhile, as spring turned to summer, I'd managed to scrape enough money together to buy a second-hand, ageing Standard 8 van, which I was going to need to undertake another business idea which I'd been chewing over for a while.

Gloucester was surrounded by some very picturesque country pubs. I'd often thought how perfect they would look printed as a line drawing onto a Christmas card, and sold to the publican as their very own personalized cards to post out. Silk screen printing lends itself to short runs and I calculated that a minimum order of fifty cards could be produced quite economically.

I worked out that if I took a photograph of the pub, then made a black and white print to the size of the Christmas card, Neil at work, who was quite a talented artist, could trace a pen and ink drawing from it. I could then use this tracing to make a photo stencil and create a silk screen frame with the image. Ken had agreed to print them, back up in his loft. Neil was charging me £1 per drawing, and Ken would charge the same to print them.

I planned on charging £5 for fifty cards netting me a princely £3 per order for my efforts. Five pounds was an enormous amount for Christmas cards working out at over two shillings and sixpence each when at the time you could buy cards for less than a couple of pennies. However, I was fairly confident that as a very personalized card, also promoting their pub, I shouldn't have too much difficulty in persuading publicans to order them.

I needed a sample to show potential customers so I chose The King's Head at the foot of Upton Hill on the outskirts of Gloucester. After photographing it and making the print I passed it on to Neil for the sketch. Within a few days he handed me back the pen and ink drawing on tracing paper from which I made the photo stencil and transferred it onto the silk screen frame. A few days later Ken delivered a few sample printed cards with the image. We also created a goodwill message from the landlord and landlady inside the card, further personalizing it.

Early the following Saturday morning I drove out to The King's Head to seek out the landlord. I must admit I was quite nervous about what his reaction might be as I'd talked the project up so much in my mind that a negative response would be a huge disappointment.

I needn't have worried. He couldn't have been more enthusiastic, not even baulking at the £5 price tag. He even asked if it were possible to have the drawing enlarged and framed to hang on the bar wall as he liked it so much. Needless to say, I was delighted and immediately booked my permitted two weeks annual holiday so I could sell my Christmas card concept.

Having fatefully chosen one of the hottest two weeks on record, selling Christmas cards during that sizzling hot summer was going to be quite a challenge! Many a landlord couldn't give me the time of day when they were running out of cold lager and their ice machines had broken down. But I persisted and I couldn't have been happier, occupying my time with my two favourite pastimes, selling and pubs!

In spite of the incongruity of selling Christmas cards in the middle of summer I had tremendous success. Travelling between Wotton-under-Edge to the south and Tewkesbury to the north, even venturing into the Forest of Dean to the west, and Bourton-on-the-Water to the east, I took over fifty orders in the two-week holiday.

A lot of the pubs required more than the minimum order of fifty cards. Some of the larger establishments like The Royal William at Cranham and The Red Lion at Wainlodes ordered two hundred cards plus enlarged framed pictures for their walls. The average order was more than double my minimum forecast. Producing all the cards took all of September and October so I was able to deliver them throughout November.

On completion I was several hundred pounds in profit, a small fortune for my efforts which ensured that we would all have a wonderful Christmas that year. The London rock band, The Kinks' currently released hit, *Dead End Street*, with which I had at first so haplessly identified, particularly the line: "…two-roomed apartment on the second floor. No money coming in, the rent collector's knocking, trying to get in,…" no longer seemed quite so applicable!

The reference to 'rent collector' in the above lyrics compels me to recall an awful tragedy that occurred that summer. Paul, our landlord, had become quite ill with what appeared at first to be a particularly nasty bout of biliousness. After several days of being confined to his bed I called his GP out, who diagnosed his illness as gastroenteritis and suggested that it would just take its course.

A week later with no sign of improvement, and Paul becoming very weak, I called his doctor out again. A different GP from the practice arrived and after examining Paul suggested he only needed "plenty of fresh fruit and fresh air" and would recover. Following another week of, by now, almost continuous nausea and vomiting I called his doctor out again. This time a third GP from the practice arrived and pronounced the same diagnosis as his colleagues.

When I informed him that the only food that Paul could stomach were the small bowls of porridge that Jan was feeding to him and we were getting very concerned, he patted my arm patronizingly and assured me that there was no cause for alarm as "there's a lot of this about" and Paul will get better.

As I mentioned earlier Paul was more than a friend, he had become part of our family. He had a brother and two sisters who all lived in Gloucester but never visited him, nor he them. He had no friends that I was aware of and since his mother had died, Jan and I were his only social contact. He always joined in our celebrations and was a permanent guest at our Christmases and birthdays. We were extremely fond of him not least for his kindness, generosity and understanding for our often dire financial situation every time our rent was overdue. It was therefore with gathering alarm that we watched his deterioration.

Finally, I called in my own GP to visit him. It was with some reluctance that Dr Bickmore arrived, explaining that it was rather unethical for him to examine someone who wasn't his patient. However, after examining Paul he also concurred with the other GP's diagnoses and assured us that it was just a stomach bug and that Paul would recuperate. A few days later, with Paul fighting for breath, I called an ambulance.

Paul was admitted to The Royal Infirmary. I visited him later that day and spoke with a young registrar who'd examined him. He told me that Paul had suffered heart failure! He said it was immediately recognizable by the curling round of his fingernails, a symptom of heart disease called clubbing. He explained very sympathetically that they suspected a diseased heart muscle and there was little that they could do for that.

Dr Christiaan Barnard's world's first heart transplant was still over twelve months into the future; Paul would have been the perfect candidate. Two weeks later, on the 3rd September, Paul died; he was only thirty-four years old.

There was little point in bitter recriminations with the four general practitioners who'd each misdiagnosed him. It wouldn't have made any difference to the outcome, except that Paul would have received professional care much earlier. For a while though, it certainly changed my opinion and shook my confidence in family doctors.

Something else that shook Jan and I was the behaviour of Paul's brother and two sisters. In the week between Paul's death and his funeral they descended on our home like a trio of vultures, rummaging through every room, squabbling over the division of Paul's belongings. At one point we heard a mighty shriek of triumph when one of his sisters found his Co-op card with his personal number which would enable them to bury Paul with the Co-op Funeral Directors and then 'collect the dividend'. It was all so shameful and added to our distress in our period of mourning.

What further distressed us was being told that they would be selling the house and that we would have to look for new accommodation. On top of this they seemed surprised to be told that we would be attending the funeral as they didn't expect there to be many mourners. I telephoned Paul's workplace, the head office of The Midlands Electricity Board, and suggested to one of his colleagues that they might like to attend Paul's funeral.

The following Saturday, the chapel at the Coney Hill crematorium was packed, with standing room only at the back. We gave Paul a wonderful send-off accompanied by exuberant hymn singing and his favourite *Enigma Variation*, much to the obvious surprise of his avaricious siblings.

When I mentioned to someone at work that Paul's brother and sisters were selling the house and we'd have to move, I learned that this was not necessarily the case. I was told that I was a 'sitting tenant'. Prior to 1989 a residential tenant was protected against eviction should the property be sold.

This was providing your landlord wasn't the infamous Peter Rachman, who'd amassed hundreds of properties around west London during the 1950s and 60s. He was notorious for overcrowding his properties and employing thugs to bully and intimidate his tenants when he wanted them out so that he could sell. Fortunately, we didn't have that problem.

I sought legal advice and had it confirmed that not only could we not be evicted but also the value of the property was worth considerably less with us in it than it would be with 'vacant possession'. It was further recommended that we make an offer for the house thereby securing it at a much reduced price to market value. This was an extraordinary opportunity for us and we decided to give it a go. I met with Paul's family and put the proposition to them.

They had obviously received similar advice regarding us being sitting tenants and had accepted that the house was worth less. With Jan and I as the buyers there was the attraction of avoiding estate agent's fees. Based on similar neighbourhood properties we agreed on a value of £2,500 but a purchase price to us of only £1,400. This represented an incredible windfall enabling us to gain our first step on the property ladder. We'd saved enough for a deposit, £70, thanks in part to my successful pub Christmas card enterprise, now all we had to do was secure a mortgage. Surprisingly, this was going to prove a lot more difficult than I expected.

Long before building societies demutualised and became banks, and banks started offering mortgages, the only organization that could assign a mortgage was a building society. The only building society that served Gloucester at that time was The Cheltenham and Gloucester Building Society from their main office just inside Westgate Street.

So it was to this august institution that I applied for our loan. They turned us down! I was shocked, we'd satisfied all the criteria regarding deposit and income, and certainly the price of the house represented excellent value; I couldn't understand why we'd failed their preconditions.

I marched into their office and asked to see the manager. He told me that he wasn't at liberty to disclose why we'd been turned down. I had my suspicions so challenged him that it was the fact that the house was in a "black area...the wrong side of the railway tracks" – there was a railway line that ran along the bottom of the street parallel with Midland Road. With that he stood up and stated in his most officious voice, "this society is not prepared to explain its lending policies". Then he showed me the door.

Accusing him of being a racist in charge of a racist organization probably didn't help him reconsider his decision. Quoting the recent Race Relations Act cut no ice either, as it wasn't until 1968 that the act was further amended to include employment and housing. It wasn't that uncommon to see signs outside boarding houses that read "No Blacks". Hard to believe in this day and age.

Fortunately, I was introduced to a mortgage broker who found us a lender in Newport, Monmouthshire; a small branch of the Bradford and Bingley Building Society. They were either unfamiliar with the ghettos of Gloucester, or simply not as racially reactive as the Cheltenham and Gloucester Building Society.

The upshot was that we were about to embark on a new year as the proud owners of our own house, and the monthly repayments of just over £10 were little more than the rent had been for three rooms. Happily, I could now relate more to a Kinks line released earlier that year *Sunny Afternoon*, "…And left me in my stately home".

Chapter 7

A New Job and Old Friends

Even though it was absolutely marvellous to own our own home; three stories, bay windows and effectively five bedrooms – if you counted the attics – the house was quite dilapidated. It had been built at the turn of the nineteenth century and needed a lot of work to bring it up to date.

As I didn't have the spare cash for these renovations it was going to be a long job. The ground-floor breakfast room and scullery were in a particularly bad state. There was a crumbling corner chimney breast above a disused fireplace, rising damp reaching up all the walls, and a floor with most of the Victorian, tessellated tiling either cracked or broken or missing completely.

I persuaded Dad to come around to help me to remove the chimney breast. It was quite a job as the brick structure continued up through the bathroom above, which needed supporting with wooden bearers hidden in the ceiling. The finished result gave the room a lot more space and could now be changed from a cramped breakfast room to a reasonably sized kitchen one day; in fact, it was another three years before this breakfast room became a kitchen!

Dad was living around the corner in a tiny 'two-up-two-down' terraced house in Twyver Street. He'd bought the house after he and Mum had separated and sold their house in Granville Street. He was in the process of building a bathroom onto it and generally improving and converting this modest abode into his 'little palace'. Pat had gone to live with him, and Dad had also got himself a girlfriend!

Florence Mather, Flo, was a divorcee with three children all in their teens. Flo had a bit of a 'reputation' as it was rumoured that during the war years she had been a bit liberal with her affections having a penchant for American servicemen. Whether true or not such gossip could be quite damaging and revealed a lot about the provincial attitudes that prevailed at the time. Now, around the same age as Dad in her early fifties she wore dyed peroxide blond hair but still carried a trim figure, so it wasn't long before she moved in with Dad along with two of her teenage children.

Dad was very fond of Flo, not least because she was a good cook, and he said she made the best gravy he'd ever tasted! Strangely this last titbit of information caused Mum not a little chagrin when I related it to her, although I certainly didn't impart to her an incident that Dad had confided to me concerning a curious bite. Evidently Flo and Dad had been having an afternoon nap after a session in the pub followed by a roast Sunday lunch, accompanied no doubt by Flo's delicious gravy. They were getting dressed when Dad noticed a rather unsightly bite on Flo's upper thigh. He told me that he remembered being quite passionate when first getting into the bed but couldn't recall committing such a carnal deed. He felt it necessary to point it out to Flo. On seeing the mysterious imprint, the puzzle was solved. "Ooh," she cried, "I've been laying on me false teeth!"

Dad's house was always busy. When my brother Pat wasn't staying over, there'd be a workmate of Dad's, Bill Turton, nicknamed "The White Hunter" as he originated from Rhodesia – now Zimbabwe – plus there'd be Flo's two teenage kids, Clive and Jenny. Clive was notorious for regularly breaking into Dad's gas meter to steal the stash of two-shilling coins; Dad always forgave him.

I enjoyed strolling round on a Sunday morning to join Dad for a few beers. Before wine bars and dining out became fashionable, pubs were the predominant venue for recreational entertainment. Much more than just places to drink alcohol, they were the social hub of a neighbourhood. Cosy and friendly, often with an open fireplace burning merrily away, patrons mingled to catch up with local news, gossip and enjoy jovial banter. They were – and still are – prolific in every town and village across the land. I walked past at least six on my way to Dad's, and he lived less than half a mile away.

Pubs have been part of British culture for centuries. Most of the storylines in the English soap operas, *Coronation Street* and *EastEnders*, centre around their two pubs, The Rovers Return and The Queen Victoria. In the 1960s women were rarely seen in pubs, particularly on a Sunday lunchtime. They were expected to be at home preparing the lunch for their menfolk; a far cry from today's liberated ladies.

The pubs at that time were only open from midday until 2 p.m. on a Sunday afternoon, so every minute was critical. Often things were a bit chaotic when I arrived at Dad's as he'd be hurrying to get himself ready. Once, having forgotten my watch, and noticing that the clock on the mantelpiece appeared to have stopped, I asked Dad how late we were running. He looked up from struggling with his shoelaces, looked at the clock and said that it was only five to twelve so we had plenty of time.

As the hands on the clock were reading five past three, I asked him how he had worked that out? He explained that the clock was still working. It was just that winding it up one morning his finger had caught the big hand and it had snapped in half, making it smaller than the small hand, so now the small hand was really the big hand and the big hand, the small hand! As a further complication an adjustment also had to be made allowing for the clock gaining up to forty minutes a day. He maintained it was still possible to tell the time from it fairly accurately. I was gobsmacked but I guess this was typical of Dad's delightfully shambolic household.

We would either walk to The Windmill, which was the old railwayman's pub I mentioned in chapter one, or around the corner in Millbrook Street to the rather disreputable County Arms. 'The County' was renowned for its cider, boasting over fifty different varieties, many of them on draught. The draught cider was stored in huge barrels behind the bar, and served by the landlady's son, Cocker.

Cocker Jones was built like the proverbial 'brick shithouse'. He had forearms like Popeye and the gait of a silverback gorilla; there was always a minor air of menace about him. It was whispered that he'd once killed a man by beating him to the ground then reversing a truck over him. This was more likely an urban myth; I wasn't game enough to ask him to affirm it!

Cocker's mother, 'Ma' Jones, chased around Gloucester on a very tall lady's bicycle. She was a tiny woman who'd lost all her teeth. At closing time in the pub, she delighted in throwing all the doors open and herding all her patrons out through them, shrieking, "C'mon, I've had all yer money, now bugger off home!" When asked how old she was she'd screech, "Forty-seven, backwards!"

The patrons themselves were a motley bunch; years of drinking cider, commonly from their own personal, pint-sized, chipped, china mugs, had given most of them impressively bulbous, blue-tinged noses and prodigious paunches.

One Christmas Eve some years later, Flo arrived in tears at The Windmill telling Dad that Cocker had not only evicted her from the pub, but he'd also barred her from ever returning. All this, she said, just for singing in the bar!

Pat told me that Dad had confessed to him that later that night when the pub was shut, Dad walked round carrying two house bricks. He calmly stood outside the public bar and hurled each brick through the two large engraved glass windows. An uncharacteristically shocking act of vandalism which, I have to say, took guts as he would have known the huge risk he was taking, with Cocker living above the pub, not to mention the man's alleged history!

****

My apprenticeship had been completed nearly eighteen months earlier in October 1965. Even though I was now earning a full journeyman's wage I still needed to supplement it by working evenings behind the bar at the Parkend Hotel.

A New Job and Old Friends

Money was still tight and there weren't many opportunities for overtime work at Priestley's as the volumes of work there had reduced dramatically. But it still came as an awful shock one morning at work when the general manager's son, David Parsons, who worked in the office, came into the darkrooms and handed me an envelope. With hardly a glance at me, he thrust the envelope into my hand, mumbled, "Sorry, Colin," then turned and scurried out.

I'd been made redundant! In the middle of June 1967 with a wife, two toddlers and a mortgage to maintain I found myself out of work. Priestley's only gave me one week's notice and not even my full entitlement to redundancy money paying only half, saying that I didn't qualify for five of the seven years I'd worked there as I was only an apprentice.

At twenty-three years old, for the first time after eight years of full employment, I found myself at the Labour Exchange – forerunner of a Jobcentre Plus – signing on for the dole; an awfully demeaning experience made worse as there were few prospects for the unusual occupation of a camera operator.

After five weeks of enduring a sense of being unwanted and undervalued my trade union found me work. Until the mid-1980s the printing industry was very much a closed shop, so employment was obtained almost exclusively by a print union. The union that I belonged to – the Society of Lithographic Artists, Designers, Engravers and Process Workers (SLADE) – had found me a job in the process darkrooms of the Evening Advertiser newspaper in Swindon.

I was very thankful for the employment and grateful to my trade union. Of course I didn't know at the time that some five years hence my opinion of trade unions would reverse when I sat on the other side of the fence.

To celebrate my new job, I decided that it would be a 'grown-up' idea to take Jan out to dinner. There were few restaurants in Gloucester in the mid-1960s; a Lyons cornerhouse teashop, a rather grubby Indian parlour specializing in curried eggs, and a Golden Egg franchise that catered for every egg platter *apart* from curried!

It Was The Best Of Times...

A few weeks previously I had run into an old friend, Dave Morris, who had been an apprentice designer at Priestley Studios, the same company where I served my apprenticeship. His father had recently bought an old pub up in the Cotswold Hills and had taken Dave out of the company to train as a chef. Dave said to me that if ever Jan and I wished to try out their new restaurant that he would look after us.

Prior to the late 1980s few provincial British pubs sold food. So for Dave's father to open a restaurant attached to a country pub in the 1960s was, as *Yes Minister*'s Sir Humphrey might suggest, "a courageous decision". The Royal William on the Cotswold escarpment was miles from the nearest village.

I had visited the pub before and even produced their Christmas cards, but I had never ventured into its rather elegant restaurant. In fact, I had never experienced dining in a formal establishment. We were shown to our table by the dinner-jacketed maître d' who addressed us as sir and madam! I was relieved that I was wearing the suit that I'd bought for our wedding, and that I'd checked myself from calling *him* sir!

Negotiating the enormous menu provided the next challenge. For the first course we eschewed the soups as too mundane – we were living on Heinz tinned soups at home –instead selecting prawn cocktails which seemed the height of exotic sophistication. The mains proved more difficult. Deciding on the sirloin steaks as the least expensive dish on offer, I was surprised when the liveried waiter asked me how I would like my steak!

"Oh, er, nice and tender please," I remember responding.

Jan added "well done" so I thought that she was congratulating me on my assertiveness before realizing that she was requesting the cooking time. When Dave stepped out from the kitchen in full chef's regalia suggesting we try our steaks medium, he ensured that we enjoyed a fabulous meal, topped off with a fashionable crêpe suzette which he personally flambéed at our table.

A New Job and Old Friends

Years later, having enjoyed hundreds of meals in some of the world's finest restaurants, I still have fond memories of my first fine dining experience.

****

Swindon is nearly forty miles away from Gloucester, so I was looking at an eighty mile a day commute for my new job. My old Standard 8 van had just about given up the ghost, so I needed something more dependable. A semi-derelict bomb site at the back of Barton Street probably wasn't the best place to look for a reliable second-hand car.

Three Cocks Motors occupied half the alleyway and part of a razed area, courtesy of Hitler's Luftwaffe. Possibly the dilapidated setting caused the shining, white Austin Mini Cooper, complete with chequered 'go-faster' stripes, to catch my eye.

I should have been a little more wary of the proprietor. Surveying his empire from his decaying caravan 'office' was the Arthur Daley[6] of downtown Gloucester; the quintessential spiv, complete with pencil-thin moustache and brown trilby hat. All he needed was a cashmere overcoat and a Terry McCann sidekick minder to complete the picture.

Nevertheless, I was hooked; a short test drive later and I was signing on the dotted line. The deposit took all my redundancy money but I convinced myself that it was worth it and that I definitely needed it for my upcoming commuting.

Before the bypass was built in 1988, the old road to Swindon began at The Twelve Bells pub at Witcombe, obliging you to negotiate the precipitous gradient of the mile long Birdlip Hill. From there it was a straight Roman road passing through Cirencester at the halfway mark. The first few journeys were uneventful, although I had noticed that the mini appeared to struggle a little on the steepest part

---

6. Arthur Daley was the lead character in a British comedy drama about the London criminal underworld called *Minder* which started in the late 70s. The name Arthur Daley became synonymous with a dishonest salesman or small-time crook.

of the hill but I paid little attention as my thoughts were always on my new job.

There were only four of us in the process department and we alternated each week in the different sections: camera, blockmaking, engraving and a klischograph which gave the work some agreeable variety. The klischograph was a very early scanner. It was a huge electro-mechanical engraving machine which cut a halftone image directly onto a metal plate, thereby producing an instant block for the press. My experience on it would prove invaluable later in my working life.

My new colleagues were a mixed bunch; two of them were good fun, one in particular, a cockney from East London, was always ready with a funny quip or an amusing line of banter. Sadly, the one charged with being our foreman was not so funny, in fact he was quite an unpleasant character. I didn't take his criticisms of me or my work personally as he denigrated everyone equally. My cockney colleague told me that the person that I had replaced had quit because of the foreman's continual condescension and abuse.

He further confided in me that his personal retribution on the foreman was to dribble some of his own piss into the man's coffee when he made it for him. I made a mental note never to upset my cockney friend or accept a coffee from him!

A more emerging problem was my car as the journey up Birdlip Hill was becoming more problematic. Although the car performed beautifully on the flat, it became apparent that it was the clutch that was slipping, noticeably on the final steep stretch of the hill.

I returned with the car to the bombsite dealer. Naturally 'Arthur Daley' feigned surprise and innocence and concluded that if there was a problem it must have been caused by my supposed rough treatment of the car!

As I couldn't afford to replace the clutch my only option was to avoid the Birdlip Hill and take the longer route via the lesser gradient on Crickley Hill. The consequence of this was my timekeeping

A New Job and Old Friends

at work became less reliable incurring further disapproval and reprimands from the foreman.

After three months and now being compelled to take the train to work, the commute became too arduous. Frequent absenteeism using lame excuses provided the company enough justification to sack me. I wasn't sorry. I sold the car to a friend of Jan's brother, Graham, who was aware of the engine defects and was prepared not only to repair it but also to soup it up and race it.

In November I managed to score two weeks work back at Priestley's for holiday relief, then, remarkably, there appeared a display ad in the Citizen newspaper for a camera operator.

The job advertised was by a company, Gloucester Design Services, located on the trading estate at Hucclecote. The company had been founded by three directors from the Gloucestershire Aircraft Company when it closed. Its main business was in the production of maintenance manuals for fighter aircraft, but it was eager to break into more commercial markets.

My experience in four-colour process work was of special interest to them and I was not only offered the job at the conclusion of the interview but was invited to attend with Jan the company's Christmas party which was to be held later that week. The date coincided with our fourth wedding anniversary, 5th December. When I mentioned this to Mr Draper, my interviewer, he insisted we come to the party, which was being held at the then fashionable Guptill Manor at Tewkesbury.

On the night, he'd organized the band to strike up the Anniversary Waltz, and Jan and I were cajoled into leading the first dance! I managed my left feet shuffle once around the dance floor consumed with acute embarrassment after which, fortunately, we were joined by the rest of the guests.

There were a good bunch of workmates overseen by the director who'd interviewed me, Ron Draper. Ron was a really nice bloke who'd had a rather unfortunate medical history. He explained to me one day that he'd been diagnosed with a tumour on his pituitary gland. Luckily, after a course of radiotherapy at the neurological hospital, Frenchay in Bristol, the tumour had gone into remission. Sadly, this was not before the tumour had caused the extremities of his body to grow unnaturally large, leaving him with huge hands and feet, and a disconcertingly long nose!

Despite a pleasant working environment and friendly colleagues, the work itself was very boring. My days mainly consisted of shooting black and white line images; repetitive batches of exploded diagrams of arcane engine parts. These uninspiring workdays were offset against a fresh social scene with the renewed acquaintance of some old school friends.

I'd bumped into my old mate Dave Whitmore who told me that he'd seen a notice in the personal column of the Citizen newspaper. The notice was for a reunion of the class of 1960 of our old school, The Crypt Grammar. I'd left the school in '59 but thought I might know some of the old boys as we went through at the same time.

The reunion was to be held at The New Inn on Northgate Street. I always thought the name 'The New Inn' was an unfortunate misnomer as the inn dated back to medieval times, so was at least five hundred years old, hardly 'new'!

In 1968 The New Inn boasted fourteen different bars; the reunion was being held in one of the smaller ones, The Olde Bar. These days this bar has been incorporated into the now fashionable real ale 'Old Tap and Barrel Bar'.

I arrived with Dave to find two faces I instantly recognised, Roger Davis and Brian Merrett. There were several others there but these two were more familiar. I'd first met Roger, or 'Podge' as he was affectionately nicknamed, at Lindon Infants School when we were five years old. We'd continued as classmates until I was moved to Widden Street School when I was nine.

It was at Widden where I met Brian; we discovered much later that we were second cousins as it was his ill-fated Uncle Alec who had been married to my homicidal Aunty Kitty!

A New Job and Old Friends

The three of us had progressed through secondary school at the same time, with our comradeship fluctuating through varying degrees of attachment as is customary in adolescence. I remember as a twelve-year-old Podge helping me with my homework one afternoon at his house.

He was an only child of very middle-class parents. They lived in a beautiful detached home on one of Gloucester's wealthiest streets, King Edwards Avenue. Their living room had French windows opening onto a manicured garden.

Podge's mum served us sandwiches made with 'real' butter! I told her that my family only had butter on a Sunday. I'm sure she regarded me quite pityingly. On one occasion Podge admonished his mother for attending to us with purple stained fingers. She apologised explaining that she had been pickling beetroots.

I recall thinking that had I reprimanded my mother similarly, I would most likely have received a slap on the backside. Sadly, Mrs Davis died very young leaving the rest of Podge's upbringing to his lovely dad, a very conservative, white-collar professional gentleman.

I'm indulging in these reminiscences as both Podge and Brian were to become very close friends over the following two years while I remained working in Gloucester. Subsequently over the ensuing years we have maintained a distant friendship but not missing any opportunity to meet up whenever circumstances allowed.

It was through this reunion with Podge that I became reacquainted with several more school friends. This circle of friends began meeting regularly on a Thursday evening in a corner of the lounge bar of the Parkend Hotel. The pub used to boast one of the finest lawn bowling greens in the country. When googling it recently I saw with dismay that ugly townhouses have now been built on this once picturesque site; even the pub itself looks like it's been converted into flats.

However, back in 1968 every Thursday evening there would be anywhere between four and nine of us together. As well as Podge and Brian, there was Tongo, Harold, Bone, Roy, Fergie and Stacker all enjoying each other's company, telling jokes, pulling each other's leg, and always ending the evening with a raucous singsong, all washed down with countless pints of Mitchells and Butler's Brew XI bitter. I think it was Podge who first named our group 'The Buds' and that moniker has persisted throughout the years.

It must be some kind of unique rarity that The Buds, to this day, still meet up for a drink together every Thursday evening! A few, like myself, have moved away; we lost one, John Collier, to prostate cancer; and there are a couple of new additions, including sons of originals! But the core group is still going strong. The venues have changed over the years and the alcohol consumption has become more moderate along with the singing, but the friendship and camaraderie are unchanged.

When we first met up at the reunion at The New Inn, I was the only one who was married. Of all the other buds only John Collier had a girlfriend even. Consequently, when I suggested that he and I go out for the evening with our partners, introducing the expression, 'a couples do' it temporarily put several noses out of joint, but may inadvertently have spurred on the others to seek girlfriends for themselves.

Those were halcyon days. Besides our Thursday evenings at The Parkend, often a group of us would meet on a Monday evening to visit a village pub up in the Cotswold hills surrounding Gloucester. The Royal Oak in Painswick, The Bear at Rodborough, The Black Horse at Cranham, The Adam and Eve at Paradise and many others all received our patronage, often with the evening ending with us stumbling through hay meadows collecting glow worms!

As more girlfriends were added to the mix there were more parties. Our home at Pembroke Street – known to The Buds as 'The Hedge' as it was the only house in the street displaying a hedge, albeit a scraggy apology for a decent privet – was the rendezvous for many get-togethers.

On winter weekends there were enough buds to field regular soccer and hockey teams; not my preferred sports so I was happy to be the official photographer. On the long summer evenings, we played limited over cricket matches and tennis tournaments. It wasn't long before the girlfriends became fiancés and the weddings soon followed.

In 2016, while visiting England for my granddaughter, Emme's wedding, I joined The Buds on their Thursday night get-together. They say that if you love someone, you don't see them age, they always appear the same to you. To an outsider we were just a group of old men, to me it was like being transported back to 1968, a band of young Turks, never a bunch of old farts.

Chapter 8

Renovations and Relocation

Although my job at Gloucester Design Services was reasonably well paid, I continued to endure mind-numbingly boring work. I managed to arrange a lift into work every day by another old school friend, Phillip Moss, who also worked for the company. He was a technical illustrator, responsible for drawing the exploded diagrams of engine parts which I had to photograph. He passed by the bottom of Pembroke Street on his way to work every morning. I used to wait for him at the roundabout opposite the war memorial to hitch my daily ride.

After several months with Phil I'd managed to save enough for my own transport. A lovely Polish man who lived opposite us was selling his old Austin A35 van. It had seen better days but it was running and it was cheap so I snapped it up. It was perfect for running around town picking up bits of building materials as I'd started renovating the house.

I had decided to create a one-bedroom flat occupying the whole ground floor. I could then enlarge our accommodation upstairs to a two-bedroom flat on the first and second floors. I had the ambitious notion that this might be the beginning of a property empire! I even imagined that renting out the ground-floor flat would quickly pay down the mortgage allowing us to buy another similar house; repeating the process until we owned five houses all converted to flats and rented out. We would then live in a mansion and I would be driving a 3-litre Rover saloon car. This was a dream I harboured and inspired me in my renovating labours.

I began by decorating the two attic rooms, Jan and I could then move into one which would become our bedroom leaving our old bedroom to be converted into a kitchen. The rear attic I converted into a bedroom for Rachel and Claire. The front attic room had been Paul's bedroom.

When we were clearing out his old bed, we found on the floor behind the headboard, disturbingly, an enormous pile of cigarette ends. Evidently Paul would lay in his bed smoking, and when finished simply drop the butt end over his head behind him. We could see that the cigarette ends had never been stubbed out, they would have been still alight when he discarded them. It was a miracle that he never burned down the house.

It was while I was working on our new kitchen that *I* almost created a major disaster. The main gas pipe ran under the floorboards servicing a gas heater in the next room. I had bought a second-hand gas stove and was intending to position it in the corner of the room. I had lifted the floorboards beneath it but realized I would need the expertise of a skilled gas fitter to connect the stove to the existing lead pipe.

As luck would have it a gas fitter was working at a house a few doors away from us. He agreed to help me with this minor undertaking, and the job only took him a few minutes. Leaving me to replace the floorboards his parting words warned me to be careful and not put a nail through the underlying gas pipe. *As if I would do anything that stupid*, I thought to myself!

Banging the final nail in, I realized to my alarm that I had carelessly positioned the nail too close to the centre of the board, below which the gas pipe was laying. Re-lifting the board to check whether I had missed the pipe, I found to my horror that I had not only hit the pipe, I had penetrated right through it and out the other side!

Stupidly, I then compounded the problem by pulling the board holding the offending nail, back out through the pipe revealing two large, neat round holes! The loud hissing sound told me that the poisonous, highly combustible gas was escaping at a frightening rate.

I ran downstairs to where the gas meter was to turn it off at the mains. The meter was located right at the back of a cupboard that ran underneath the stairs. Piles of accumulated household junk lay in front of me. Crawling over cardboard boxes, a broken ironing board, an unwanted clotheshorse and other domestic debris I found the meter. At the side of the meter is a small metal handle which turns the gas off. It was missing!

I struggled backwards out of the cupboard and raced back upstairs. Already the first floor was reeking of gas. I charged up to the rear attic room where the girls were having their afternoon nap. I scooped them both out of their beds, much to their distress, tore back down the stairs, sprinted out through the back door and deposited them, confused and crying at the bottom of the garden, well away from the lethal fumes.

Running down the street to the telephone kiosk only to find it occupied by a large gentleman. He gaped at this wild-eyed, frantic looking lunatic demanding to use the phone. The man looked so startled he made way for me immediately. The calm voice at the other end of the emergency gas number instructed me to bind some sticky tape around the holes in the pipe, and an engineer would be on his way.

I burst into the grocery store next to the kiosk, barged in front of a queue of elderly ladies and beseeched the surprised shopkeeper for some sticky tape, "urgently"! She didn't sell any! In the forefront of my mind I remembered that my brother-in-law, Graham, was popping round to visit that afternoon. I had left the front door wide open to allow the gas to escape. I pictured him arriving in my absence, walking upstairs to our flat and lighting a cigarette!

"Any type of sticky tape, anything!" I screamed. The ladies in the queue were all edging away from me, eyeing me nervously.

As the shopkeeper was shaking her head and backing away from the counter I had a moment of inspiration, "Sticking plasters, Band-aids"?

Snatching the box from her and shouting over my shoulder that I'd be back to pay later, I skidded out of the shop and dashed breathlessly back home. Fortunately, there was no sign of Graham, and the girls had remained at the bottom of the garden, albeit both in floods of confused tears.

The house was full of the noxious odour of gas. Holding my breath as best as I could, I crouched down to the damaged pipe, ripped open the box of band-aids and managed to attach a couple around the holes in the pipe. Immediately the loud hissing stopped. I threw open all the windows and went down to the garden to comfort the girls.

While explaining to them what a silly daddy they had, the engineer from the gas company arrived. I couldn't believe it! It was the same man who had helped me install the stove, and who'd warned me about nailing the floorboards. The look of bemused pity across his face said everything.

Reappearing from the cupboard under the stairs, he pointed out that the handle to turn the gas off had simply slipped off and was laying on the floor beside the meter! Had I not been in such a blind panic I would have seen it, and not needlessly upset the gentleman in the telephone kiosk, the shopkeeper and her startled customers, not to mention two shivering toddlers at the bottom of the garden.

While there were no further *major* incidents, tackling the ground-floor breakfast room and scullery did prove a lot more arduous than I had expected. I planned to convert the scullery into a bathroom, but first I wanted to make a kitchen out of the breakfast room. The walls were sodden with rising damp and both the floor and the old lath and plaster ceiling needed replacing.

Having helped Dad to hack down an old ceiling in Granville Street I knew how to go about it. Fixing the new large plasterboard sheets was a different matter. I enlisted the help of a builder friend of Dad's, Tommy Broadhurst.

I vaguely knew Tom as I'd seen him around, mostly in the local pubs. He was a small guy, probably in his late fifties, with the flushed, wizened face of a heavy drinker. He never looked strong enough to lift and manhandle the heavy eight by four-foot sheets of plasterboard which he had to attach to ceiling joists.

He squinted out through permanently bloodshot eyes which he said were caused by the amount of plaster dust constantly getting into his eyes. I rather imagined it was caused by the amount of grog that was constantly getting into his stomach. As part of the deal I'd agreed to act as Tom's labourer helping hold the sheets to the ceiling while he nailed them to the joists.

Tom was a chain smoker and kept a perpetual cigarette between his lips. Taking this as a signal I was also smoking a cigarette when we lifted the first sheet to the ceiling. I'd placed a long plank on two milk crates to enable us to reach the height we needed. I had both arms outstretched above my head holding the plasterboard sheet.

With a hammer in one hand and a bunch of nails in the other, Tom was about to hammer in the first nail. Positioning himself he backed towards me and his head knocked against my outstretched hand which was holding the board. It was also holding my cigarette!

At the same moment that his head knocked my hand, it caused my cigarette to drop from between my fingers onto his head. The large heavy sheet of plasterboard that I was struggling to hold tilted downwards to hold the burning hot, red-tipped, king-size Rothmans cigarette firmly against his thinning scalp.

Why he didn't drop the hammer and nails he held in his hands and push the board upwards and away, then simply brush the offending ciggy off, I don't know. Instead, belching bestial grunts and snorts he swivelled his head backwards and forwards attempting to dislodge it.

I was a helpless observer, standing at the other end of the sheet using all my strength and energy just holding it above my head, watching this amazing firework display as red-hot embers and sparks burst out from between his head and the board showering around his shoulders like a mini volcanic eruption.

Eventually after much cursing and head gyrations he succeeded in extinguishing it. When examining his charred and blistered scalp afterwards, it didn't really help when I suggested he was lucky I didn't smoke big cigars!

Renovating the breakfast room continued over a long time, the walls had to have the old plaster stripped away, then coated with a black sticky tar-like substance to hold back the damp. Batons could then be attached and fresh plasterboard installed and skimmed over with thistle plaster.

Jan's brother, Graham, helped me replace the old floor. The broken tiles were all dug up and replaced with aggregate then concreted over. Finally, a cheap linoleum floor covering finished the job. The result probably wouldn't stand up to the scrutiny of a current television renovation programme's standard, but for its day it fit the bill. The conversion of the scullery into a bathroom would take a while longer.

Meanwhile my heart sank every morning as I prepared to drive to work. I'd been with Gloucester Design Services for nearly three years and was now desperate for a change. I still cherished a strong ambition to break into sales.

I started writing unsolicited applications to all the major photographic film companies; Kodak, Ilford, Agfa, 3M, Fuji and DuPont. Most of the replies stated that they only employed salesmen with experience and a proven track record. I was in a catch-22 situation. Finally, the sales manager from 3M offered me an interview. Even though he couldn't offer me a job he appreciated my dilemma and advised me to read as many books on sales as possible, suggesting that this could count in my favour at future interviews. I had no idea that there were any books on selling.

A visit to the library opened my eyes. There was an entire section devoted exclusively to selling. Being a regular and avid reader, I devoured them all. I even waded through the incredibly comprehensive *American Textbook of Salesmanship* (7th edition!) which included such details as the ideal salesman should be a minimum six feet tall, well-manicured and coiffured, with a whole chapter devoted to the perfect handshake.

I learned much later that a lot of this was nonsense as of the two best salesmen that I employed, one was a short, tubby, Indian gent with a goatee beard, and the other was medium height and balding. I've since discovered that the best attributes for a salesman are product knowledge and sincerity.

Around June 1970 a full-page display ad in the trade journal, *Printing World*, caught my eye. It was for sales demonstrators for a company called Crosfield Electronics which was based in Archway in North London. The advertisement stated that the company was launching its revolutionary Magnascan film scanner and was recruiting camera operators and retouchers. I wrote off immediately. Within days I received a reply inviting me for an interview.

The address was 766 Holloway Road. I planned the route from my treasured *A-Z of London* atlas and set off with some excitement in my A35 van. From the Caledonian Road I joined Holloway Road about halfway along its length and scanned the buildings for numbers. Having no idea what to expect I was looking out for a small workshop.

Being the main A1 in and out of London, the Holloway Road is one of London's busiest thoroughfares. Passing through Holloway the road is lined with major stores and numerous smaller shops. There is a massive art deco Odeon cinema, then seemingly miles of period terraced housing interspersed with the occasional church and pub.

Suddenly to my utter amazement, ahead of me standing apart from its surroundings was a six-storey magnificent modern building with the eponymous company name in huge letters emblazoned high up on the south facing side of the structure.

I'd never been inside such a lavishly appointed building before. I learned that this building housed just the offices and the demonstration suites. Where all the scanners and press controls were assembled was across the road in the main factory. I presented myself at the reception desk and was invited to take a seat. I settled myself onto one of the many leather sofas and took in my surroundings.

The stylishly hessian-lined walls of the spacious area were hung with a collection of large colour photographs of the exciting range of equipment that the company produced. The centrepiece of one wall consisted of two impressive plaques signifying the company winning the Queen's Award to Industry; one for technological innovation, and the other for export achievements.

After years of backstreet sweat shops and trading estate factories I recognised that I was at the focal point of professionalism and opulence. This company was at the forefront of my industry's creativity and ingenuity; it was intoxicating.

After a few moments I was greeted by the head of the photographic department, Brian Banks. Brian was about my age, twenty-six, with an attractive affable manner which immediately put me at ease. He showed me to his office on the first floor. During our introductory small talk, it transpired that Brian was from Bristol and had even attended the same school of printing that I had, albeit a year ahead of me. This affiliation certainly seemed to do no harm to my prospect of employment, quite the opposite.

Towards the completion of the interview Brian was encouraging me with the affordability of house prices out in the suburbs where he himself lived, although £6,000 for a semi-detached house in High Barnet seemed a fortune to me. However, the starting salary on offer was £1,900 pa, nearly twice what I was currently earning. But it came as a bit of a blow when Brian informed me that the job on offer was not exactly in sales, it was for a demonstrator, specifically for the company's recently unveiled Magnascan scanner.

He sensed my disappointment and hastened to explain that nearly all the company's salesmen had first been an equipment demonstrator. He went on to add that due to the high cost and technical complexities of their products it was essential that their salesmen had a comprehensive knowledge and expertise on the machinery. He then offered to show me this latest revolutionary Magnascan.

Back down on the ground floor, through a doorway off the main reception was the Magnascan demonstration suite. The entrance foyer was furnished with black leather settees surrounding a coffee table. There was a well-stocked drinks fridge and a coffee percolator. A long modern light box displaying several sets of sharp looking, four-colour film separations was fixed to one wall. Beneath the light box was the outlet of the drying unit of an automatic film processor.

At the end of a short hallway was the door to the Magnascan room itself. By the time Brian had finished enthusiastically expounding its many functions, I was completely overawed. This machine could produce in forty minutes what it took me, using the old gallery camera at my present firm, three days to complete, I couldn't wait to get my hands on it!

I shook hands with Brian and headed back to Gloucester. He had told me that he did have more applicants to interview but he was looking to recruit at least three or four candidates and would write to me soon. I felt cautiously optimistic.

Back home in Gloucester Jan was as excited and enthusiastic as I was about the possibility of moving to London. Finishing the conversion of the ground floor to a self-contained flat became a priority.

I calculated that I needed about £100 to decorate and install a bath, wash basin and toilet in the old scullery, and I thought I knew where I could raise that amount.

Opposite the Gloucester Leisure Centre on Eastgate Street – what is now a Salvation Army second-hand clothes store – used to stand a branch of Lombard Banking Ltd, at the time the largest chain of finance houses in the UK. Their window carried posters of happy couples simpering over fistfuls of five-pound notes, with copy lines extolling the simplicity of raising a loan.

I met the manager and explained what I needed the loan for. I filled in the required paperwork and he said that they would review the application and let me know in due course. I mention all of this as it forms the genesis of one of the spookiest coincidences I have ever experienced in my whole life. More will be revealed shortly.

About a week after my interview in London I received a letter from Brian. He was pleased to inform me that I was a successful candidate and I could commence work with Crosfield Electronics in early August. Our next challenge was to find somewhere to live in London. We decided to spend a weekend exploring the areas around Crosfields to find out what was available and how much the current rents were. To do this with six and four-year-old little girls would have been very difficult, so Jan's mum, Gladys, offered to have them stay with her.

Gladys – Nana Bullock – had divorced Jan's dad some years before, and he had returned to Australia. She had remarried a lovely chap called Stan Bullock, whose surname was quite appropriate as he earned his living driving cattle trucks. They lived in a small cottage on the banks of the River Severn on an outlying farm at the edge of the remote Rea Village.

On a sunny Friday afternoon after work I drove Jan and the girls out to her mum prior to us heading off to London for the weekend. I still hadn't heard back from the manager at Lombank as to whether my loan application had been approved. This information was vital as it would affect not only what we could afford to pay in rent but also how soon we could commit to a lease in London.

Leaving Jan for a while to get the girls settled with their nan, I headed back towards Gloucester in search of a telephone kiosk to phone him. The Rea Village is at the termination of miles of single-track no-through road, which runs between open farmland following the course of the River Severn half a mile to its north.

I was convinced there was a kiosk at the next village, Hempsted, several miles away. I was mistaken; not wanting to be driving to London too late in the evening I gave up and headed back to the Rea Village to collect Jan.

Halfway back in the middle of nowhere a car had pulled over and there was a man looking over a gate into a field. On the off chance that he might be a local and would know where the nearest telephone kiosk was, I stopped to ask him. I called out to him and he turned and came towards me.

I could hardly believe my eyes! Of all the weirdest serendipitous occurrences, this had to beat them all. It was the manager of the finance company, the man who I was desperately trying to reach by phone! Sadly, there's no happy end to this story. He was quite indifferent to the amazing coincidence and advised me that from his recollection my application had been turned down.

Despite this setback Jan and I carried on with our trip to London. We needed to see what was available in the residential rental market. It might have been an option to sell our house in Pembroke Street and look immediately to buy in London, but we felt we wanted to test the water first.

We stayed with Jan's brother Derek and his wife, Sheila, who had moved to a house in Sidcup, South London. He suggested we sign up with various rental agencies. We spent all Saturday and most of Sunday looking around areas close to Crosfield in Archway. We had no idea of the geography of North London, nor the social demography, so it was a bit dispiriting discovering that this neighbourhood and its surrounds in the Borough of Islington in this period before gentrification, was rather disenchanting.

Many of the endless rows of Victorian terraced housing were cracked and decaying, telephone kiosks were vandalised and stank of urine, and the pubs seemed populated with ugly, surly customers. It became apparent that this would take more than a weekend to resolve. Crosfield had offered to put me into a guesthouse for the first week, after that I'd be very much on my own.

We returned to Gloucester with mixed emotions. On the one hand I was on the threshold of fulfilling a lifelong ambition to work in London with the opportunity of finally getting into a sales career. On the other, the move presented all sorts of challenges and difficulties, not least the prospect of being separated from my wife and young family. I had already handed in my notice to Gloucester Design Services so now there was no turning back.

Chapter 9

Another Baby Another Job

London in the late summer of 1970 had an entirely different appearance and mood to the London of 2019. A glance at any footage of 70s London will give the predominant impression of a bad hair decade! Footballers wore their hair long and their shorts short. Fashions had changed. Mary Quant's famously designed daring mini skirt – named after her favourite car, the mini – was disappearing. Clothes were more colourful. Floral crop tops with big collars worn over high waisted, wide bottomed slacks, revealed high-heeled, platform footwear; and that was just the men!

The political scene had also recently changed. Against all the opinion polls a new Conservative government under the leadership of the youthful bachelor Edward Heath, had replaced the old Labour government of Harold Wilson on a mandate to reform the anarchic trade unions. The miners, dockers and postal workers had all carried out disruptive strike action for outrageous wage claims, forcing the new government to declare a 'state of emergency'.

None of these matters were on my mind on a balmy Sunday afternoon in August, as I drove away from my home and family in Gloucester in my little A35 van towards London. Crosfield's had arranged for me to stay for my first week at the home of one of their senior employees, Mrs Stevie Rogers and her family, in East Barnet.

Their house was an impressive detached, stone-faced building set back from the road and fronted by a large, neat, lawned garden. I arrived in the early evening to find no one at home. I parked my van on the street outside the house and waited. About an hour later their car pulled up. Full of apologies they explained that they had been held up driving back from their holiday home, a cottage in North Wales.

I'd never met anyone who owned two houses before, so they were obviously very comfortably off. Apparently, Mr Rogers was someone quite high up in the London Underground. I did amuse myself pondering his exceptional levitating skills to achieve that feat! They were both extremely welcoming which helped to settle my understandable anxiety. Next morning, I followed Stevie's car through the heavy rush hour traffic to Archway to begin my first day.

There is a saying 'bad start, good ending' which was certainly the case for me working at Crosfield. Knowing nobody in London except Jan's brother Derek, and his wife, and they had moved way out to Sidcup, I was expecting a company the size of Crosfield would have a huge social club, maybe supporting several sports teams. This would have provided an immediate introduction to new friendships and leisure pursuits.

Unfortunately, as the personnel manager explained to me on my first day's induction meeting, the sheer scale of London and the lengthy commuting times made after work get-togethers very difficult. Once staff had left work "they scatter in all directions" and apparently were reluctant or unable, due to distance, to backtrack for social gatherings. This was a real disappointment particularly as I was going to be on my own away from my family until I could find somewhere for us all to live.

Added to this initial letdown, Brian Banks, the manager from Bristol who had interviewed me was on holiday and away from the company for two weeks. I was placed in the charge of a Swiss installation photographer who, while a very pleasant guy, was obviously not too sure what he was meant to do with me.

I was also to discover that London pub patrons were not the friendly welcoming folk that I was used to. I put their reticence down to the fact that Londoners see so many people during the day on buses, trains and the underground, that when gathered in little cliques in their local pubs in the evening, they've no desire to expand their social networks any further, or maybe they just didn't like the look of me.

However, the five years that I was to spend working at Crosfield Electronics was certainly life changing and set me on the pathway to a more financially rewarding and exhilarating future than I could ever have hoped for. Sadly, it was to be at the expense of my provincial innocence, and eventually my marriage to Jan. But during those first heady months training on the scanners and meeting so many engaging colleagues, I could not believe how lucky I was to have landed such an interesting and stimulating job.

Nearly fifty years later I am still in contact with three other young recruits who joined at the same time as me – Pat Brownrigg, Dick Tibbitts and Pete Rogers. Dick, Peter and I worked together intermittently over the following thirty years and I cherish them among my dearest friends.

Although he was born in North London, as opposed to being born within the sounds of Bow's church bells,[7] Pete Rogers appeared to me to be the typical cockney. His broad London accent and confident manner coupled with the ability to articulate his strong opinions on most subjects immediately attracted me to him. At that time Pete was still single and living at home with his parents.

One day when leaving work, Pete and I were passing a local menswear shop. Pete stopped and pointed to a pair of trousers, "Nice strides," he said, "I think I might treat myself to a pair of those." I could only look on enviously. With a young family to support and a mortgage to pay I could only dream about the impulse purchases that Pete could make, but my time would come.

When Pete and I completed our training period we were assigned to training the staff of companies who had chosen to send their operators to Crosfield for in-house instruction. These

---

7. To be born within the sound of Bow Bells is the traditional definition of a London Cockney.

trainees, who were each with us for at least two weeks, came from all over the world. They often had only a smattering of English, so communicating was a challenge, resorting to sign language and even drawing pictures.

It was during this period meeting so many people from foreign countries that gave me a much broader outlook on life. This may sound strange but it came as quite a surprise to me that basically all people are the same. We all want the same things out of life; a family, a roof over our heads, food in our bellies and an occasional holiday. We even share the same sense of humour, laughing at the same things.

Coming from such an insular and parochial background this struck me quite profoundly and led me to believe that if we could only remove the bigotry and ignorance of each other the world would be a much happier place. This revelation all seems a bit naïve now but at the time it was quite an eye opener.

After my first week in London I moved out of Stevie Rogers' house and took lodgings at a friend of hers while I desperately sought a more permanent home that we could all move in to. Eventually, after a couple of months searching, I found an unfurnished flat in Burnt Oak just south of Edgware. It was on the first floor of a three-storey purpose-built block on the tree-lined posh *sounding* Montrose Avenue.

It was a small but self-contained unit which we soon decorated and made comfortable for ourselves. The second bedroom was so tiny it could only accommodate bunk beds for the girls, which fortunately they were very happy with. Their walls were soon covered with posters of Slade, Donny Osmond and the now infamous Gary Glitter – who would have forecast his ignominious demise along with the likes of Jimmy Savile and Rolf Harris?[8]

---

8. Glitter, Savile and Harris were international entertainers from the 70s disgraced with convictions of varying degrees in connection with child pornography or assault.

The block backed onto the abandoned Hendon Airdrome – now the sprawling and not too salubrious Grahame Park Estate – but at the time we were surrounded by lots of parkland and greenery.

Burnt Oak's tube station was only a five-minute walk away, so working in Archway everyday was fairly hassle free. My little A35 van had long since given up the ghost after the many weekend trips back and forth to Gloucester visiting Jan and the girls before I found the flat. The extra money I was now earning allowed me to complete the downstairs bathroom and kitchen in our house in Pembroke Street.

We could now rent out the property as two flats and had no problem finding tenants for them. The upstairs two-bedroom unit we rented to an acquaintance, David Ward, who I'd met when he was a customer of The Mason's Arms pub, when I was working behind the bar. I was to learn much later that I should have been more discerning and less trusting when renting to that tenant. The ground-floor flat went to a nice young newly married couple. We charged £5 a week for each flat which just covered our rent in London.

Those early days in London were quite special. The girls were happy in their new school, Goldbeaters Junior, which was only a two-minute walk away, and Jan had found a part-time job serving at Sketchleys, a drycleaner in Burnt Oak, plus I was earning good money and loving my work. We had the occasional visit from friends in Gloucester and nights out in London's West End; the original Marquee Club in Wardour Street and the 100 Club in Oxford Street were favourite haunts of ours. It even snowed on our first Christmas Day there!

Prior to celebrating our second Christmas in London Jan and I had decided to try for another child. By that Christmas her pregnancy was confirmed and we were excited to break our good news to Rachel and Claire. We waited until all their presents had been opened then sat them down to tell them what we thought would be the highlight of the day.

To our surprise they both seemed unimpressed as though our big announcement was matter-of-fact and happened every day. The news, that come the summer they would be having a new baby brother or sister left them unmoved, even impatient to get back to playing with their new Christmas toys.

Meanwhile I had grown in confidence in my work at Crosfield, although one training programme had tested me. Pete had moved on to the demonstration suites, and I was left in charge of training programmes. The company had invited a group of science undergraduates from the London College of Printing to attend the firm. They were to spend a week studying typesetting, one week in the press control division and finally a week in the graphic equipment division learning about scanners. I was assigned to educate them on the latter.

There were about eight or ten of them, all very bright and in their early twenties, not much younger than I was at the time. I was very apprehensive and nervous about my capability to command the attention and interest of such academic and knowledgeable students. On the first morning of the programme, Jan pointed out that my side of the bed was a mess of wrinkles and creases where I'd tossed and turned during a sleepless night.

As it transpired the week went very well. The company even received a letter from the college thanking me personally as their week with me on scanning had been the most rewarding of their visit. The praise was passed on to me by my divisional director, Ray Box. I could not have been prouder. Shortly after this I was asked to join Pete, working in the prestigious Magnascan demonstration suite.

The 1970s is often documented as a period of economic strife and social turmoil, which is only part of the story. Despite the many strikes, power cuts, high interest rates and inflation, working-class people were better off than they'd ever been. This was certainly the case for Jan and me. Colour televisions were replacing black and white sets. Fridges were standard, and many houses boasted the new-fangled microwave oven.

Aspiring middle-class suburban wives could wheel out the latest in-home entertaining, the hostess trolley, from which they could serve their guests a glass of Blue Nun white wine, before gathering around the shared fondue set. Long-playing vinyl records (LPs) were being superseded by tape cassettes. Motor cars were fitted with stereophonic tape decks allowing young drivers to listen to the likes of T. Rex's Marc Bolan or David Bowie's androgynous Ziggy Stardust.

Families could now afford to take a package holiday to Spain, unheard of in previous years. Like most other children at that time, Rachel and Claire's toy of choice was the ubiquitous 'space-hopper'. A large rubber ball with handles that they could sit on and bounce around the local play areas. Their favourite confectionery was a stick of chocolate coated caramel from Cadburys called a 'Curly-Wurly'. Getting the Japanese girlfriend of my brother to struggle pronouncing it sent them into fits of giggles.

Looking back, it appears a time that good taste had bypassed. Attired in a wide lapelled suit with loud floral shirt and its matching floral tie, sporting a Frank Zappa moustache, was the uniform I wore to work.

Even though Magnascan demonstration days followed a pattern, no two demos were the same. The day would begin with a salesman arriving with his customers who had flown into Heathrow airport earlier that morning. They would unpack their briefcases containing the colour transparencies they wished to have reproduced. These were taped to the large wall-mounted light boxes and Pete or I would select the first one to be scanned. Our objective was to generate a colour separation and have it up on a light box within forty minutes.

By the time the customers had taken their coats off, settled into one of the comfortable leather sofas and were enjoying a cup of freshly percolated coffee, their first scan would be in front of them which was hugely impressive and generally knocked their socks off. The day continued with a steady stream of their work appearing on the light boxes before them. When they all returned from a long lunch, normally lubricated with generous amounts of alcohol, we had completed the balance of work that they'd brought with them. A wink from the salesman let us know that another order was in the bag.

Demos didn't always run so smoothly. With a highly complex piece of electronic, optical and mechanical engineering there were inevitable breakdowns and 'technical hitches'. It was not uncommon to secretly smuggle an engineer through the back door into the darkroom to fix a problem. This would often be accompanied by Pete ferociously slamming a door, or a vicious punching of a wall! Although this last violent act was more likely due to his fiancé Fran's ultimatum to "set a date for the wedding or the engagement's off!" (Pete did finally marry Frances but the marriage didn't last long!)

At the end of a successful demo the salesman would often bring drinks to celebrate with us. The sales manager of the French office, an Englishman, Tom Webb, delighted in returning with literally armfuls of bottles of vintage Moët & Chandon champagne; a wonderfully amusing and entertaining man who I met up with again in Paris in 2016, some forty-five years after we had worked together. Although then in his eighties he hadn't lost his sparkle and his gregarious hospitality, nor indeed his love of champagne!

The salesman responsible for Spain, Michael Raif from Germany, was particularly generous to Pete and me. When taking his customers to lunch he would regularly interrupt his meal to drive back from the restaurant up the road in Highgate to deliver a meal to us.

One week he had booked six demos in six days – Monday through Saturday – for Spanish customers. Pete and I had our most successful week ever, six Magnascan orders in six days! A record that to my knowledge was never broken.

All this excitement paled behind an event that occurred two days after Rachel's eighth birthday with the arrival of our third daughter Louise. Jan and I were both convinced that she was expecting a boy. This was only because her pregnancy was so different from her previous two. She experienced far less morning sickness and there was much more stirring and activity from the baby. In fact, we joked that the baby was destined to become a great footballer if the amount of violent kicking was anything to go by!

In the final weeks of her confinement, while crowded into the tiny Marquee Club listening to a particularly deafening rock band, Jan took my hand and placed it on her bulging tummy to feel the baby moving to the throbbing rhythm of the music.

On the evening of the birth at Middlesex Hospital in Edgware, I decided that I wanted to be present having not been allowed at the first two. The nurses got me dressed in a hospital gown in readiness. Sadly, I discovered that I was not very capable in hospitals and was overcome with queasiness to the point of almost fainting.

The nurses had to help me back to the waiting room where they helped me hang my head out of a window to get some air until I recovered. When the news came through that it was a girl, I was astonished but no less delighted. I was now the proud father of three beautiful daughters.

****

Back at work, it was during this period that one of the UK salesmen, Kevin Smith, left the company to set up his own graphic equipment sales firm, Europa Graphics. Dick Tibbitts, who'd been working overseas installing Magnascans, had successfully applied for his job. I was a bit peeved as I thought I had made it known to everyone that I was keen to join the sales force.

Dick explained to me that he had simply written a formal application for the position to our divisional director, Ray Box. Meanwhile a vacancy had opened for a salesman to market and sell the company's range of Gretag densitometers. These pieces of equipment, imported from Switzerland, were used to measure the density of coloured inks on the printed paper. It enabled the printing machine minder to control the quality and consistency throughout the print run.

Early small offset colour printing was often produced on single or two-colour presses. A densitometer was invaluable for guaranteeing the finished four-colour job would reproduce the required colour accuracy. However, they were expensive, around £600 then – £9,000 in 2019 money.

Following Dick's example, I wrote a formal application for the position to our divisional director. Ray Box was a lovely man of medium height and build with a wide forehead, dark wavy hair and an engaging smile; he had a confident manner and a natural ability to put you at your ease. When I had joined the company two years previously, he had greeted me on our first introduction with a friendly "Welcome aboard, Colin".

At a subsequent Christmas drinks get-together when I was regaling the gathering with stories of the mishaps when helping my dad to renovate, Ray in particular was roaring with laughter. Whether this had influenced his decision, or whether it was my unbound enthusiasm for the job, I don't know, but either way I was ecstatic when he awarded the position to me.

The salesman that I was replacing, David Smallman, another lovely man, was leaving to launch his own reprographic brokerage. Before he left, he was very helpful to me suggesting that I should organize a reply-paid mail shot to be printed and distributed to all the major UK printing companies; this advice proved invaluable.

The company arranged for me to attend a sales training organization for a week's intensive coaching in preparation for my new responsibility. They also coordinated my very first overseas trip; I was to visit the Gretag factory in Zurich, then fly on to Frankfurt to visit the enormous Drupa printing exhibition that was showing at the time.

For a 28-year-old who'd led a fairly sheltered life, this was all heady stuff, plus, within a few weeks the company supplied me with a brand new Ford Cortina motor car, so I was 'suited and booted' and ready to go! I had finally achieved my lifelong ambition to become a professional salesman. All I needed to do now was to accomplish some successful sales, easier said than done!

Encouraging replies from the mail shot began arriving on my desk, however, my very first sales visit included a moment of considerable embarrassment. In response to one of the enquiries, I had made an appointment with the manager of the printing department of the massive pharmaceutical group, Glaxo, in Brentford, West London.

The packaging of their products was printed with their corporate colour blue in a panel across the front of the cartons. They were having trouble maintaining the exact hue. If the density of the ink was not up to strength it gave the appearance of a faded look. On pharmacist's shelves, they not only lost their impact, it also made the products look old and out of date. Pharmacists were returning them in their hundreds.

While I was demonstrating the densitometer which would solve their problems, the printing manager asked me a technical question to which I didn't have the answer. Ever since I was a child, I have had a distressingly embarrassing blush when confronted with a discomfiting situation; this was one!

Instead of confessing to not having an answer, my lack of experience led me to waffle. I started to feel my cheeks burning, I sensed them turning from pale pink to puce. In an attempt to disguise my discomfort, I contrived a violent coughing fit. It began with a gentle throat clearing and developed quickly into heaving, doubled over, chest racking, hacking convulsions.

I suspect that the manager saw through my ruse although he did run to fetch me a glass of water. Luckily by the time that I had recovered my 'composure' the problematic question had been forgotten, or maybe he decided to embarrass me no further. I vowed to myself never to waffle again.

Not all my sales calls were so bad. On a visit to the huge De La Rue Corporation, one of the world's largest printers of securities and banknotes, I was greeted with a sight that almost had me salivating. At the far end of the cavernous press room were rows of wooden pallets stacked high with wasted run sheets, all various country's currencies, and all due to poor colour variation.

After a short demonstration of the benefits of the densitometer to the printing manager and the technical director they immediately signed an order for three machines. On top of my salary I was also earning three per cent commission on my sales. The De La Rue order would buy me a black, suede leather trench coat that I had been admiring in a Bond Street boutique window.

Throughout 1973 I continued to travel around the country on sales calls, overnighting as far afield as Glasgow and Edinburgh in Scotland, and all the major print centres in England; Liverpool, Manchester and Leeds in the north, and Birmingham in the midlands. I was rarely away from home for more than two nights a week although I was beginning to enjoy the freedom and independence of the travelling salesman, especially with a generous expense account which allowed me to stay in nice hotels and eat in good restaurants.

I was unaware at the time that excursions to nightclubs and discotheques, behaving like a single man, were gradually undermining my marriage. Jan had been my first and only girlfriend before we were married. I'm ashamed to admit that I took advantage of my lone status while away from home and cheated on Jan, betraying her loyalty. I convinced myself that these liaisons were harmless fun, a perk for being away from home.

Several colleagues who I had confided in warned me that I was playing with fire, that I could destroy my relationship with Jan. I argued that this was absurd as nothing would affect my love for Jan and my family. However, these trysts were having an insidious effect on me and would eventually cause irreparable damage.

It was during this year that Dick Tibbitts got married to Frieda, a Dutch girl he'd met in Beaconsfield where she was an au pair. The wedding was to be held in a beautiful church in Chalfont St Peter in leafy Buckinghamshire with the reception in the historic Bull Inn at Bisham and he'd asked me to be his best man. I was extremely flattered but also very nervous about my first attempt at public speaking. In the event it went quite well.

Sadly, some years later Frieda was to abruptly leave Dick for a scanner customer of his, a somewhat shady businessman, Eammon Barrett. It happened on the eve of the family's intended move to Singapore, where Dick had committed to a Crosfield offer of a transfer to head up the sales for the whole of Southeast Asia including Australia, when Frieda dropped her bombshell. Luckily, Dick honoured his commitment to the company and, sometime later in Australia met the lovely Ann, who he married and still lives happily with in Sydney.

Recalling Eammon Barrett, I remember that Dick and I were the innocent accessories to one of Barrett's nefarious business transactions. He had ordered an expensive film drying appliance from Crosfield and Dick and I delivered it. After buying us a lavish lunch in a local restaurant he offered to show us a new repro factory that he was setting up in Brixton in South London.

He asked us to carry his new piece of equipment out of his firm and deliver it to the new premises. Unbeknown to us he was liquidating the original company from which he'd ordered the equipment and was secretly transferring the asset to his new operation. I don't think Crosfield ever got paid or recovered their machine.

During my work selling the densitometers I attended several seminars and conferences. It was while at one of these in the East End of London that my car was broken into. Not only did the thieves steal my new suede coat that was on the back seat, they also took my demonstration densitometer. It was obviously no use to them so they discarded it in a doorway near Piccadilly Circus.

The contraption was an odd-looking piece of hardware. With a large dial on the front, many wires protruding and a very visible red circuit breaker, it was mistaken for an explosive device! This was at the time the IRA were setting off bombs all over London. The police cordoned off a large area of the West End and called in the bomb disposal squad. Fortunately, they didn't perform a controlled explosion and blow it up and it was returned to me at Crosfield undamaged, albeit to red faces all round.

It was towards the end of this year, 1973, that Pete left the company to join a repro firm in Southwark in south London. He left to operate the Magnascan that the owner of the company, Tad

Laskowski, had ordered. Tad's company, Colour Precision, was to feature large in my working life a couple of years hence.

Dick also left the company to expand the sales of a repro company in Slough, though he rejoined Crosfield a few years later. The vacancy in scanner sales created by Dick's departure was offered to me. A considerable step up, with an accompanying salary increase and commission on sales. It was my dream job and included the whole of the UK and Ireland as my exclusive territory. I wasn't to know that Britain's economy was about to collapse, and sales would become few and far between.

Chapter 10

Sales and Betrayal

The National Union of Mineworkers had called for industrial action in their pursuit of a thirty-five per cent wage increase and in November their members enforced an overtime ban. On the 1st January 1974, the Conservative prime minister, Edward Heath, placed the country onto a three-day working week to conserve electricity. In February, the miners upped the ante and went on strike. Edward Heath then called a general election under the slogan "who governs Britain"?

Surprisingly, he lost his majority and Harold Wilson's Labour government was returned to power. The miners got their pay rise and went back to work and the three-day week ended. However, inflation was running at sixteen per cent and was set to rise to almost twenty-five per cent. The Bank of England's minimum lending rate was thirteen per cent, with the cost of borrowing averaging five points above this. To put this into perspective, in 2019 the minimum lending rate was 0.75 of one per cent!

For a company to raise the finance and be able to service a loan on equipment costing £35,000 – £355,000 in 2019 – presented a formidable challenge. Most of the larger, more financially robust repro companies had already purchased their scanners in the preceding four years, those remaining comprised what was described as a cottage industry.

Nevertheless, there were many hundreds of these small operations, often working out of dingy warehouses and owned by a couple of tradesmen partners, employing few staff and producing repro on gallery cameras in the old conventional way. Unfortunately, their bookkeeping and financial records often were not of a standard or strong enough to support a large bank loan.

To get around this problem I connected with a young finance broker, John James. John was about my age and had spent his working life in the banking and finance industry. He had enormous expertise coupled with a dry sense of humour, developed I imagined from years of examining company accounts! He had also recently established his own brokerage and was eager for new business. We struck a deal to help each other.

I would introduce him to potential buyers, in return he would inform me of any finance enquiries for our competitor, Dr Rudolf Hell's scanning equipment. Dr Hell's colour scanner was manufactured by the German engineering conglomerate, Siemens. headquartered in Munich. Their machine was launched shortly after the Crosfield Magnascan and up until then had none installed in London. The nearest Hell scanner was in a trade house in Birmingham. The last thing I wanted was a competitor's machine on our doorstep.

As my territory also included Ireland, I took the opportunity to follow up on some sales enquiries from the republic. I flew into Dublin where my first call was at ten-thirty in the morning. It was at a large but conventional repro company near the centre of the city. I was shown into the managing director's office, and after pleasant introductions, I went into my sales pitch.

I'd barely uttered a few words when he stopped me and asked if I was "a drinking man". I replied that I quite liked a beer, so he suggested that we adjourn our meeting, and continue it at a nearby public house! It was barely 11 a.m. and I was about to discover the truism of the Irish drinking culture. The pub was already quite busy as we found a space at the bar, and I attempted to persevere with my sales pitch. It was a lost cause!

My potential client was far more interested in hearing about London; how Harold Wilson, the prime minister, was dealing with the trade unions, my background and origins, as my surname was Irish, in fact he wanted to talk about anything apart from scanners. I enjoy a good conversation so I soon allowed myself the distraction and threw myself into the hearty discussions and deliberations that grew more ardent as the pints of Smithwick's Irish ale flowed freely.

As 2 p.m. approached, he informed me that the pub would soon be closing for 'Holy Hour'. I made to finish my drink and leave.

"Oh no," he said, "'tis alright, we'll be having the lock-in!"

Prior to the late 1990s, Irish pubs had to close for an hour after lunch, supposedly to allow their patrons some time to indulge in ecclesiastic contemplation. In reality, landlords simply locked their doors so that their customers could continue imbibing in peace. It was known as the *in*famous Holy Hour, and the famous Lock-in!

The Lock-in meant that there was no escape for me, for while potential patrons couldn't gain access to the pub those within couldn't leave either! As I was in no fit state to keep the afternoon's appointment that I'd made, I telephoned from the pub and rearranged it for the following day and continued drinking with my new drinking buddy. By early evening he suggested we leave, pick up his wife and all go out to dinner.

At his home he introduced me to his family, collected a couple of his neighbours and we all piled out to a restaurant. It's all a bit of a blur in my memory. I do remember that at the end of the evening as we were saying our goodbyes and rejoicing in what a great day it had been, he stunned me by asking, "Now what was it you came to see me about?" adding, "Maybe you'd better come in again tomorrow morning!"

I had planned on four meetings in Ireland, thinking they could be accomplished in two days. In the event I was there for over a week. The Irish reputation as a nation of drinkers was certainly confirmed in my experience. There were several other novel encounters and amusing incidents during my trip, and one stands out in memory.

I was driving over to Galway, the city in the west of Ireland on Galway Bay. It was late afternoon and I decided to stop at a small lounge bar for a beer and a bite to eat. Irish lounge bars in the 70s were quite unlike the modern, themed Irish bars that are seen all over the world these days. Back then they could be quite austere places, but they were everywhere. In all the small villages and towns that I drove through, almost every other building was a lounge bar.

Picking one at random, I walked into the empty room. Greeting me with a smile, the landlord asked me what I'd like to drink. The only draught beers on offer were the ever-present, Smithwick's ale, or Guinness. Having never drunk the dark stout before, I decided to try a pint. The landlord then surprised me by asking, "Would you like a fast one or a slow one?"

"What's the difference?" I replied.

He went on to explain that a slow one is more traditional.

"I only pour about two-thirds," he said, pronouncing 'thirds' as 't'irds'.

"Then we wait a while for it to settle, it'll take a couple of minutes. Then I top it up, wait another little while, then I scrape off any excess bubbles and it's ready."

"What's a fast one?" I queried.

"Well, I just pour it straight up, and fill it to the brim."

"I'll have a slow one." I said.

"Jolly good," he said, and proceeded to pour 'two t'irds' into the glass. He placed the part filled Guinness onto the bar between us, and we both waited, watching the black, foaming drink settle. After about a minute or so, with the drink still in the process of settling, he looked up at me and asked, "Would you like a fast one while you're waiting?" I thought to myself that this could only happen in Ireland, what a wonderful country!

****

Unlike the market for the densitometer which was spread over the whole country, the primary market for the scanner was the smaller trade houses and was concentrated around London. Jan and I had been renting our flat for over four years and now determined that London would be our future. House prices were increasing dramatically so we decided to sell our house in Gloucester and look to buy in London.

I informed our two sets of tenants of our plan, explaining that there was no immediate rush. The ground-floor couple accepted the situation and told me that they were looking to move anyway as they were having 'trouble' with David Ward upstairs. David Ward was more difficult, telling me that he wouldn't move unless he had a court order to do so.

A court order would enable him to gain a council house for him and his wife and their two small children. I discovered that the residential rental laws in 1974 were far more favourable to the tenant than to the landlord. I sought legal advice and was told that the only way to evict Ward was to apply to the court, and for Jan and me to 're-establish residency' in our old home.

On the day of the court hearing I presented our case to the magistrate which was accepted and the decision was granted in our favour. Talking with the solicitor on the steps of the courthouse afterwards I was approached by Ward. He could be quite truculent and aggressive at times; this was one of them! He was barely coherent, cursing me about unfairness and threatening to 'get' me.

I was flabbergasted as he had told me some time before that he *wanted* a court order. He also understood that the rental wasn't permanent and had originally accepted that one day we would want our house back. The solicitor was as shocked as I was, saying what a dreadful man, and how lucky we were to be rid of him.

At least now we could move forward with our plans to move back! We gave notice to leave on our London flat and on a sunny early summer's day, Dick and Frieda helped us with our removal. I hired a box van and we managed to cram all our furniture inside and drove off to Gloucester.

We arrived to find the damage left by Ward. Most of the upstairs walls were covered in graffiti, and he had taken Rachel and Claire's two little nursery chairs that had been a Christmas present from their Uncle Derek.

Jan also noticed that a floorboard in the kitchen appeared to have been disturbed. On her insistence, I prised it up to see underneath it. It was unbelievable what the little bastard had done. Directly under the floorboard lay the main gas pipe. He had not only cut a hole in it he had also severed an electric cable leaving the bare wires exposed next to the damaged gas pipe.

Had we turned the power and the gas on, a spark from the 'shorting' cable would have ignited the escaping gas, causing a fire or an explosion. Jan wanted me to call the police but I decided it would only be our word against his and as none of us were hurt I was happy to have nothing more to do with him.

Having had the move back to Gloucester forced upon us we chose to make the best of it and convert the house back from two flats into one large family home. I had builders knock through the front sitting room into the ground-floor middle room creating a fabulously large living room.

We changed the first-floor front sitting room into our main bedroom, and Rachel and Claire had a bedroom each in the attic rooms. I was back to driving home at weekends but at least I had a better car to do it in. For the first few weeks I was sharing friend's flats around London until I found a tiny bedsit in Highgate that would suit as my pied-à-terre.

Living on my own in London during the week I must confess to behaving like a bachelor. Many of my colleagues were unmarried and it was all too easy to slip into the life of a single man with no responsibilities. Drinking after work with customers or workmates became the norm. Regular parties and nightclubs were the constant entertainment. With only my tiny garret to go home to in the evening it was all too tempting to look for excuses to stay out late, although I came to regret one late night celebration.

George Walker was a character and a half! A short, stocky Liverpudlian with a wicked sense of humour and an endless supply of jokes and anecdotes. He was the assistant production manager for the mighty National Magazine Company, publishers of *Cosmopolitan*. I met him at a printing conference and we hit it off immediately.

He'd invited me to one of his local pubs near Putney in south London where began a marathon pub crawl. George fancied himself as a gourmet cook and insisted that I return with him to his flat for dinner. He was preparing a huge roast leg of lamb, which took hours before it was ready. We passed the time while it was cooking by finishing several bottles of Burgundy… each! By the time dinner was ready it was after 1 a.m. and being too drunk to drive back to Highgate I spent the night on a rug in his living room.

Next day I had an early morning appointment with a large repro company in east London, Tower Engraving. I had overslept and woke up with a throat and tongue furrier than the rug I'd slept on, and a brain even more woolly. I had the mother of all humongous hangovers. It was too late for me to get to my bedsit to get a fresh shirt, so I drove straight to the meeting.

I had made the appointment with the technical director on the telephone, he had sounded a reasonable guy. I planned to explain to him about my previous late night, beg his forgiveness for my demeanour and tardiness, and maybe suggest another appointment; I didn't get the chance. While seated waiting in their reception, he rushed past me with a breathless, "Won't be long Colin, just getting a few people together!"

After a short while the receptionist led me through into a massive boardroom. Seated round the long table were about a dozen, suited, serious-looking gentlemen. My contact, the technical director, an enthusiastic, bubbly guy introduced me with a flourishing, "And this is Colin Fitzgerald from Crosfield Electronics, who's going to excite us with all the benefits of colour scanning, okay now Colin: shoot!" Needless to say, I didn't get the order.

Following my embarrassment at Tower Engraving I tried to temper my future revelries with some degree of success, though finding customers for Magnascans became increasingly difficult.

John James was a great help putting financial packages together for the very small operations, but even his assistance was thwarted by opposition from an unexpected quarter.

I had half a dozen assorted companies on the point of signing. I'd had them all in for demonstrations and delighted them with the speed and quality of the results. I had taken them to installations where they had listened to the scanner's praise from third parties. And John James had, often miraculously, found them finance. But then the trade unions intervened.

This was the period when the trade unions were at their most militant. The National Graphical Association was no exception. There were many cases where an order was about to be placed when the company's house chapel, under the direction of the local branch, would make demands that were completely unrealistic. In return for 'allowing' the scanner into the company, they wanted a reduction in working hours to thirty-five per week, an increase in holidays from five to six weeks per year all paid at time and a half – the equivalent of nine weeks per year!

But the demand that put the kibosh on most of my prospective customers was that the union wanted *everyone* in the company to have the opportunity of operating the scanner. This was totally unacceptable. The union's argument was that if the company was going to add to its wealth, then all the workers should benefit. The reality was that often the installation was meant to save the company from decline and bankruptcy. Sadly, most of these companies did fold soon afterwards.

Despite these setbacks I had managed to secure two orders for the Magnascan. One of them was definitely helped by Tad Laskowski who by now had two scanners running in his company, Colour Precision. I had been negotiating with F. E. Burman Ltd who were a medium-sized repro company based in Bermondsey in South London. They had been in for a demonstration but still needed convincing.

I asked Tad if I could show them his operation at Colour Precision in Southwark. Tad was a very successful businessman.

A larger than life character, ebullient and effusive in the extreme. He was very obliging and agreed immediately to me inviting Freddy Burman and his son Michael along.

On the day Tad was his usual exuberant self, lavishing profuse praise upon the scanners. His clinching remark was to the effect that having bought one scanner, its performance was so far beyond his expectations that he had to rush out and buy another. When we returned to Freddy Burman's office, he signed the order!

Sam Roubini was a different kettle of fish altogether. Often mistaken for being Italian, Sam told me that actually he was Jewish. Short in stature and extremely shrewd he ran his company, D. S. Colour International, with brutal efficiency. His factory was a showcase, beautifully presented in a prominent position on City Road in Finsbury, a stone's throw from Crosfield. He confided to me that his staff joked behind his back that even the partition walls in his factory were portable so that he could take them with him if he moved premises.

I'd had him into the company where he had been shown a first-class demonstration. I had wined and dined him and finally he was convinced to buy. However, he was also attracted to our competitor, Hell's DC 300 colour scanner. Late one afternoon Sam called me to his office where he gave me his decision.

He would place an order for *two* Magnascans, but he not only wanted ten per cent off *both* machines, he only wanted an option on the second machine until the first had proved its worth. There was no longer a ten-month waiting list for a scanner as there had been in the past. In fact, the factory was stockpiling them, so I thought it was a good deal, especially as we didn't want our competitor's machine literally on our doorstep.

Ray Box agreed with me and we took the proposal upstairs to the new managing director, Rowland Dunkley. He rejected the offer saying that he thought Roubini was bluffing and would pay the full price if pushed. I told him that I didn't think so; Sam had already told me that he'd had a good demo on the DC 300 and Perschke Price, the UK agents, were offering him a good deal.

Ray supported me in the argument but to no avail. I drove back down the road to Sam to give him the news. I felt he was as disappointed as I was, but it made no difference, he ordered our competitor's DC 300. Over the following years he was to purchase *seven* DC 300s!

Meanwhile my social carousing continued. I shared my office with the technical manager of the Graphic Equipment Division, Edward Dobouney. Edward was an interesting man. He was about my age and originated from Iraq. He was very ambitious and good-looking in the Omar Sharif mould. It was late summer and we had arranged to go out for an evening partly to help me drown my sorrows after losing Sam Roubini's order.

It transpired that Edward was more of a ladies' man than a hearty drinker like me. We started our evening in a Hampstead pub, The Horse and Groom. The pub was tied to Young's Brewery who sold their very strong Young's Special beer. I must have drunk around six pints of it when Edward, who had only been drinking halves, suggested we change pubs and move on to The Old Bull and Bush. We arrived to find several of our Crosfield colleagues there, so the drinking continued in earnest.

Edward's attention was distracted when two beautiful young women entered the bar. He suggested I accompany him to 'chat them up' at the bar where they were ordering their drinks. He started talking to the darker haired girl whose name was Sandy. I was standing next to Sandy's friend who had bewitching blue eyes, was from Sweden and had an exotic name, Birgitta.

I could not have made a worse impression, unsteady on my feet as I was quite drunk, and making nonsensical conversation. I attempted to roll a cigarette for Sandy from her tobacco pouch; tobacco, filter tips, and cigarette papers were dropping all around me before I gave up. Obviously completely unimpressed the girls finished their drinks and made to leave.

I told Birgitta that I had better conversation when I was sober and asked her to 'meet me here for lunch tomorrow'. She readily agreed but without much sincerity. She admitted later that she had no intention to keep the appointment. It wasn't until I fell back into a chair as she was walking out of the door and I cried out, "Please don't let me down, everyone's letting me down!" that she took pity on me and kept the assignation.

Over a sober lunch the next day, I lied to Birgitta telling her that I was separated from my wife. She told me that she was divorced and that her husband had left her for another woman. I couldn't imagine why he would have done that. To me, Birgitta was the most beautiful woman I had ever met. She was tall with long curling auburn hair and pale blue eyes. She spoke softly with an endearing Scandinavian accent. At thirty-three, she was three years older than me and seemed so cosmopolitan and fashionable. I was completely captivated by her.

Throwing caution aside I began seeing her regularly. She invited me to her home for dinners where I met her young children. Eventually we started spending nights together and I realized that I had fallen deeply in love with her. When I finally confessed to her that I *hadn't* separated from Jan she was horrified and tremendously upset, wanting to break off our relationship. By now I was certain that I wanted to spend my future with Birgitta, so I reassured her that I was about to tell Jan that I was leaving her. It was a confrontation that I was dreading, consequently I kept postponing the distressing encounter.

The year 1975 began with some disturbing news. One of the Crosfield press controls salesmen had heard that a printing company in South London was installing a DC 300 scanner. I had heard nothing nor could find out who the company was so I rang John James.

John called back the next day to say that he had found out that the company was a small offset printer with a small repro department called Hogan Colour Plates and that it was based in Deptford. I rang them and spoke to the owner John Hogan. He agreed to a meeting but was adamant that he was ordering our competitor's machine.

John Hogan was in his early thirties, a Mancunian who could be both genuinely charming and disturbingly uncouth, a complete enigma. I drove down to his factory. Deptford in the mid-70s was a declining if not derelict suburb. Grimy deserted buildings on grimy roads that were mainly a thoroughfare to the elegant areas of the adjoining Greenwich.

His factory was off a small yard at the back of a Victorian warehouse. He had a four-colour offset machine, some miscellaneous printing machines and an assortment of repro equipment, all crammed into a tiny section of the building. As he showed me around, I warmed to his self-deprecating humour and his self-evident ambition.

We went for a beer in a nice pub in Greenwich, and after much persuasion he agreed to come for a demonstration, even though he insisted that I was wasting my time as he was completely sold on our competitor's DC 300.

The demo, which we did a few days later, went extremely well. He arrived with a bag full of transparencies which were all completed by the end of the day.

It was still a huge shock to me the following week to receive his call saying that he was still ordering a DC 300. I was shattered as I really believed that we had converted him to our machine. I was also disappointed as I liked John and was looking forward to seeing more of him. I told him how sad I was but fully accepted his decision. I went on to say that aside from him not buying from us, how about we meet for a beer anyway, he agreed.

Like myself, John liked a beer. He could be enormously funny and entertaining, also acutely embarrassing, but he was fun to be with. I got the impression that he liked me too and found me equally good company. We had a great day's drinking session, beginning at lunchtime, going through the afternoon into late evening. Not being able to help myself, I continued to enthuse about the merits of the Magnascan.

Next day John called me to invite me to meet in his office. He told me he would order a Magnascan if I would come and work for him. My first reaction was to tell him that he couldn't afford me.

He shocked me by offering me *twice* what I was earning plus a generous commission on sales.

I had worked for Crosfield for five years, maybe it was time to move on. The scanner market was becoming tougher, my territory had been halved with the recent employment of a northern salesman, Ken McHale. Plus, as the charming, tall, Swedish director designate, Lars Janneryd, had said to me after a sale, "Okay Colin, that's history now, where's the next one?"

At least with selling print and repro, once a new customer has been won, you didn't have to keep selling to them to get repeat business; I was tempted.

In the late spring of 1975 after several days of giving it all my thoughts, I telephoned Ray Box with the news, good and bad. We'd got the sale but I was leaving the company, I'd made my choice. I thanked Ray for everything but told him that I wouldn't ask him to match what John was offering me. Looking back now, despite my disastrous time with John, I would still make the same decision.

Chapter 11

Debacles in Deptford

The eight months that I worked for John Hogan were the most instructive yet turbulent months in my entire working life. The saying 'bad start: good ending' could be rewritten to 'bad start: bad ending'!

I have never been a wholehearted advocate of 'image over substance' but I do recognize the importance of presentation, so from my first morning when I saw the beat-up, rusting old Hillman Imp that John wished me to use as a company car, I thought that it did not project the appearance of a successful, young, go-ahead company!

Also, I didn't know that I would have to answer to John's father who he also employed. John Hogan senior – *Mr* Hogan – was of the old school 'muck and brass' brigade. A stocky northerner whose own repro company in Manchester had collapsed and he was now working for his son. He had no time for good employee relations, "Chop his legs from under him if he's nowt good!" was his constant refrain. Neither was it unusual for John to be heard screaming abuse across the factory floor to an unfortunate worker for some minor wrongdoing. I discovered that I had signed up to a netherworld workhouse.

However, I kept my focus on obtaining new business for the company. One of the first sales calls I made was to a repro brokerage, Mullis Morgan, in their tiny offices above a 'greasy spoon' café just off Clerkenwell Road in EC1. I persuaded them to place some work with us. The job they gave me was a large, colourful wine catalogue.

It was already running late when I was examining the proofs with John; it was awful! Not only were the colours bad, the job didn't even fit, it was out of register giving the colour pictures a blurred look.

I told John that I couldn't submit this to my new customer, especially as it was the first commission from them. John got quite angry and told me that as I was a salesman to "go and sell it to them". Stupidly I did try. To say that John Mullis, one of the partners in the firm was upset is putting it mildly, he was apoplectic. He almost threw the proof sheets back at me. I scuttled out of his office with my head down.

The re-proof was produced and was much better quality. John said he wanted to accompany me to Mullis Morgan to re-present it. This second attempt was received much more favourably, then John astounded me in front of my customer by accusing me of submitting the first shoddy proof, saying that had *he* seen it, it would never have been presented! I was gobsmacked but beginning to comprehend what a two-faced tyrant I was working for.

After the meeting we invited John Mullis, along with his tall, attractive receptionist for drinks around the corner in The Crown, a pub on Clerkenwell Green. We were all standing at the bar when John displayed what an unpredictable animal he could be.

Looking up at John Mullis's receptionist he asked her how she could ever get a boyfriend being so tall. She looked down at him and replied that she would never go out with a small squirt like him. With that, John reached over the bar, grabbed a soda siphon and proceeded to squirt soda water into her face! Amazingly she took the incident quite well although I don't think she ever accepted a drinks invitation from him again.

Even more surprisingly, sometime in the future, John Mullis was to join John Hogan setting up a colour scanning company, Brunswick Scanning. I have a suspicion that it all ended in tears.

Another incident that depicted what a volatile and cowardly person John could be, happened as we were leaving work one evening. I was in my car following behind his car as we were waiting to exit the factory yard. There was heavy rush hour traffic flowing in both directions on the busy street that we were attempting to cross.

When a short break in the westbound traffic occurred, John edged his car halfway out across the road while waiting for a gap in the eastbound stream. A small sports car travelling west took exception to being held up by John's car, and the driver tooted his horn.

While I watched from my car behind, John got out of his car, walked to the front of the beeping car, lifted his leg and brought his boot hard down on the car's bonnet denting it. He then raced back into his own car and sped off down the road. The sports car managed a U-turn and chased after him.

I found John shortly afterwards hiding behind a nearby service station, waiting until the angry motorist had passed by. He wasn't so brave under threat of retaliation.

It was during this distressing work period that I was seeing more of Birgitta even though I still hadn't found the courage to tell Jan. I started staying in London over the weekends instead of driving to Gloucester to be with Jan and the girls. I lied to Jan telling her that I was either too busy with my new job or occupied looking for a house for us all to live in.

Looking back, I squirm with guilt over my lies and brutal selfishness. I had virtually moved in with Birgitta, only visiting my bedsit occasionally to collect mail or pay my rent. It was on one of these occasions on a Saturday morning that I'd driven from Birgitta's to Highgate to buy groceries for our dinner and had called into the flat.

I was talking with two old colleagues from Crosfield who also rented there when there was a ring at the front doorbell. I couldn't believe my eyes and was momentarily in a state of shock when I saw Jan standing at the front door!

My mind was racing as Jan was telling me that as it was so difficult for me to get to Gloucester, she decided to surprise me and had caught an early train to London. I couldn't let her see inside my bedsit as all my clothes were at Birgitta's. I suggested she freshen up and we would go out for lunch.

I ran a bath for her in the shared bathroom and told her that I had arranged to see a mate for dinner, so I would just need to pop around to his flat to let him know that I wasn't going to make it. Once I had ushered Jan into the bathroom, I made a mad drive back to Hampstead to collect my clothes and let Birgitta know what was happening.

Even in this hour of high drama there was a moment of comedy. As I entered the house, Birgitta's nine-year-old son, Bobby, was in the hallway. As I rushed past him telling him that I was sorry that I couldn't linger as I had an emergency, he dashed off calling out, "Mum! Mum! Colin's got an emergency!"

I raced upstairs to empty my clothes from the wardrobe when Birgitta stopped me and insisted she accompany me back to Highgate to confront Jan with the truth.

"No, no, no!" I cried. "Let me do it my way, today is not the time to do it."

I promised her that I would tell Jan once this weekend was over. She was not happy.

I sped back to my flat and crept passed the bathroom carrying all my suits. I managed to get them all into my wardrobe just before Jan stepped out from the bathroom. After showing her my tiny room with its cot-size single bed I suggested we go out for lunch. I was terrified that Birgitta might arrive at the flat at any moment.

We drove into the West End and spent the day sightseeing with me constantly looking over my shoulder for fear of the sudden appearance of Birgitta. I can't remember what we did the following day. I only know that I trembled with anxiety in case of an unthinkable encounter. I was also exhausted and guilt-ridden from leading this deceitful double life. Eventually, in the late afternoon I saw Jan back onto the train to Gloucester. I then drove back to face the music with Birgitta.

Understandably she was angry and very upset. She again wanted to end our relationship. Again, I implored her to be patient, promising that on my next visit to Gloucester I would confess to Jan and tell her that I was leaving her. Mollified to a degree she finally accepted my pleading was genuine, and our life returned to a level of normality, notwithstanding my awful sense of foreboding.

A few weeks later I drove to Gloucester. I took Jan out on the Saturday night to a local pub, mainly to give myself some Dutch courage for the task that lay ahead. I had obviously been distracted the whole evening, and when we returned home Jan asked me what was wrong.

I finally blurted out that I was seeing another woman. The expression 'pole-axed' doesn't come near Jan's traumatic reaction. She physically dropped to the floor, emitting a heart-wrenching howl. She sat sobbing, continually bawling, "No, no, no, no." Eventually she composed herself and I helped her to her feet.

Jan was a petite, slim, passive woman, so it came as a bolt from the blue when she suddenly swung a huge kick at me. No doubt there was justification where her foot connected with my body; it was my turn to drop to the floor! She then raced upstairs to bed screaming at me to get out of the house and that she never wanted to see me again.

Next morning, having spent the night on the sofa, I ventured upstairs to see if Jan was alright. She had calmed down but was now begging me not to leave her. To say that I felt a complete bastard is putting it mildly. Seeing Jan so distraught I felt utterly despicable. I wouldn't want to hurt someone so much who I didn't like, let alone someone I had loved.

Writing this now, nearly fifty years after the event, I am reliving the guilt. Knowing that there are millions of other couples who have gone through similar break-ups doesn't help. My total infatuation with Birgitta was sweeping all sensitivities aside. Even though my future with Birgitta was to prove less magical than I had anticipated, with hindsight I would adopt the same course.

Over the years, Jan never denied me access to my daughters who I visited nearly every weekend, nor, as far as I'm aware, ever poisoned their minds or attitudes towards me. She remarried a couple of years after our break-up and had another daughter, but I don't think she ever forgave me for my unfaithfulness.

Now that my relationship with Birgitta was out in the open I vacated my bedsit in Highgate and moved in full-time with her. Much as I was besotted with Birgitta, living with her and her three children had its problems.

Birgitta's children, Daniel, Bobby and Rebecca were similar ages to my three. In fact, the boy's birthdates were within days of Rachel and Claire's. Rebecca was only two years older than my Louise, but sadly Rebecca always resented me being there. As a four-year-old little girl, she harboured the innocent hope that her dad and mum would somehow get back together again, therefore I was an obstacle to this. It was an animosity that I was never able to overcome even as she grew older.

Bobby was a different kettle of fish. A lovely easy-going lad who wore a constant smile. I always felt that I enjoyed a great relationship with him, unlike his elder brother.

Of all our children, Birgitta's and mine, Daniel could be the most difficult and problematic. He was probably the brightest, but always seemed the most troubled. He was never as happy-go-lucky as his younger brother Bobby or my girls. I spent more time trying to encourage him than any of the others. I urged him to take up piano lessons and applauded his achievements. I introduced him to photography, helping him to create a darkroom, and showing him how to do his own developing and printing. Sadly, despite the extra attention and care, I never seemed to be able to get close to him.

Even though I was earning reasonable money it was never enough to support my family and contribute to my new home. Birgitta's ex-husband, David, who lived around the corner with his partner, Yael, and their young daughter, Naomi, continually berated me for more contribution. He was a less than successful songwriter who lived off the largesse of his famous brother, the singer, Cat Stevens.

David was a towering, dark, formidable figure who had inherited his violent temperament from his Greek father, Stavros. His sister, Anita, was married to a lovely Albanian man, Alex Zolas, who was Cat Stevens's bookkeeper and general factotum; Alex was to help me a lot when I eventually set up my own business.

At work at Hogan Colour Plates it was becoming more difficult to hold on to any new business that I was winning. John laughingly likened our relationship to a car panel-beater's sign he'd once seen which read, 'YOU BEND'EM WE MEND'EM'. He said that in his case it would read, 'I BEND'EM *YOU* MEND 'EM'. I didn't find it that funny!

One day I received a phone call at work from Alex. He told me that Steve – as we called Cat Stevens before he embraced Islam – was going on tour again and could I quote on producing the souvenir programmes. He said that the tour was being promoted by Harvey Goldsmith, and could I meet them to discuss it.

At that time Harvey ran his company from a dingy basement in Wigmore Street in the West End. This was long before he became the legendary, global producer of stadium events from Pink Floyd to Pavarotti. Harvey introduced me to his merchandizing partner, Mick Worwood.

Mick would not have looked out of place in the front line of a heavy metal band. Tall and wearing his hair below his shoulders, he was covered in jewellery. Heavy silver necklaces and turquoise bracelets and rings to complement his rhinestone shirt, which was held at the neck by a braided, leather, Navajo Indian ornamental shoestring tie.

On top of this he was wearing a luxuriant wolf hound overcoat that reached down to his hand tooled Stetson cowboy boots. Saville Row he was not! I felt quite bland standing next to him in my two-piece beige suit from Lord John's on the Kings Road.

The design of the programme, *The Majicat Tour*, was already complete, but I gave them a very competitive price for the repro and printing. Mick wanted to see the factory before he placed the order, so I volunteered to drive him down to it.

He brought with him his PA, a very pretty, blonde-haired girl, whose moniker was Muffin – from the 50s TV show *Muffin the Mule*. It transpired that Muffin was Mick's sister who got her nickname from regularly kicking people when she was a little girl. As we were hitting the rush hour traffic heading out of London, it seemed to take forever to reach Deptford, prompting Muffin to ask if we were still in London.

I was getting increasingly apprehensive as to John's reaction when I would arrive with this bizarre duo. Luckily the mercurial John was at his most charming, and Mick and Muffin left the factory duly impressed.

On the drive back to Mick's office he surprised me by offering me an immediate job producing the souvenir programme for another band that was about to go on tour, The Sensational Alex Harvey Band. The finale of Alex Harvey's act was taking centre stage and eating a bunch of red roses! One day I was at Harvey Goldsmith's offices where one of the young female assistants was sitting patiently picking the thorns off the bunch of roses that Alex Harvey would later be eating.

Following our completion of the Alex Harvey and *Majicat* programmes, Mick awarded us a much bigger contract, The Who's calendar. The Who were performing three Christmas concerts at London's Hammersmith Odeon, and instead of a conventional programme, they would be selling a large format calendar.

As usual with the music business everything was running late. I was waiting at the designer's studio in Oxford Street for every single piece of artwork, then racing back to Deptford for scanning. It was not a simple job. The designer was producing some very complicated compositions, each taking us lengthy times to produce the plates for printing, consequently the job ran late.

There wasn't time to have the calendars properly spiral bound. Mick had to arrange for a team of assistants backstage at the concerts to collate the single sheets, bind them with cheap plastic binders then rush them round to the auditorium for sale; he was not happy!

Inevitably, the sub-standard result did not sell well and Harvey refused to pay the full amount of the invoice. Subsequently, after I had left his company, John Hogan sued Harvey for full payment. At the court case a couple of years later, Harvey called me as a witness in his defence.

The oak-panelled court room at The High Court is an austere and intimidating chamber. I entered to see John Hogan in the witness box telling the court that Colin Fitzgerald was a liar and no one should believe what he said. Mick arrived having just flown in on the 'red-eye' from Los Angeles. The only concession he'd made to his normally outrageous apparel, was to swap his shoestring tie for a borrowed one which happened to be a bright silver wedding tie. The judge took one look at Mick and the case was lost!

****

I had located a medium size offset printing company in Southwark called Vinalith. It was run by a couple of very engaging guys with whom I had become quite friendly and I had been getting a lot of work from them over the previous months. I was delivering a set of litho plates to them when John decided to alter our terms of payment from them.

He instructed me not to release their work unless they paid their invoices up to date, and in cash! This was an extraordinary demand and placed me in a dreadfully invidious position. The invoices amounted to several thousand pounds and, as their company's majority shareholder and cheque signatory was a financier based in the city, it would take some time to arrange the cash, not to mention the disruption this outrageous demand had caused.

I had no hesitation in releasing the plates to them while I waited for the money to be delivered. I returned to John later that afternoon with a bag full of cash and told him that I thought he'd done a shameful deed. He was unrepentant and even tried to blame me for his cash flow situation; I stormed off.

It Was The Best Of Times...

At home that evening I told Birgitta that I didn't think I could carry on working for John. I couldn't even contemplate another day with his company. I had no other job to go to, I would be unemployed but I'd had enough of his vicissitudes.

I rang him at his home and told him that I had quit. He seemed unbothered by my decision and I hung up. Some years later I heard from a third party the heartening acknowledgement that John had said that the worse mistake he ever made was to let Colin Fitzgerald leave. I had no such regrets.

As well as changes in my employment, the spring of '76 also brought changes to the political landscape. The prime minister, Harold Wilson, quite suddenly and unexpectedly announced his resignation. He was replaced by the avuncular James Callaghan, 'Uncle Jim'.

Harold Wilson said that he was 'exhausted' following his successful campaigning for the European Economic Community referendum, the forerunner of the European Union. It later transpired that he had been diagnosed with early stage Alzheimer's disease and had decided to quit before it began to affect him adversely.

On the opposition benches, the shrill Margaret Thatcher had beaten Edward Heath for the leadership of the Conservative Party following his defeat at the general election. An unsociable, taciturn man, he withdrew to his seat in parliament from where he sat glaring at her for the next fifteen years.

Talk of global warming began as it was about to become the hottest summer for three hundred years, and the young MP Dennis Howell was appointed the first Minister for Drought. When the heatwave finally broke, he was appointed Minister for Floods, really!

While I was looking for work Birgitta was enjoying her new business. When we had met, she had just started working for a sales company selling men's shirts. Lugging a heavy suitcase full of her wares, she tramped the high streets going from door to door seeking out customers to whom she could directly sell.

It just happened that one of my customers, a small repro company in the East End, was next door to a wholesale shirt distributor. I met with the two young Turks, Harold and Chris, who owned the business and asked if they would supply Birgitta with shirts for her to sell; they were agreeable. We purchased a range of shirts for samples, and I gave Birgitta a long list of my contacts in the repro and printing industries. This proved far more successful than arbitrary high streets.

Young tradesmen in these firms were extremely well paid and very susceptible to an attractive young woman offering high fashion shirts at wholesale prices. She did exceedingly well, taking orders and getting paid up front, then buying the goods from the two likely lads, Harold and Chris.

Meanwhile, I was not having much luck looking for work. I had been unemployed for two weeks when I decided to see Tad Laskowski. Tad had just set up another business, a large colour printing company in Greenwich, Boss Colour. Unfortunately, he had just taken on a salesman, an ex-insurance salesman, Peter Marmet, so he wasn't looking for anyone.

I suggested a repro company that Tad had a financial interest in, Spectraplan, but Tad assured me that they didn't need anyone as *he* was the salesman for that company and that he was currently generating £360,000 of sales a year, more than they could handle.

I mentioned another of his companies, the scanning company Colour Precision, where Peter Rogers worked. This drew a blank as Tad explained that it was really a service company to Spectraplan; it was in the same building. I left disappointed but with an idea.

I ran my thinking passed Birgitta who suggested that I should treat myself to a new suit, take one of her very fashionable shirts, and arrange to see Tad again. I had been getting quite despondent and having doubts about myself, but Birgitta's advice and urging was just the tonic I needed.

I bought a very stylish, dark blue wool suit from Pierre Cardin, and a new tie to go with the new shirt. This all sounds a bit vain, but I found that looking good is halfway to feeling good, and I certainly felt optimistic and enthusiastic when I next met Tad.

We had arranged to meet in the infamous Crown pub in Clerkenwell Green, the scene of the squirting soda siphon. I ordered Tad his favourite drink of the time, a double Canadian Club and soda, and put my idea to him.

Tad always came across as larger than life; big in stature, assertive, and expansive in himself and his investments. I liked him a lot. I felt my confidence growing as I outlined my plan. Tad had two colour scanners at Colour Precision which I felt were under-utilized. Putting them on shift work would create a lot more production space.

The main thrust of my proposal was that I was convinced that there was a big market for scanned sets of separations. No one was producing them, yet there were hundreds of small repro companies and trade shops that were enduring sub-standard, poor quality work conventionally produced in-house.

Given the opportunity to purchase standalone, high quality scanned separations I was not only sure would sell well, I also had all the contacts to sell to. The more I enthused the more I sensed Tad warming to the idea. Finally, he nodded his approval, he'd go for it and I could start working with him on Monday; I was back employed again!

Chapter 12

Blackfriars to Broadway

Following the traumas of the previous eight months it was a joy to be among rational people, particularly again working alongside Pete Rogers for whom I had enormous affection and respect. Colour Precision, which Pete ran, occupied most of the third floor of a four-storey Victorian warehouse in a narrow alleyway, Valentine Place, off Blackfriars Road in South London.

The remainder of the floor was rented to a small offset printing company, Duxford Press, which was owned by Tad's brother Andy Laskowski, a heavily moustached man who could have doubled for the Polish trade union leader Lech Walesa.

Downstairs on the second floor was Spectraplan, the planning and platemaking company, of which Tad was a director. Tad had three partners there, the brothers Alan and Tony Easton, and the lugubrious 'Nobby' Clarke. Alan, a retoucher by trade, had film star looks and was very affable; his brother, Tony was less fortunate.

Having lost a leg in a motorbike accident as a young man, and constantly battling an ex-wife in never-ending recriminatory divorce proceedings, Tony did not have a happy disposition. Aesop's *Dog in a Manger* fable could have been written with Tony in mind as he refused to move out of the marital home.

One day I noticed the time on the meter on the only parking bay outside the building had expired with Tony's car parked on it. I rushed upstairs to ask him if he'd like me to 'feed' it for him. He said, tapping his prosthetic leg that he didn't need to feed it as he was displaying a disabled sticker.

I was shocked that he would occupy the only parking bay when he could have legally left his car on the yellow line leaving the bay for someone else. Not knowing what to say next I blurted out, "Oh, er, yes of course, only one leg, that's lucky!"

He snarled back at me, "I'd rather have *two* legs and have to feed the meter!" He always frightened me.

Spectraplan bought their colour scans from Colour Precision and had ran up a huge debt over the years, which I was keen to reduce by offsetting against repro work that I could introduce.

Colour Precision was basically two Magnascan 460s, one apprentice, Robin Cannon, and one customer, Spectraplan. Pete agreed that he was underemployed and was excited with the prospect of expanding the business to its full potential.

The first task that I had to do was to re-establish contact with all the customers that I had lost through the indifferent service at Hogan's. Two companies that I approached first were the guys at Vinalith who'd had to find the cash for Hogan's sudden change in his terms of payment, and Arch Press, whose works manager, Ray Benwell, was to help me enormously later when I set up on my own. Both these companies immediately supplied me with work for my new employer.

The biggest customer that I wanted to win back was Harvey Goldsmith as his work also involved printing which would feed Tad's new printing company, Boss Colour. I visited Harvey and his partner Mick Worwood at their new offices in Welbeck Street in the West End.

They were not only pleased to hear about my new appointment but they also offered me the official souvenir programme for the forthcoming Rolling Stones tour of Europe. This was a massive job; 36 colour pages with a 70,000 print run.

Mick Jagger specifically wanted the programme to be printed on an ultra-lightweight paper so that fans could fold it over twice to fit in their pockets! This was quite a coup for me to win as one of my first jobs to bring into the company.

As a highlight of the tour, the band were performing six nights at Earls Court in London and Harvey had gifted me six tickets for one of the nights. I can't remember who I took with me or indeed much of the show, as someone had handed me a very strong joint causing me to spend the evening in a haze of anti-social introspection! Come to think of it, it was probably from Mick, as he was quite the expert at rolling a five skin Camberwell Carrot![9]

During that summer the rock band The Who were headlining at three concerts held at the football stadiums in Swansea, Charlton and Glasgow. The events were titled *Who Put the Boot in* and Mick Worwood had given me the posters to print. They were all-day concerts supported by the bands Little Feat, The Outlaws, Widowmaker and The Sensational Alex Harvey Band – of the thornless roses diet!

I went along to the Swansea gig. The Who were performing numbers from their new musical, *Tommy*. At the end of their act, different coloured laser lights – a new technology at the time – were fired at reflectors high up on the ground's floodlights. They gradually created a lattice work of coloured beams covering the entire stadium; it was quite spectacular.

In October that year Black Sabbath were kicking off their world tour from Tulsa, Oklahoma and Mick wanted us to do the repro for the souvenir programme which, to avoid excessive freight charges, was to be printed in Tucson, Arizona.

The tour was promoting their latest album, *Technical Ecstasy*. The artwork was designed by Richard Evans based upon the album sleeve designed by the illustrious Storm Thorgerson from the famous design company, Hipgnosis. Ozzy Osbourne is quoted as saying that the theme of the design was like "two robots screwing on an escalator" which is pretty much what Storm was alluding to.

---

9. A joint consisting of twelve papers that's around 18 in (45 cm) long and filled with pure weed – the term comes from the cult classic film *Withnail and I*.

It Was The Best Of Times...

It was a complex 48-page colour programme with a large size square format to match the vinyl album cover. The plan was for Colour Precision to produce the colour scans and Spectraplan to assemble the films ready for platemaking, then ship it all over to Tucson for printing.

As we approached completion of the job I was concerned about the delivery. If it was held up in customs or any other freight delay, the printer would miss the deadline for the opening concert. I suggested to Mick that it ought to be couriered over.

Mick's response was to ask me if I would take it myself. He went on to say that I could then not only supervise it on press, but also fly on to Tulsa with the first batch to be sold. He said that his company would organize and pay for my flights, and that I would be doing them a great favour – how could I refuse?

Tad acknowledged the logic in this and agreed to me going. We also saw an opportunity for me to meet up with an old colleague, Claude Kersh, in New York, he was the agent for Crosfield scanners. I could then ascertain the market for scanned separations in the United States.

It was arranged for me to fly out from Heathrow, change at Kennedy Airport for a flight to Phoenix, where Rodger Ford, who owned the printing company, would meet me and fly me in his private plane to Tucson.

At the last minute, we realized that I didn't have a visa for the USA. This was at a time when you had to apply directly to the US Embassy in Grosvenor Square, a procedure that could take several weeks to accomplish. I arrived at the embassy where a sea of people was sitting waiting their turn to be called.

I went straight to one of the desks and showed them letters stating that I was taking work to be produced in the USA while waving my plane ticket for that afternoon! They were incredibly helpful issuing the visa within minutes and I caught the flight.

The Brazilian Airlines ageing Boeing 707 may not have been the most glamorous way for my first crossing of the Atlantic to the USA, especially with inordinately strong headwinds creating a frighteningly bumpy ride, but I was way too excited to care too much about such discomforts.

Unfortunately, the headwinds caused the flight to be delayed into Kennedy and I missed my connection. I managed to contact Rodger Ford and rearrange a flight direct to Tucson. He was at the airport to meet me when I arrived around midnight local time. He drove me straight to his factory where we unpacked all the films.

Due to the square format of the pages creating a very large layout, Spectraplan had produced the work on very thick seven thou' film rather than the conventional four thou'. The American platemakers had never seen such thick film and joked that they may not need to make plates, they could just 'strap the *film* onto the cylinders'! Rodger got me to a hotel, and after twenty hours travelling and all the visa excitement, I crashed out straightaway.

The next few days were spent in the factory overseeing the Black Sabbath print run. Rodger was a very hospitable host. He invited me to his ranch-style home for an evening barbecue, where we sat around an open fire and he cooked the biggest T-bone steaks I'd ever seen.

He insisted I stay the night, and early next morning we saddled up two of his horses and went riding in the foothills of the Santa Catalina mountains.

He also took me to an instant printshop that he'd just opened, Alpha Graphics, next to the University of Arizona. He had taken a photograph of me on horseback and had it printed onto a T-shirt for me.

I was to meet up with Rodger again in the mid-80s when he'd expanded his instant printshops to number over 150, all based around a new, clever little desktop computer called an Apple Macintosh! Eventually there numbered over 400 shops spread across the world before he sold out; a true entrepreneur!

When the souvenir programmes were printed and bound, we boxed up several hundred and I flew with them to Tulsa, Oklahoma, to deliver them to the first gig. I was met at the airport by one of the roadies and we drove to a huge sports arena, the Tulsa Assembly Centre.

He took me backstage and asked me if I'd like to meet Ozzy. I had heard and read so many hair-raising stories about Ozzy Osbourne, the infamous 'Godfather of Heavy Metal' that I must admit to being a tad unnerved. He couldn't have been more charming as I showed him the programme. He was lavish in his praise, betraying his thick Birmingham accent, "It's groit, oi loik eet." He thanked me effusively as we shook hands when I left. I stayed to watch the concert during which Ozzy encouraged the thousands of fans to stand on their seats, much to the displeasure of the management of the arena.

It was not long after this tour that the band sacked Ozzy who, despite his legendary drinking and substance abuse, managed to continue a very successful solo career; an amazing man. Next day I caught a flight to New York to meet up with Claude from Crosfield Electronics.

Mayor Rudy Giuliani's 'Zero Tolerance' campaign during the 1990s which cleaned up New York created an almost Disneyland compared to the New York that I saw in 1976. What I arrived to was more Schlesinger's *Midnight Cowboy* or Scorsese's *Taxi Driver*.

From the plumes of steam rising from the sewers and subways, to the massive yellow Checker taxicabs cruising passed the porno cinemas, massage parlours and sex clubs that burgeoned around Times Square, to the no-go areas of Harlem and The Bronx, it was dirty, vulgar and in parts, dangerous, but wow! was it exciting, and I loved it!

The incumbent mayor of New York at that time was Ed Koch. He had been elected on a law and order platform and had promised to 'clean up the streets'. The joke at the time was that the only cleaning-up he achieved was introducing fines for not picking up your pet dog's faeces.

This led to the invention of the 'pooper-scooper', a small plastic trowel with which to scrape it up. A smart marketing company had come up with a deluxe version. It was a contraption which combined a plastic bag for the mess, and a sliding handle to assist in the scooping. They called this the 'super-duper-pooper-scooper'! I just had to admire the ingenuity of American creativeness, and so often with a sense of humour.

I had checked into The Drake Hotel on Park and 56th, courtesy of Claude's credit card. I had used up the small amount of dollars I had brought over with me and only had English Travellers Cheques left which only the banks were interested in exchanging for cash. Not possessing a credit card myself I would have been stranded if it weren't for Claude.

Sadly, Claude wasn't willing to help me in any other way as he explained it wouldn't assist his scanner sales if Colour Precision were offering cheap colour separations to the US market. We had a pleasant lunch together then split up.

The Drake Hotel was a famous landmark in Midtown Manhattan. In its past, it had hosted such notable guests as Frank Sinatra, Judy Garland, Jimi Hendrix and the rock bands Led Zeppelin, The Who and Slade.

The hotel was eventually sold in 2006 for a remarkable $440 million, only to be demolished to make way for the tallest residential building in the Western hemisphere, the eighty-four, high-ceilinged storeys of 432 Park Avenue, where studio apartments cost $18 million, and the penthouse sold for a staggering $95 million; it could only happen in New York! Meanwhile, I had expenditure challenges of my own.

I had arrived on a Sunday, then discovered that the Monday was a public holiday, Veterans Day, so the banks would be closed. I had no money and it was pouring with rain. As I mooched about my hotel room idly pulling open drawers in search of something to read, I came across a large heavy plastic bag stuffed full of coins.

I tipped them out onto a small side table. There were hundreds, mainly from foreign lands; Italian lira, Spanish pesetas, German marks, English florins, but also American currency. There was a stack of quarters, nickels and dimes that added up to around $30. I could only guess that the previous occupant had been globetrotting and, getting fed up with carting all this shrapnel around had discarded it.

The American coinage that I had collated would keep me in beers and coffee until I caught my flight back on Tuesday. The rain had stopped, leaving me to explore this noisy, frantic, extravagant metropolis that I was falling in love with. It didn't disappoint; after two days of striding the streets and avenues of this awe-inspiring city, I felt my batteries were fully recharged, and my head was buzzing with new ideas as I boarded the flight back to London.

Back at home my life with Birgitta and her children settled into an incongruous arrangement. As I often worked late or chose to go for drinks after work with Pete, Tad or clients, I was rarely home before eight o'clock at night. Birgitta would give the children their evening meal early, then cook again when I arrived.

I was still experiencing some resentment from Rebecca but assumed she would soon grow out of it and come to accept me. Daniel was often absorbed in his darkroom with his new hobby, photography, and Bobby was ever the easy-going pleasant company.

Every weekend I drove to Gloucester to visit my girls. Gloucester is a small provincial town, so quite limited for family entertainment, especially for a single father with three young daughters. It did have one cinema though, as well as a magnificent twelfth century cathedral, and is surrounded by the beautiful Cotswold Hills. Our weekends together followed a regular pattern, most often involving one or more of its three main attractions.

After checking in at a small hotel on the outskirts, I collected the girls from their mother early on the Saturday morning and drove to one of the Cotswold beauty spots. We would climb one of the hills and generally lark about for an hour or two.

The Cotswolds is a designated Area of Outstanding Natural Beauty (AONB). From its rolling hills the views over the escarpment towards the Severn Valley below are breathtaking. From the meadows edged with drystone walls to its many medieval villages, all built from local pale, golden limestone, the area is a delight for weekend strolls. It was probably more enjoyable for me than the girls, although it was always fun to scramble up one of the local beacons.

Most Saturday afternoons we spent at my mum's. Following her divorce from Dad she had bought a large, three-storey house in Southgate Street. She rented out the top two floors as self-contained flats, while she occupied the ground floor. She loved to provide a lunch for us all, which was generally fish and chips from the local 'chippy'. Invariably we ended up sitting round chatting, then watching an old black and white film on her television set.

Sunday mornings we visited my dad. Dad and Flo had recently been rehoused. The Local Authority had slapped Dad with a compulsory purchase order on his "little palace" in Twyver Street. They were demolishing the entire row of terraced cottages under a "slum clearance" order.

His house was small but certainly no slum. He had extended the house at the rear to accommodate a new bathroom and toilet and had completely redecorated the house throughout. The council only paid him the land value of his home, a pittance, then rehoused him and Flo in a tiny council flatlet some distance away from their previous neighbourhood.

Their new flat was heated by two huge, ugly night-storage heaters – they're called 'heat-banks' in Australia. These were supposedly cheap to run using off-peak electricity at night to heat internal ceramic bricks which stored the thermal energy then released the heat during the day. As they became more widespread, the 'cheap' off-peak electricity became more expensive.

Dad was finding it increasingly difficult to make ends meet. He was in his mid-sixties. He had been a painter and decorator all his working life. He was now suffering back problems from years spent lifting heavy wooden ladders and planks. Having been self-employed most of the time he had no pension or superannuation to fall back on.

He had spent twelve years serving his country in the Royal Navy, which included the six years of Second World War. He had survived *three* sinkings – twice torpedoed and once bombed. He had experienced horrors that are hard to imagine, yet now he was being pushed around and treated shamefully by the local council and ripped off by the energy company.

He told me that his weekly electricity bill *alone* was more than his entire outgoings in his previous Twyver Street home. He had written to the council and the energy company complaining of his excessively high bills, informing them of his distressing financial situation. They replied that they would send one of their 'domestic economists' to visit him to assess his situation and advise him what economies could be 'implemented'.

When he recounted this visit to me, I was appalled. He said that a young 'chit' of a girl arrived, went through his flat with her notepad and pencil, then sat down with him and Flo to discuss her findings.

Her only recommendation for saving energy and reducing their bills was that when they were boiling a kettle for a pot of tea, the remaining hot water in the kettle should be poured into a thermos flask to use for future cuppas! If it hadn't been so tragic it would have been laughable.

I vowed to myself at that time that I would work to get myself financially secure, to be invulnerable to such treatment when I reached Dad's age.

Despite Dad's situation he was always cheered to see his grandchildren. We'd arrive to find him and Flo bustling around their tiny kitchen preparing their Sunday lunch. Fortunately, Flo's children had now left home, so at least Dad's gas meter was safe from her son, Clive's, thieving hands. Once the roast was in the oven, we'd all walk round to the local pub-garden to sit and chat.

Dad loved hearing my stories from London, and on occasions I could get him reluctantly talking about his wartime experiences. He related one story of a ship he was serving on, HMS *Hermione*, a light armoured cruiser, being torpedoed in the middle of the night in the Mediterranean Sea.

The sailors who had survived the blast and the fire were given the order to abandon ship as the vessel keeled over before sinking. They lined up along the edge of the deck, preparing to run down the side of the ship as she turned turtle. As they climbed over the rail, many men slipped on the slimy surface beneath the water line, crashing their backs against the sharp metal ridge that ran along the hull. Dad said he was lucky. As his feet skidded and slipped on the slime, his heals hit the ridge and propelled him into the sea away from the sinking ship.

I know that it was very difficult for him recalling these events, but I was extremely proud of him and always pressed him to tell me more.

Once in the water he said you were besieged by panic-stricken shipmates who couldn't swim. Huge areas of the surface water were on fire from oil spillage. Clinging to some floating jetsam, he struck out away from the ship and the flames. All night he trod water, listening to the shouts and cries from other survivors of the attack.

As dawn began to light the horizon, he could see the silhouette of a naval destroyer heading towards them. He imagined that thankfully they were soon to be rescued. As the ship neared them, they heard mighty blasts. The destroyer was firing depth charges as enemy submarines were still in the area. He said that the sea erupted around them. He witnessed ill-fated seamen, who had survived the ship's sinking, being blown to bits.

Great chunks of metal and body parts were falling all around him. Eventually the shelling stopped, and the destroyer heaved her bow towards them and he was picked up safely. Mum told me that years after these traumatic events she would wake Dad from horrific nightmares, when he was yelling and thrashing around in bed.

These days there's a far better knowledge of post-traumatic stress disorder. Sadly, in Dad's day there was little understanding and no help. When Dad finally left the navy in 1948, along with other ex-servicemen, he was given just £10 in financial aid and a new suit. This, presumably, was something onto which to pin his chest full of medals!

Dad didn't wear a suit when we visited the pub-garden on those Sundays. But he was always smartly dressed. Most often wearing a dark blazer with the Royal Navy badge sewn onto the breast pocket. For years he also wore a trilby hat, which he always lifted when encountering female company – an old-fashioned courtesy which in these days of feminism would seem comical if not ludicrous.

After a couple of beers with Dad and lemonades for the girls we would leave him to his lunch and I would take the girls to a steak bar in town. This was always a lovely part of my visits and one that the girls always enjoyed. With their ages ranging from only six to twelve years old they all felt quite grown up to be sitting at a restaurant table ordering their lunch from a menu.

There was a middle-aged waitress, Margaret, who had worked in the dining-room for years. She always made a wonderful fuss of the girls, especially little Louise. She often sneaked the girls extra desserts to take home with them.

On a visit later in the year, Margaret was nowhere to be seen. A young waitress told us that Margaret had been sacked for 'technical theft'! It was obvious that the management had wanted to replace her with a younger employee. To avoid paying her the entitled redundancy money, which would have been substantial, they had spied on her favouring certain customers and used it to dismiss her. We never ate there again.

Following our lunches, we would either spend the rest of the afternoon watching a film at the local cinema or, if there was nothing showing that was suitable, we would occasionally visit the cathedral for evensong.

I am not a religious person but sitting at the back of the nave on a winter afternoon, seeing glorious sunbeams shining through the high stained-glass windows, listening to the spectacular sound of the magnificent organ was truly awe-inspiring. It lifted us all. After returning the children to their mum late in the afternoon, I would make the long drive back to London.

****

At Colour Precision business was expanding daily and Pete was hiring more scanning staff to cope with it. Among the new recruits we had managed to poach a very skilled and experienced scanner operator with whom I'd worked at Hogan's, Ron Brown. Ron was to play a very important anchoring role when I eventually set up my own business.

Crosfield's had recently launched a new scanner, the Magnascan 550, which could produce all four separations in one scan, supposedly making it four times faster than our existing 460s; Tad ordered one, the first to be delivered and installed in London. Unfortunately, we were to discover that the model had been launched prematurely.

We encountered numerous teething problems and it never lived up to the high-speed machine that Crosfield had proclaimed. To compensate Tad, they supplied us with a further machine. Colour Precision ended up with three 550s all being operated around the clock on three shifts each.

As our production capacity increased, I needed to employ more help on sales. I didn't think that it was necessary to employ a person with proven experience in print or repro. Based on Birgitta's success selling primarily to colour repro companies, I understood how susceptible to a pretty face that the predominately male customers could be.

Armed with just a price list, a calculator and some superb scanned samples, I felt an attractive woman would be equally successful. These days this sounds terribly non-PC, but I am writing about the late 1970s!

After several interviews a young woman, Sonia Everett arrived. Sonia was vivacious and a single mother with a young daughter. As Pete and my office was occupied at the time, I was attempting to interview her in the busy corridor outside when she suggested we adjourn to the local pub for a beer; immediately I was won over!

Sonia joined the company and proved to be extremely successful; she was a real diamond with a lot of front, winning us some major accounts.

Sales were constantly increasing and came from a variety of sources. We were still getting work from the music business. In the late spring of '77 we won the repro for the progressive rock band Yes's album *Going for the One*. Designed by Storm Thorgerson of Hipgnosis, this was a break from conventionally designed album sleeves. It presented as a six-sided gatefold sleeve, and the record marked the return of the keyboard artist, Rick Wakeman, to the band.

In March of that year I dragged a reluctant Pete to join me driving up to Birmingham's Bingley Hall to be enthralled by Pink Floyd performing tracks from their albums, *Wish You Were Here* and *Animals*, complete with huge inflatables including the infamous pig, retrieved after it cut loose above Battersea Power Station when shooting the album cover!

Much as I was enjoying my time working at Colour Precision, and the work and clients that I was introducing, I was also hankering to expand our sales overseas. My trip to the States had whet my appetite for foreign travel, and I believed that there were fresh markets to seek out in Europe and beyond.

An unexpected visitor was to provide the opportunity to explore these new challenges.

Chapter 13

Marrakech to Manhattan

One morning at work Tad introduced me to his visiting brother-in-law, a charming and courteous Moroccan man, Said Zine. Said was eager to establish a repro company in Casablanca and had already contacted several potential customers. A few weeks later Tad asked me to fly to Casablanca to meet up with Said and visit the contacts he'd made and suss out the general situation there.

Said met me at the airport and drove me straight to a hotel he'd booked for me. After checking in Said suggested, in his heavy French/Moroccan accent, "Now you make a nice show*er*, 'ave a nice rel*ax* and I meet you in one 'ow*er*."

The Hotel Transatlantique was a mixture of French Colonial and Moorish architecture and stood on the corner of a busy intersection. My room had a balcony overlooking a small courtyard. It was the first time I'd seen palm trees, or the bougainvillea and hibiscus that decked out the terrace below.

I freshened up and couldn't wait to see more of this seemingly chaotic city. While waiting for Said on the steps of the hotel a shoeshine boy offered to polish my shoes. The price of seven dirhams seemed reasonable enough. Later when I told Said what I'd paid he was horrified, he told me the rate was only *one* dirham.

The next morning, I again allowed the shoeshine boy to polish my shoes. When he finished, I informed him that I had already paid in advance for a week's worth of shoe shining. He smiled his acknowledgment of my bargaining prowess and cleaned my shoes every morning at no charge. I was learning the Moroccan way of conducting business.

Said and I made about half a dozen visits to potential clients and managed to win a small job from Royal Air Maroc. Said confided to me that he was more interested in Tad committing to installing a scanner in Casablanca, and less him becoming a mere agent. I don't think that this was ever in Tad's consideration.

Said and his wife Uget had three daughters, the eldest two were similar ages to Rachel and Claire, who were eleven and nine years old. The family were very welcoming to me and took me to their beachside club at the weekend. They suggested that I might like to visit with my daughters and offered us to stay with them in their house.

Since working for Tad, I had been on a temporary tax code as I was in dispute with the tax office over expenses going back to my time at Crosfield. I had finally resolved the issues and had just received a healthy rebate. I decided to accept Said and Uget's kind offer and blow it all on a holiday with Rachel and Claire. As Louise was only three years old, it was decided that she was a bit too young for all the travelling, so she stayed at home with her mum.

Apart from a week in a friend's caravan at Tenby in North Wales, when it rained most days, we had never had a proper holiday together. We flew into Casablanca where Said met us with his youngest daughter, Hin, and drove us to his home.

Said was an executive at an oil company and lived a middle-class life in a very nice large, modern bungalow in the suburbs of Casablanca. The girls had never been abroad before so it was all wonderfully different and exciting, though Casablanca, or 'Kasa', as it's nicknamed, is really a busy, noisy and rather grubby city.

However, the second week of our holiday we took the Marrakech Express from Kasa down to the ancient Moorish city of Marrakech. We checked into the Hotel El Maghreb opposite its sister, Hotel de la Menara, which shared all its facilities. The hotels were next to the nine-metre high, reddish pink clay ramparts of the old city which date back to the twelfth century.

The girls spent most of their days enjoying the hotel's swimming pool, also venturing out for a ride on the nearby horse-drawn carriages. The locals were fascinated with Claire's shoulder-length, luxurious mop of red hair, which sadly she's never found so attractive herself.

We strolled to the bustling ancient square, *Jamaa-el-Fna*, in the medina, with its snake-charmers, water-sellers and storytellers, surrounded by miles of crowded souks where hundreds of merchants and vendors were selling sacks of saffron and cumin and baskets of mint, dried fruits and olives; I was intoxicated with this place.

The holiday ended all too soon. Over the following few years I returned many times to this amazing medieval city with its palm and orange tree-lined streets, but on a recent return in September 2016, I was sad to discover that it had lost its allure. Where once the only traffic was donkeys and mopeds, now the hot, dusty streets are congested with motor cars. Street vendors selling dates and mint tea are being overtaken by Burger King and the ubiquitous McDonalds. It is now almost indistinguishable from any European city with its shops selling all the international brands each with identical signage; the forfeit that's paid for progress and globalization!

Later that year at Dusseldorf in Germany, the printing and repro trade's biggest exhibition, Drupa, was being held. It was organized only once every four years and Tad agreed that he, Pete and I should go. He suggested that we invite some customers to come with us. I chose a couple of guys who owned a repro company in EC2 who'd been giving us a lot of scanning work, Tony Austin and John Morley.

They had bought their company, Web Offset Repro, from the colourful Bob Gavron when he'd split his St Ives printing group to focus solely on printing. Sadly, Bob Gavron died in 2015. He had been created a life peer for all his philanthropic charity work and generous donations to the Labour Party.

Tony and John were good customers and good fun. I'd had several lunches with them in the past and enjoyed their company. Tad invited three of his customers and together we were a party of eight. All the hotels in Dusseldorf were booked out due to the show, so we ended up in rather meagre lodgings in Cologne, some thirty miles away.

Luckily, when Pete and I, along with Tony and John, visited the Crosfield stand at the Expo, Lars Janneryd, now the company's managing director, offered us two twin rooms in the nearby Hilton Hotel. We all had a great couple of days, not least in the Hilton's bar one evening where I met a couple of Americans who owned printing companies in downtown New York. They expressed an interest in buying separations from us in London; a casual meeting which was to influence our export ambitions later.

Another source of new business came from an introduction by an old colleague at Crosfield. Steve Hicks was the young marketing manager who was also a very talented designer. He had redesigned our corporate stationery creating a brilliantly clever cylindrical shaped logo with the words 'COLOUR PRECISION and COLOUR SCANNING' wrapped around it. He introduced me to the then art director of *Vogue* magazine, Terry Jones.

Terry was designing a beautiful coffee table book titled *Masterpieces of Erotic Art* to be printed in Italy, but he was looking for a local company to do the separations and proofs.

Colour Precision produced the work and after it had been printed and bound, we had a superb sample which was a great sales aid to getting further work from the book publishing sector. Terry was later to create the famous style magazine, *i-D*, and we became quite close friends working together.

For some time, I had been renewing and cultivating old friendships from Crosfield with the view to expanding our sales overseas. Roy Warras was based in Oslo, Norway, and acting as our agent introduced us to several Norwegian clients. Towards the end of October, I visited him and together we made about a dozen sales calls.

I was struck by the incredible cleanliness of the repro companies that we visited, completely different to the embarrassingly untidy and generally grubby state of our own in the UK. Roy was an extremely sociable character, one evening at dinner he introduced me to the local speciality, reindeer, assuring me that I wasn't eating Rudolf. I can't say that I preferred it over a more familiar beef steak.

Travelling on from Norway I flew to Frankfurt to meet another ex-colleague from Crosfield, Michael Raif, who had also agreed to act as our agent. Together we attended the colossal annual Frankfurt Book Fair, the largest gathering of book publishers in the world.

We had enormous success, especially showing our impressive sample *Masterpieces*. Following the Expo, we drove to Stuttgart and visited the massive Mair printing company. Michael introduced me to many repro and printing companies that he was visiting on our behalf.

It was around this time that Birgitta's ex-brother-in-law, Cat Stevens, had purchased two apartments on the top floor of a five-storey block in Limassol, Cyprus. The apartments were adjacent to each other, so he had them knocked together to form one enormous flat. He had bought them for his mother to holiday there as it was next door to the hotel where his mum and dad had spent their honeymoon. Birgitta and I were considering a short holiday and he had offered us the use of it for our break.

Cyprus had recently been invaded by the Turkish army who had partitioned the northern part of the island. Thousands of Turkish Cypriots who had inhabited Limassol in the south, had been 'repatriated' to the north. Consequently, the region at that time was not commercialized and was free of tourists.

The apartment building was situated at the end of a country track off a minor thoroughfare right on the seafront. It was a wonderfully quiet area with only a few hospitable tavernas nearby. We had such a fabulous time that we planned to return in the future.

In the event, a couple of years later, we did return, taking with us my mum and our two youngest daughters, my Louise and Birgitta's

Rebecca. We landed at the airport in Larnaca, about forty miles from Limassol, and I gave the taxi driver the address of the apartment.

I thought there was some mistake when he delivered us to an unrecognizable destination. He had pulled over on a busy dual carriageway, lined with high-rise apartment blocks and hotels. He insisted that it was the correct place and pointed out the directions for our apartment building.

Gone was the narrow country track leading to it. Where there had been open fields, trees and rich shrubbery, there were now souvenir and gift shops, bars and even a rollerblade discotheque! In the intervening years, displaced Greek Cypriots from the Turkish occupied north of the island, had descended on Limassol and developed the entire region. It was a nightmare. As it turned out, Mum and the children loved it, exploring the shops and the 'entertainment', but for Birgitta and me, it was the longest three weeks in our lives.

****

As 1978 dawned I was impatient to secure more sales from outside of London. I placed an advert for a salesgirl in the *Manchester Evening News*. There were dozens of applicants so I hired a small conference room in the grand, red-brick, baroque Midland Hotel in the centre of Manchester, and spent a day interviewing the most likely candidates.

We employed the successful young woman but unfortunately, she didn't last long. After only three months with no orders she gave up. Maybe Mancunians were more resistant to young sales ladies, or maybe she just didn't try hard enough, I don't know.

However, my attention had been turned across the English Channel to Paris. I had re-established contact with yet another old Crosfield colleague, the urbane and amusing Tom Webb; he of armfuls of vintage champagne fame.

Tom was the manager of the Crosfield French office and had contacts all over France. He was also keen to act as agent for us. It wasn't long before work started to flow from him and I found myself on trips backwards and forwards to Paris.

This was a period when the only regular flights to Paris were shared between British Airways and Air France, and only flew out of Heathrow. They alternated airlines every hour on the hour. The first flight, Air France, left Heathrow at 6 a.m. followed at 7 a.m. by British Airways then back to Air France, changing throughout the day. The last flight, a British Airways, left Paris for London at 8 p.m.

Many times, I caught the first flight out in the morning to deliver work to Tom and caught the last flight back. Unfortunately, both airlines flew from different terminals. Having left my car parked at Terminal Two, the European terminal, I'd arrive back late and tired at Terminal One, the British Airways terminal. Half the time I didn't know where I was! This went on for several months.

Occasionally Tad drove over in his bright red Porsche Boxster, taking the finished work with him. This was long before the channel tunnel was built, so the journey involved the tiresome ferry crossing route between Dover and Calais. Tad kept us amused with stories of breakdowns, traffic hold-ups, customs problems and a myriad of other frustrations that occur when you are trying to improve Britain's balance of payments deficit!

I'd long had a bee in my bonnet about getting work from New York, the city I had fallen in love with two years previously. By now Tad had three Magnascan 550s operating around the clock; when they were all working efficiently, we had an enormous production capacity, so we were always searching for new markets.

The American contacts I had made at the Drupa exhibition, plus the gigantic potential from the New York book publishing industry persuaded us to give it a try. We decided to set up a new company, Color Precision, and we commissioned Steve Hicks from Crosfield to design new business stationery and a beautiful 12-page glossy brochure exemplifying our best work.

Tad, Pete and I all committed to investing £2,000 each to get the new company started. I wasn't sure how I was going to raise my share of the capital as my bank, Barclays in Hampstead, had already turned me down for the loan. My friend in Germany, Michael Raif, had offered to lend me part of the amount, but only on a very short term.

Mick Worwood from Harvey Goldsmith's office told me that they had an office in New York, which was also a small apartment that would be coming available shortly. It was on the sixth floor at 130 West 57th Street, right next to the Russian Tea Room, and a couple of floors above the Rolling Stones' New York office. I told him that we would certainly be interested in taking over the lease.

With the brochures and stationery all printed, and my suitcase packed, I said long goodbyes to Birgitta as I might be gone for a couple of months and set off for The Big Apple.

I had booked into The Sheraton on Seventh Avenue opposite Carnegie Hall and just around the corner from Mick's office. My first disappointment came from Mick's staff who told me that they didn't know when or even *if* they would be vacating the office. This was a big blow as the office was to have doubled as a small flat for me.

The Sheraton, although reasonably priced, was going to be too expensive to stay in for long. After the first week, I decamped to the rather tired, even shabby, but much cheaper, Wellington Hotel opposite.

My next disappointment came with the subject matter that we had chosen to illustrate our brochure. We had used photographs by the renowned photographer Sam Haskins, whose signature shots often had an apple in them – photojournalists nicknamed him 'Sam the apple man'!

The front cover of the brochure showed a partial back view of a nude woman wearing a body stocking and clasping an apple between her elbow and her waist. The shot was intended to illustrate the scanner's ability at reproducing the fine detail of the stocking mesh, while maintaining full colour saturation in the red apple.

Originally, the copyline beneath the photograph was to read 'Big Apple's latest babe'! a reference to our young company moving to New York. Subsequently, we decided to replace this line with just our company name, 'Color Precision'.

Unbeknown to us, most of the production managers in the publishing houses in New York were women. In 1970s' New York the women's liberation movement was in full swing, with writers like Gloria Steinem and Germaine Greer leading the feminist crusade. In some cases, our front cover was regarded as derogatory and demeaning to women, with some prospective clients receiving it with disdain, if not outright revulsion. My presentations often started on the back foot!

Despite these setbacks, I was enjoying my days selling, or attempting to sell, but the evenings could be very dull and lonely in Midtown Manhattan. Happily, Birgitta's ex-brother-in-law and uncle to my stepchildren, Cat Stevens, was often in town.

He very kindly invited me out on several occasions to have dinner with him and his manager or his lawyer. He got me front row seats at Madison Square Gardens to see one of my favourite bands, Electric Light Orchestra. He was staying at the luxury Carlyle Hotel on the Upper East Side, where the hotel management had organized a powerful hi-fi system and a grand piano in his suite. He had just recorded what he said would be his last album, *Back to Earth*, as he had just converted to the religion Islam, and was changing his name to Yusuf Islam.

He took this repressive religion very seriously but was quite tolerant of my intemperance and atheism. We had very passionate arguments about the origin and meaning of life. He tried very hard to convince me of the truisms of the Bible and the Koran, without success. He came in for a lot of criticism and even ridicule for his newfound faith.

A member of the paparazzi had photographed him walking in New York carrying his rolled-up prayer mat under his arm. The New York Times printed the picture on their front page under the heading 'The Cat Sat on the Mat'.

I felt very privileged to be sharing his company. He was an extremely generous, sincere and interesting man, whose music and lyrics had influenced millions of people across the world. I thought that it was very sad that he was turning away from it all.

I had been working in New York for a few weeks but still hadn't managed to raise my share of the seed capital, £2,000. I decided to try to sell my share in my ex-marital home at 14 Pembroke Street.

Jan had met a nice guy, Geoff, who worked in middle management and had moved in with her. I rang him to ask if he would like to buy my share, fifty per cent of the house, so he and Jan could own it together. The house was valued at around £17,000, an amazing gain considering we had only paid £1,400 a few years earlier.

There was probably desperation in my voice as Geoff drove a very hard bargain. He pleaded penury but suggested that if he sold both his car – he drove an impressive, classic Sunbeam Tiger – and his camera, he might be able to raise about £1,500! I think we settled around £2,000, but I was grateful as I was at my wits' end.

After I had been working in New York for a month or so, Pete flew out for a long weekend to keep me company. On the Saturday morning, we were sitting outside a coffee shop on Seventh Avenue; Pete was gazing thoughtfully skywards at the impressive high-rise buildings that were towering above us. I asked him what he thought of it all. He turned his gaze to me and said that he was just "marvelling at the vulgarity of it all". New York wasn't his cup of tea! The next day we were to find out how dangerous and scary New York could be.

It was a beautiful autumnal morning and we had decided to go for a stroll in Central Park. After a short walk into the park we came across a bicycle rental stall, so we hired a couple of their distinctive, white-painted bikes and peddled off to the north-west corner of the park, where Central Park West meets 110th Street, the outskirts of Harlem.

This was long before Harlem became gentrified. Everyone I had met in New York had warned me that the only safe way for a white person to enter Harlem was to be accompanied by a black person of the same gender.

On that sunny Sunday morning, it all looked so peaceful. While standing by our bicycles contemplating venturing further, several groups of young black guys were strolling by carrying enormous 'ghetto blasters' on their shoulders, rhythmically jiving happily along the busy boulevard.

We decided that it looked very friendly and took off to explore more. Within a couple of blocks, the entire landscape changed. Gone were the wide tree-lined boulevards, replaced with narrow, dark terraces, lined with seemingly derelict tenements. Burnt-out cars and upturned garbage bins littered the streets. From smashed doorways, squatting groups of vagrants gave us surly looks.

Looking the quintessential tourists – Pete even had his expensive camera dangling round his neck – I suddenly felt terribly out of place and conspicuous. A startling smash of breaking glass directly behind me caused me to stop and turn to look, thinking that Pete had crashed into something. He indicated that it had come from one of the upper tenement windows.

Another crash and I realized that someone was throwing bottles down at us. At that moment a gang of young black guys, also on bicycles, rode up and started to encircle us menacingly. I didn't wait to see if maybe they were just local Sunday School students offering to act as our guides. I just took off and didn't stop peddling frantically until I reached the safety of the busy Central Park North.

When Pete caught up with me, he reckoned that I had performed a bicycle wheelie leaving a 20-metre long skid mark! I wasn't sure where the skid mark that he was referring to was. When I recounted the incident to some of my customers, they were shocked at our stupidity, telling me that the previous year there had been almost 2,000 homicides in New York, *half* of them in Harlem!

A few days later Pete returned to London and I continued with my canvassing. After a couple of months of traipsing the streets I had lost nearly two stone in weight and I reckoned my arms had grown two inches carrying my briefcase and heavy samples bag.

The flat at Mick's office didn't eventuate and I'd pretty much had enough. I had only opened a couple of accounts, I was missing

Birgitta and my daughters. The money had just about run out so I decided to head back home for Christmas.

Back in London we managed to recoup a portion of our costs by me writing a marketing report on sales opportunities in New York, for the British Overseas Trade Board (BOTB), a government initiative. But otherwise, sadly, the venture was a complete failure.

There was an amusing footnote to the report that I'd had to write for the BOTB to recover all our expenses for flights and hotels. The document had to include the names of all the companies that I had visited and provide the names of their management personnel and details of the books that they had published. We were to be attended by an officer of the BOTB to check that we were a bona fide company. The gentleman duly arrived and Pete and I gave him a tour of the company, extolling its modern equipment and portraying what dynamic and progressive young executives we were.

Immediately after we had escorted the official out of the building, I suggested to Pete that we might like to listen to a new tape cassette of the group Manhattan Transfer that I had just bought. We ducked into my car that was parked outside, reclined the front seats back to full tilt, turned on the car stereo to full volume, sank back and closed our eyes to enjoy the fabulous harmonizing of this talented group.

No sooner had we immersed ourselves in the overwhelming surround-sound than there was a loud knocking on the car window. Startled, we opened our eyes and bolted upright to see our visitor from the BOTB who'd returned with a question he'd forgotten to ask. Looking down at the pair of us prostrate, listening to deafening music must certainly have challenged his views of us being the highly motivated, energetic executives that we'd attempted to portray. Maybe he saw the funny side as he approved the report and the BOTB paid the grant in full!

****

Meanwhile, London was experiencing one of the coldest winters on record. Freezing temperatures bringing with it blizzards and deep snow. It wasn't only the weather that was freezing; in an effort to control escalating inflation, wage rises in the public sector were frozen causing widespread strikes across the country.

Hospital ancillary staff, lorry drivers, refuse collectors and, in Liverpool, even grave diggers were on strike! Rubbish was piling up in the streets, and hospitals were accepting only emergency patents. It was rumoured that bodies were piling up in the mortuaries in Liverpool.

It was into this chaotic situation that the prime minister, Jim Callaghan, returning from a summit on the Caribbean island, Guadeloupe and sporting a conspicuous suntan, proclaimed that there was no chaos, prompting *The Sun* newspaper to splash the famous headline, 'Crisis? What Crisis'? and historians to label the period 'The Winter of Discontent'.

This also began my own period of discontent. I was disappointed with the outcome in New York, and generally dissatisfied with my employment situation. Even though Tad was an exemplary employer, and Colour Precision had become a thriving little business with great colleagues to work alongside, I hankered for something else. A couple of incidents prompted my next move.

When leaving the factory one evening I bumped into one of the salesmen from our local graphic arts merchant, who was delivering a box of film to Spectraplan. His grey hair betraying his retirement age and wearing a slightly crumpled suit and a harassed expression as he bustled past me to run up the stairs and make his delivery gave me pause for thought.

That evening I mentioned the encounter to Birgitta who jolted me with the accusation that I also might end up as 'an ageing rep'. I realized that she was right, I had lost sight of my original ambition. The three years that I had been working for Tad had totally engrossed me.

While I was very proud of our accomplishments at Colour Precision, I recognized that at thirty-five years of age, having been employed for twenty years it was time to strike out on my own before I lost my self-confidence. Late that same evening, Birgitta's ex-husband, David, called around. Over a few drinks I unburdened my employment frustrations.

He suggested that what I had achieved for Hogan's and Colour Precision I should be doing for myself. He went on to say that all I needed was an order book, take the orders then place the work with a variety of sources adding a percentage onto the bill for myself. It was just the encouragement that I needed.

I was very upfront and honest with Tad, explaining my dissatisfaction and aspirations. He was very understanding and even supportive. Pete wasn't ready to join me at that time but enjoyed assisting me in choosing a name for the new venture. He still claims the credit for coming up with 'Latent Image'; my recollection, of course, is slightly different!

I needed a new office to work from as I felt it was important to break away from Colour Precision. The two friends and clients, Tony Austin and John Morley at Web Offset Repro, not only offered me an office in their factory, but also volunteered to pay me a stipend of £100 per week to secure first option on my work.

Although I gratefully accepted their offer, their address of 'Scrutton Street' did not have the cachet to which I aspired. Cat Stevens had a lease on a five-storey building at 27 Curzon Street, Mayfair, where he kept an apartment and his offices. He agreed to me using this on my stationery and for my postal address. These days the building is occupied by the exclusive, private gambling club, Aspinall's.

Alec Zolas, who worked from the address, was Cat Stevens's brother-in-law and his bookkeeper. He introduced me to their accountant, Jose Goumal. Jose, or Joe as he preferred, registered my new company and supplied me with a cash book, and purchases and sales ledgers.

Not knowing a thing about corporate governance or financial administration, Joe reassured me that my forte was selling, and that was what I should go out and do, leaving all the admin stuff to him and Alec.

So there I was, 'the winds of change were blowing'. There had recently been a general election and Britain had its first woman prime minister, Margaret Thatcher. Jim Callaghan's 'winter of discontent' had blown him off his pedestal.

There was to be enormous conflict ahead as the new Conservative government took on the powerful and militant trade unions, leading to over three million people unemployed and the worst recession since The Great Depression of the 1930s.

Fortunately, I was oblivious to all of this on Monday 1st October 1979 as I drove towards Tunbridge Wells. It was the inaugural day of my new business, Latent Image Limited, and I was driving to pick up the first job for my new company.

It was only seven small scans to be separated, but to me it represented a whole new beginning and a good omen to be bringing in work by 9 a.m. on my first morning, finally working for myself in my own company.

Chapter 14

A Wedding and a War

After twenty years of virtually continuous employment and having worked for eight separate companies always enjoying a regular income, it was quite daunting to leave all this security to go it alone. From my very earliest entrepreneurial endeavours selling bundles of firewood, pub Christmas cards, wall prints, etc. I had always wanted to run my own business, and now here was my opportunity.

Tony and John made me very welcome in the new office they'd made available for me at Web Offset Repro – which they were soon to re-name as Argent Colour Ltd. Tony had just treated himself to a new Porsche 911 sports car which he was keeping hidden around the corner from his factory. He told me that he was worried that if his employees saw him in it, they would think he was making too much money and demand increases in their wages.

I needed transport, so I offered to buy his former wheels, a beat-up, two-door Opel Kadett. I generously say *two* doors, as the passenger door was broken and remained locked shut throughout the twelve months or so that I drove the old banger.

This was more of an embarrassment than an inconvenience, particularly when I once had to collect a visiting German customer from Heathrow Airport. Fritz Rudiger was a very large man, fortunately he had a sense of humour as he struggled to get his massive frame and suitcase through the driver's side and across the seat and protruding gear stick to the front passenger seat.

The car also possessed a very unpleasant smell, not unlike the rancid, sour stench of fresh vomit. I'd appealed to Tony several times as to the origin, but he always pleaded ignorance. It was in this mode of transport that I charged around London drumming up business for my new enterprise.

During the first few months in my new company I was fortunate to meet several people who were to have a big impact on the business. The tall, young, curly-haired Ray Benwell from Arch press in Southwark was a huge supporter, feeding me with as much repro work as he was able, which I tried to repay by placing my small offset printing requirements with his company. Ray and I became very good friends, but sadly lost touch when he left the printing industry to open a guest house on the Isle of Wight.

Another person to help me enormously was the engaging Alex Zolas, Cat Stevens's brother-in-law and bookkeeper. Originally from Albania – or Bulgaria, I can't remember which – his moon-faced countenance and Mediterranean features complemented his jovial and generous nature.

Alex and I shared an enthusiasm for modern fiction and red wine, spending many evenings together sharing both! At the start of my business Alex organised my bookkeeping and introduced me to the concert promoter, Mel Bush.

Although thinning, greying and receding, Mel Bush still wore his curly hair fashionably long in keeping with the famous musicians and rock bands that he promoted. Always in blue jeans over stylish cowboy boots, he worked from his large first-floor apartment on Hyde Park Square.

Mel had promoted all the big bands; from Bowie to the Bay City Rollers, from the Osmonds to Elton John; Led Zeppelin, Queen, you name them, he'd promoted them. He was a quiet, unassuming, unflustered man whose only outward sign of wealth was his Rolls Royce Silver Shadow with personalized numberplates.

He was currently negotiating with Oxfam and the United Nations children's humanitarian organization, UNICEF, to produce a concert that November to raise money for the International Year of the Child. Alex had suggested to him that I was the man to produce the official souvenir programme for the event.

This was a massive job and a huge feather in my cap, a great start, and only my second month in business. Mel was assembling a wonderful variety of famously talented artistes and bands including, among others, the singer David Essex, the soul group The Real Thing, the progressive rock band Wishbone Ash, the classic/rock fusion band Sky, even persuading the now reclusive Cat Stevens to come out of retirement and perform.

Mel wished me to handle everything from design, typesetting, repro and printing, even wanting me to secure the display adverts in the programme. I had no hesitation where to place the design work. My old friend, the marketing manager from Crosfield Electronics, Steve Hicks, had since left the firm, joined forces with the ex-manager of Crosfield's typesetting division, Glyn Hayes, and formed a creative design agency, Hicks and Hayes.

They had only recently started their business and were still operating out of Glyn's flat in Earls Court. It wasn't long before they were moving to a trendy loft style studio in a warehouse in Paddington. Steve was a very talented designer, extremely professional and an absolute pleasure to work with.

He conceived a design which illustrated perfectly the sentiments of the event. Everyone was delighted with the final printed programme; it cemented my association with the Mel Bush Organisation for many future concert productions.

I was still managing to visit my girls at weekends, although as Rachel and Claire were heading towards teenagers, they were finding our routine of visiting their grandparents etc. increasingly tiresome. I arrived one Saturday morning to find them in a mood of shuffling unease; they had made other plans.

They told me that they would rather meet up with their friends and hang out in town than join me walking in the Cotswolds and visiting Mum. I was taken by surprise and remonstrated that I had driven from London to be with them. I was hurt but accepted that it was their weekend as well, and it would be pointless to compel them.

As they turned to get ready to depart, my seven-year-old Louise took my hand, looked up at me and said, "Don't worry Dad, you've still got me," and my heart melted.

There were times, particularly over school holidays, when I brought them all to London with me. It was much more fun for them, taking in all the sights and visiting West End shows. Having six children in the house was a bit of a handful; stepbrothers and sisters don't always make for perfect sibling relationships.

We were hardly The Brady Bunch, but by and large, except for a few minor spiteful childish incidents, they all got on fairly well. One Saturday morning, Yusuf – as Cat Stevens now called himself – turned up and offered to cook all the children his 'speciality' breakfast. I can't remember whether it was scrambled eggs or eggs Benedict, but whatever it was, it was a success, and everyone around the table enjoyed it.

During the meal, Rachel asked Yusuf what *his* favourite song that he'd written was. It was a question that I'd never thought to ask him. Without hesitating he said, "Father and Son", which I thought was interesting as it wasn't his most famous, yet evidently it was his most personal.

Birgitta was always very welcoming to my girls. I know that she enjoyed watching them choosing what to wear when we were all going out, unlike her boys who, like all boys, aren't at all interested in selecting an outfit to step out in.

Over the years we had all my girls living with us for periods of time. Young Louise stayed with us and attended the local school with her stepsister Rebecca while Jan was in hospital in Gloucester undergoing and recuperating from a complicated hysterectomy operation.

Claire lived with us when she became a particularly rebellious teenager and was too much of a handful for her mother. Finally, Rachel lived with us when she had joined the Civil Service in Gloucester, then successfully applied for a transfer to Westminster.

As we entered the new 1980s decade, Britain was heading towards a deep recession, the worst since the depression of the 1930s. Unemployment was approaching two million and destined to climb to over three million as the Thatcher government wrestled to control inflation which was rising above twenty per cent.

The interest rate was above seventeen per cent which was hitting manufacturers particularly hard. Fortunately, this didn't appear to affect my endeavours as I was finding myself getting busier and busier. But I was spending more time organizing, placing, collecting and delivering work than gaining new business. I needed someone to handle the production side while I looked after and obtained new sales; I needed Pete Rogers.

Pete and I had kept in close touch since I had left Colour Precision. On several weekends Pete had joined me when I was visiting my girls in Gloucester; they grew up knowing him affectionately as 'Uncle Pete'. It was during one of these trips away that I put the idea to him about joining me at Latent Image.

I must admit I probably painted a rather rosier picture of the success of my one-man-band, but I was confident of its future potential. In the event, after offering Pete a forty per cent shareholding he agreed to join me, taking up residence in my little office at Web Offset Repro early in March that year.

With Pete now taking care of all the production and admin, it allowed me to develop our sales. Within weeks we'd won the repro for four heavily illustrated coffee table books from two separate book publishing houses. Also, Mel Bush had given us orders for the souvenir programmes for two major tours, the Scottish singer/songwriter B. A. Robertson and the band Sky.

Work was also piling in from the small printers that I'd found. I felt confident enough in our immediate financial future to suggest to Birgitta that as we'd been together for over six years it was time that we got married.

Opposite the Grade 1 listed Victorian Gothic masterpiece that is St Pancras railway station on London's busy Euston Road stands the pillar-fronted neoclassical Camden Town Hall. This beautifully impressive building is nowadays where couples, resident in Hampstead Garden Suburb, which was where Birgitta and I lived, can attend the local Register Office there to legally pledge their nuptials.

However, on that bright but windy May Day afternoon in 1980 the register office was in the adjoining 1970s Brutalist style town hall annex. It was here in its austere utilitarian interior, that Birgitta and I, in front of twenty friends and family, swore our marriage vows. Following the legalities, we all took off to the historic Spaniards Inn on Hampstead Heath where I'd booked the upstairs Dick Turpin Room for our reception.

At thirty-nine years old – only three years older than me – Birgitta looked beautiful. She was wearing a pale, dove-grey fitted suit over an open-neck white blouse. She carried a small bouquet of white roses and carnations with a tiny matching posy in her hair, I couldn't have been happier.

Mum and Dad and my brother Pat and his wife Louise all made the journey to London for the occasion. Pete and his new partner Rosemary, plus Alex and his wife Anita with her famous brother, Yusuf and their mother, Ingrid, the grandmother to my three stepchildren all joined the party.

Even Birgitta's ex-husband David put in an appearance. Along with a few customers of mine who had all become friends, it made for a brilliant afternoon. The next morning Birgitta and I flew off to Agadir in Southern Morocco for a two-week honeymoon, lazing on its pristine and almost deserted beaches.

*****

Back in London approaching summer, Pete and I were so busy that we were placing work with several other companies apart from Tony and John's Webb Offset Repro. One of the companies we supplied was a small three-man outfit, Capricorn, owned and run by the prickly John Young.

I'd known John since my days with Crosfield when he'd set up his business in an attic five storeys above a NatWest bank on the corner of Goswell Road and Old Street in The City. It forever amused me that his young apprentice, Tony, always answered the phone with, "Hold on a minute, I'll see if he's in," which was funny as the firm was only one room, and John was always standing next to him!

John had since increased his business and had relocated around the corner to a ground-floor studio at 1 Crescent Row, a definite step up in the world. I liked John, often enjoying a beer or two with him, although he could be touchy and outspoken when things displeased him.

I had mentioned to John that the volume of scanned separations that I was outsourcing was enough to keep a scanner occupied full-time. He suggested that were I to buy a scanner he would be very interested in participating in a joint venture.

Pete was very keen on the idea even though it would entail him being the scanner operator, to begin with at least. He also knew where there was a second-hand Magnascan 460 for sale. The company wanted £25,000 for it – over £100,000 in 2019 money. We didn't want to pay the asking price, so we were offering £22,500; this wasn't accepted, so disappointingly we reached an impasse.

It was during this period of negotiating that I was producing a booklet for Yusuf. I had placed the printing work with Tad's printing company, Boss Colour in Greenwich. I'd invited Yusuf with Alex to visit Boss Colour to see his job on the presses. It was a small order but important to Yusuf as it illustrated his embracing of Islam, narrating the story of his conversion. The finished copies were to be mailed out to his fan club which, despite his withdrawing from recording more music, still numbered in the many thousands.

After we had finished at the printers, I offered to drive them over to see the scanner that I was negotiating on. Gordon, the director, was very accommodating, but did look askance at my anomalous looking guest.

It Was The Best Of Times...

In the early days of his conversion, Yusuf had immersed himself totally in Middle Eastern culture, learning Arabic and wearing traditional Arab clothing. A backstreet repro company wasn't used to seeing a visitor dressed in an ankle length *dishdasha thawb* over open leather *najdi* sandals, topped off with a rounded, white, crochet skullcap; this piqued Gordon's interest.

That evening Gordon telephoned me asking me about my curious companion. When I disclosed that the 'Arab' gentleman, Yusuf, was in fact the singer, Cat Stevens, Gordon was so overwhelmed to have had such a famous visitor in his factory he proposed accepting my offer price of £22,500 for the scanner, if maybe I might be able to persuade Yusuf to visit his house one evening for dinner?! I accepted his proposal with a proviso that it was unlikely that the less-than-sociable Yusuf would accept the invitation.

On a Saturday morning some months before, Yusuf had called by our house with the surprising news that he intended getting married. When I asked if we knew his 'intended' he shocked me by saying that *he* hadn't met her yet! She was the daughter of a fellow worshipper at the local mosque and Yusuf was on his way to ask her father for his daughter's hand in marriage.

In the event, Yusuf and Fauzia married and moved into a modest house around the corner from us, next door to his mother, Ingrid.

Occasionally they came around to join Birgitta and I for dinner, but I never got to know Fauzia. She was extremely reserved, never even raising her eyes through her face-covered *niqāb* to look at me. One day her restrained serenity almost caused me a monumental embarrassment.

It was pouring with rain and I was dashing to collect my mail from Yusuf's offices in Curzon Street in Mayfair. I'd had to park my car some distance away, so I was soaking wet as I entered the hallway of the building. As I was struggling out of my wet mackintosh and was about to throw it over a well-laden hat stand that was standing in a darkened alcove to my left, I was momentarily distracted by a voice ahead of me at the top of the staircase.

It was Yusuf on his way out of the building. I stopped at the foot of the stairs to say hi. We exchanged a few brief pleasantries then I asked after Fauzia.

"She's well," he said, beckoning to a sudden movement on my left.

I hope he didn't notice the startled look on my face when I realized that the dark, stationary object that I'd mistaken for a weighted down hat and coat stand, was in fact the motionless, floor-length, black *jilbab*-clad Fauzia! I was eternally grateful that I wasn't wearing a hat!

Now that we'd agreed a price for the scanner, the next problem was how to pay for it. When I'd started Latent Image, I'd opened a bank account with a small branch of Barclays near Waterloo railway station. With revenues in excess of £100,000 in less than ten months, I naively imagined that the bank would fall over itself to lend us the money.

Nevertheless, Pete and I were quite apprehensive on our way to our appointment with the bank manager. Pete had typed up some numbers on an A4 sheet of paper illustrating our current corporate income along with our projected sales and profits forecast.

Arriving at the bank we realized neither of us had a pen. I stressed to Pete that it was much more professional, when talking someone through our figures, to point to the columns of figures with a pen rather than an ugly, nicotine-stained index finger! We quickly ran to a local newsagent, purchased a 10p biro then hurried back to the bank, arriving sweaty and dishevelled!

The elderly, dour manager, seated behind his rather grand desk listened patiently to our enthusiastic presentation. As the meeting wore on, I sensed he wasn't sharing our excitement for the proposal. Finally, to clarify our projections, I walked around to his side of the desk, slid our sheet of figures in front of him, took out our 10p biro and attempted to hold the point of the pen against a column of sales figures.

Embarrassingly, my hand was nervously shaking so much that the pen was rat-tat-tatting against the paper. I had to rapidly exchange the pen for my index finger, stabbing it down hard on the desk to prevent it quivering.

After silently staring at our figures for a few moments, he leaned forward in his chair, unfolded his arms which had remained crossed across his chest throughout the meeting and got to his feet, signalling that our meeting was over. He shook our hands and told us that we had "a nice little business happening" but that we shouldn't risk it by investing in expensive equipment that he thought we didn't need.

He went on to say that we should stick at being agents which was proving to be successful. Pete and I left feeling quite dejected. Back at Capricorn, John suggested we try his bank across the road, a branch of NatWest. We made an appointment to see the manager for the following morning.

Fred Tongue was a completely different kettle of fish to our man at Barclays. A very tall Yorkshireman with sparkling blue eyes and a mop of prematurely grey hair, who addressed everyone as 'Pal'. He made us feel very welcome from the moment we stepped into his small office at the rear of the bank, even offering us a glass of whisky, although it was only ten-thirty in the morning!

He listened intently to our story, looked over our crude figures, then announced that he'd be happy to take over our account and arrange a small business loan to buy the scanner! Over the ensuing years I grew very fond of Fred; he was extremely supportive of me and the business, and we were destined to enjoy many happy hours socializing together until his early retirement some twelve years later.

Pete and I arranged with John to install the scanner on the ground floor of his factory. We formed a new company for it, Kindpoint, a name taken 'off the shelf' which we intended to change to 'Scandal', but for reasons that I can't remember was never used. It was agreed that Latent Image would hold two-thirds of the new company and John, by virtue of supplying the premises and some of the work and labour, would hold a third.

Pete got the scanner up and running, maintaining his boast that he was still the best scanner operator in London, and on Wednesday

6th August 1980 Kindpoint produced its first job, the front cover of the London listings magazine, *Time Out*.

Initially the scanning work trickled in, but soon there was a steady flow. Within months we were almost inundated, with Pete flat out working long hours keeping up with it. At that time the bulk of the work was coming from John's company, Capricorn. He had created a small office area for me to work from so I moved out of Web Offset's studio and settled into No1 Crescent Row.

It was approaching Latent Image's first anniversary; I had progressed from being a lone agent. I had partners, a full order book with many regular customers, our own scanning equipment and every reason to feel satisfied and happy.

Business was going from strength to strength, we were doing all our own scanning but placing a large amount of planning and platemaking with outside sources. We decided to employ our own planner.

I'd first seen Terry Harry when he was a young apprentice at a small trade planning company, H&L Planning in Goswell Road. I was delighted when he applied to join us as I knew he would be an excellent tradesman having learned from two guys whose work I really respected.

Terry did not disappoint us. His work was not only faultlessly accurate, he was exceedingly fast. Leaving his bench at the end of the day would see him covered from head to foot in bits of masking and Sellotape, and pieces of sticky Rubylith material, with his fingers stained brown from the opaque lacquer.

After many months working with us Terry politely, but sheepishly enquired if it would be possible for him to have a stool to sit on at his bench. He was finding the old dustbin that was all that I'd provided him to use, both uncomfortable and unhygienic. Terry definitely was not a whinger!

The top floor of our three-storey building housed the studio where the illustrious designer, Pearce Marchbank worked. Pearce designed the layouts for the weekly *Time Out* magazine. He was responsible for creating its iconic 'glowing neon' logo which embellished his famous, and often infamous front cover designs. The magazine was now including a four-page colour section in the middle which meant more work for us.

Unfortunately, the youthful owner of *Time Out*, Tony Elliot, was soon to encounter staffing problems which would force him to stop publication. But before this, Pete delivered his own bombshell to me.

He told me that Tad had teamed up with Andrew Petit, the owner of the printing company, Brandprint, and they were setting up a new repro company specializing in producing press-ads. They were installing a Hell DC300 colour scanner, plus all the ancillary planning and platemaking equipment. Pete told me that they had offered him a third of the business if he would join them. He said it was an offer he couldn't refuse.

I was shell shocked! It was the spring of 1981, we were extremely busy, particularly on scanning, and I was losing my partner. No amount of pleading, persuading or cajoling could change Pete's decision, he had made up his mind. He signed back the forty per cent of Latent Image that I'd given to him, and within a week he had left.

While *Time Out* had temporarily ceased publishing due to its staff being on strike the opportunistic Richard Branson of Virgin Music – this was at a time when the Virgin empire was in its infancy, long before he set up Virgin Airways – had seized the moment and was launching his own weekly listings magazine called *Event*.

He had persuaded Pearce Marchbank to join him as its art director, and Pearce channelled the cover and colour work through to us at Capricorn and Kindpoint. Although I was very sorry for Tony and his problems at *Time Out*, I had loans to repay and wages to find so didn't hesitate in accepting this work from Branson. It was a much more colourful magazine than *Time Out*, not only a colour cover but also eight pages of colour inside and numerous duotone – two-colour – images that would keep the scanner extremely busy.

A Wedding and a War

With Pete gone, John was still able to help a bit with scanning, but he had his own business to run. The only option was for me to operate the scanner myself. For many weeks I was not only collecting and delivering work during the daytime, I was also spending the nights working on the scanner, grabbing moments of sleep whenever I could. Birgitta often brought food to the factory for my dinner; it was a tough period.

Fortunately, come the summer, I managed to persuade Ron Brown – the scanner operator with whom I'd first worked at Hogan Colour Plates who had then joined us at Colour Precision – to come and join me at Kindpoint which relieved me of a huge amount of pressure. Ron proved to be an outstanding operator, and a stalwart pillar of the company for many years to come.

In late August there was the much-anticipated party for the first edition of *Event*. Richard Branson was holding the reception at his newly acquired nightclub, Heaven, which was in the vaulted arches underneath Charing Cross railway station. He had bought the club from Jeremy Norman, the chairman of Burke's Peerage, boasting that the half a million pounds he'd paid for it was funded by the brewery supplying the beer!

The club was the first sizeable gay club in London; it displayed a spectacular light show with Super Trouper spotlights rotating at the ends of the cellars and laser beams bouncing off the walls. John and I were invited to the party along with hundreds of guests including many celebrities, numerous journalists and assorted television crews.

Before the first printed issues arrived from the presses, Richard, Pearce and Al Clark, the editor, gathered around a long table which was bearing a massive, iced, sponge cake, baked in the shapes of the five letters that spelled the title 'Event'.

No sooner had Richard cut a huge slice from the cake, living up to his exuberant, mischievous style, he hurled it at Pearce, followed quickly by another piece at Al. Exactly as Richard was hoping, an enormous food fight followed with dozens joining in. Wearing a decent suit, I managed to avoid the flying food; when things had settled down, I congratulated Richard on the magazine; he thanked me for all our efforts and wrote a complimentary message on my copy of the launch issue.

Sadly, it wasn't always to be so friendly. As the months wore on with competition from *Time Out*'s sacked staff's rival magazine, *City Limits* and *Time Out* eventually reappearing on the newsstands, the circulation of *Event* gradually fell until its closure within the year. Prior to its final demise, Richard began scrutinizing all our invoices to him; it was not pleasant to be summoned to his houseboat on the canal at Little Venice, which he also used as his office, to have every minute item queried and negotiated downward!

It was also in late August of that year that a seemingly routine job would have such portentous consequences. I had been called into Arch Press to meet a client of theirs who was producing a colour calendar. I was introduced to the gentleman and shown about a dozen colour photographs that he wished to have reproduced. There were pictures of penguins, sea lions, elephant seals and a Royal Naval icebreaker.

I was told that the gentleman was producing the calendar on behalf of his community. They were concerned that a recent government Defence Review white paper was proposing naval cuts including the decommissioning of the pictured ice breaker, which they were convinced offered their community some protection from invasion. They hoped that the calendar would publicize their concerns and persuade the government to change its mind.

It transpired that the gentleman was not a regular client of Arch Press; he had flown into London that morning, consulted the Yellow Pages in the telephone directory, and Arch Press was the first printer to catch his eye. He had a slight brogue, so when he told me where he was from, I assumed it was somewhere north of Scotland, close to the Shetland Isles, Orkneys or Outer Hebrides. "Oh no," he explained, "it's in the South Atlantic, the Falkland Islands"!

A Wedding and a War

The calendars were produced and dispatched and I thought no more about it until the following April when the devastating news was announced that the Falkland Islands had been invaded by Argentina.

Memories flooded back to my meeting with the Falkland Islander, listening to his anxieties and warnings which I had dismissed, like so many others as hysterical paranoia. Sadly, his fears were all justified.

To try and divert attention from their stagnating economy, the Argentinian ruling military government had decided to invade the Falkland Islands, which they had always asserted was Argentinian territory. Unfortunately for Argentina, they hadn't reckoned on the iron will of Britain's prime minister, Margaret Thatcher.

As a lifelong Labour voter, I'd had many disagreements with Margaret Thatcher's policies, particularly economic ones. However, I would be the first to admit that she was absolutely the right person to take on the Argentinian military junta.

While the Foreign Office were advising her of all the difficulties and potential disasters of any military conflict, the Chief of Naval Staff, Sir Henry Leach, marched into her office and told her that he could assemble a task force within 48 hours to retake the islands!

Three days after the Argentinians had invaded, a task force set sail. Headed by two aircraft carriers, it included eight destroyers, fifteen frigates, six submarines and dozens of auxiliary minesweepers and supply ships. It carried over fifty warplanes and thousands of marines. Even so, everyone, including the United States, initially suspected that the whole operation was doomed, mainly due to the logistical difficulties of mounting a conflict 8,000 miles away.

Seventy-four days after the invasion, with the tragic loss of over 900 men, including 255 British soldiers and sailors, and three women islanders, the Argentinians surrendered to the British forces. The 1,820 island residents, not to mention the 500,000 sheep, would maintain their British sovereignty, and Margaret Thatcher would go on to a second election victory the following year.

It Was The Best Of Times...

****

In the spring of '82 major changes were developing. I felt that the business was growing large enough to stand alone in its own factory, so I set about searching for premises. A brand-new development of small factory/warehouse units just off the Caledonian Road, opposite HM Prison Pentonville caught my eye.

They were in the London Borough of Islington and the local authority was under the control of the Social Democratic Party who were endeavouring to encourage businesses into this run-down deprived area. To this end they were not only offering a six-month rent-free period, but also £1,000 for every employee a business introduced into the borough; a very attractive proposition.

Meanwhile, John was considering selling a third of his share of Kindpoint as he was seeking to raise money to install a large colour proofing press. I mentioned this to Ron who was interested in buying John's share. First, we had to agree on a valuation for Kindpoint. Naturally, trying to keep the price as low as possible for Ron to afford I opined that it wasn't worth much more than the value of the scanner, currently around £20,000. Obviously, John took the opposite view that with its revenue and profits it was worth twice that much. From memory we settled somewhere in between and Ron sought a loan to buy in.

It was around this time that Birgitta and I were out to dinner with Pete and his partner, Rosemary. I hadn't seen Pete for almost a year so was looking forward to hearing how he was getting on with Tad and Andrew. Pete was normally a contemplative, taciturn man, but that evening he seemed more withdrawn than usual. He said that his work was going ok but didn't want to expand on it, so I didn't pursue it.

Later in the evening, with Pete distracted, Rosemary took me to one side and told me that Pete was desperately unhappy, neither the promised scanner nor the partnership had happened. She felt sure that if I offered him his job back, he'd jump at it.

I didn't mention anything to Pete that evening but called him later in the week to suggest getting together for a beer. When I told him that I was looking to move into a new factory away from Capricorn he got very excited. I mentioned there may be a possibility to raise money to install platemaking equipment to provide a full repro service.

I really wanted Pete back working with me, he was my perfect foil; we had always worked so well together. Pete always regarded himself as a pragmatist, but he was also very thoughtful, even philosophical. He was conscientious and meticulous in his work practices and most of all, he was a lovely bloke and I loved him.

So I was ecstatic when he accepted my offer to return and work with me again. He insisted that he didn't want his shareholding returned to him, stating that he was happy to be an employee, adding that he would be more comfortable without the responsibility. So it was on that agreeable basis that Pete and I joined forces again.

With the combination of my two eldest daughters, Rachel and Claire, leaving school and starting jobs and work still pouring into Latent Image and Kindpoint, I felt confident enough to suggest to David, Birgitta's ex-husband, that I buy the house, our home at 4 Hill Rise, Hampstead Garden Suburb, from him.

It was valued at £50,000, so I would have to raise £25,000 for his half. When I discussed the loan with Fred at NatWest, I proposed the idea of borrowing the full £50k and using half to purchase equipment for the new factory that I was looking at in Islington.

Fred hesitated at this suggestion, saying that it was highly unorthodox as mortgages were meant to be just for the home. This was at a time when banks were beginning to compete with building societies in the mortgage market to combat the building societies' recent incursions into the banking sector by issuing cheque books.

I stressed to Fred that those regulations were only *guidelines*; I then exaggerated and said that I'd heard that building societies were turning a blind eye to these rules. After a phone call to his regional superiors relaying what I'd just said, he agreed to write the loan.

It Was The Best Of Times...

The final piece of this reorganization and transformation of Latent Image was about to fall into place. My old friends, Steve and Glyn at Hicks and Hayes had recently employed a young, attractive Irish girl assistant, Jenny. She had a girlfriend also from Ireland who had a university degree and was looking for a job. I needed someone to do our administration work so agreed to meet with her.

Joanne was lovely, totally unqualified for what we required, but so eager and bright that she won me over. She admitted that her only bookkeeping skills had been learned as a teenager looking after her parent's newsagent shop. What she lacked in experience she more than made up in enthusiasm.

Many people, particularly Prince Charles and Princess Diana, would rejoice on Monday 21st June 1982 for the birth of their son, the new heir to the throne, Prince William the Duke of Cambridge; others, simply because it was the longest day of the year. I would always remember it as the day that I got the keys to my new building at 6 Balmoral Grove.

Accompanied by a gang of builders who were to erect darkrooms and a staircase to a large mezzanine floor, I was excitedly envisaging my own self-contained, streamlined and productive factory; I wasn't to be disappointed.

Chapter 15

A Bad Debt and a Good Deal?

It had taken almost three years to finally establish myself in my own repro factory; it was even better than I could have imagined. It not only housed the Magnascan but all the new equipment for a fully operational repro company and it looked spectacular. In the first few weeks while we all settled into our new environment, work continued to flow through the door, we were attracting new business and our equipment was performing superbly, but there remained one cloud on the horizon.

Birgitta's son Daniel often appeared a troubled and cheerless lad. He was clever but not academic. I'd continued to encourage his hobbies. I'd even taken him away on his own, just the two of us, hiking on the Malvern Hills in a vain attempt to get closer to him. He was now sixteen years old with no idea what work he'd like to do.

Birgitta had persuaded me to employ him so he had joined Pete and me some months before, when we were based at John Young's Capricorn Repro factory. There were difficulties from the very beginning. Just trying to get Daniel to get out of bed in the mornings to join me on the drive into work was an everyday effort.

One of his duties as the youngest and designated apprentice scanner operator, was to fetch the snacks from the local café, for the morning's break; this he refused to do! He complained that he couldn't cope with the traffic's exhaust fumes along the City Road. He showed little interest in becoming a scanner operator, in fact John had joked that Dan wanted to start as company chairman, then work his way up!

Now, in our own premises, an apprentice's duties were even more important, but sadly, Pete, a normally patient, tolerant man had had enough, Dan would have to go. In fact, he told me, "It's either him or me!"

It was not easy to sack your own stepson. It caused no small problems at home with an unsympathetic Birgitta, who felt he hadn't been given a proper chance. David, Daniel's dad was none too happy with me either. Luckily Dan's Uncle Yusuf came to the rescue and employed him, doing what I'm not sure, but he seemed happier.

Dan's departure created a vacancy for an apprentice which I mentioned to two friends Steve and Chris who owned a scanner servicing company, Centerfax; they told me a story which I found hard to believe.

They said that they purchased their electronic parts, resistors, transistors and capacitors etc. from a one-man specialist retailer in North London. He worked on his own and his shop was always busy; always a queue of people, the phone always ringing and the owner up and down stepladders searching for electronic components to complete orders. The owner could obviously have done with some assistance. Steve suggested to him that he should employ a young lad who could at least answer the telephone for him.

The man told Steve that he had been advertising for months and had interviewed dozens of youngsters. He went on to say that the first one who could answer one simple question would get the job; so far no one could answer the question correctly.

Utterly intrigued, Steve asked, "What is the question?" His answer stunned Steve and me when he told me. The shop owner simply asked, "What's three times nine?"

I found it very hard to believe that sixteen-year-old school leavers didn't know their times tables. Pete was as shocked as I was at the story and determined to ask the same question to the young applicants that we were due to interview. We decided that the correct or incorrect answer to the question wouldn't necessarily be the clincher for the job, but that it would be extremely interesting and enlightening nevertheless.

Over the course of three days in mid-August, Pete and I interviewed nineteen young school leavers, none of whom appeared to have received any guidance towards presentation for a job interview. Several turned up with friends, some of whom were carrying large 'ghetto blasters' with them. As to the cardinal question, it was generally received with a blank stare, or a scratched head and a mumbled, "Er, I wasn't very good at maths."

One lad volunteered "Twenty-four?" to which Pete said, "So if I pay you nine pounds a day and you work for three days, you'll be happy with twenty-four pounds?"

We did have one candidate who stood out from the rest. He had worked for a short period for a bookbinding company which had recently closed. However, he'd had the foresight to request a reference from his employer which he'd brought with him.

It was extremely complimentary, extolling the lad's work ethic and his capabilities. Young Steven Szekely was indentured as our first apprentice; he certainly lived up to the testimonial that he'd shown us.

I had become aware of the difficulties for school leavers to enter the printing industry due to the prevailing restrictions operated by the print unions. Jan's brother, Derek, a schoolteacher and careers master in South London, had told me that it was impossible to get any of his students into the printing industry in London.

When I mentioned this to Pete, he acknowledged it telling me that the only way that he had entered the trade was because his father was a retoucher, working at the gigantic, rotogravure factory, Odhams Press. His dad had also got Pete's brother, Steve, into the trade as a planner.

I had paid my union dues and kept my union card up until my time selling the scanners for Crosfield. When I realized that the union movement had become too strong and militant and it had cost me sales, I stopped my subscriptions. This was a period when trade union powers were at their zenith. The 'closed shop' system forcing companies to employ only union members – made illegal in 1990 – was bad enough, but I considered the pervasive nepotism to be completely repugnant.

I recognized the print unions as both sexist and racist as there were no women or black people working in the trades at that time. Pete and I both determined to do our best to change this situation whenever we could. This gave me great satisfaction over the years as we employed many young people. Many became apprentices who completed their four-year indentures going on to become skilled tradesmen.

We had completed our six-month rent-free period but as yet I hadn't claimed the £1,000 for each employee introduced into the borough. Including Pete and myself we numbered just six of us, but even so, £6,000 would make a huge difference to our cash flow which was always pretty stretched due to the 90-day credit given to clients which was the standard period at that time.

I made an appointment to see the local government officer in charge of our area. As I presented my request to him, the incredulous expression on his face did not bode well! After rummaging through his filing cabinet, he withdrew a sheaf of papers. He said that he was surprised that I had not heard that in the recent local council elections, the Social Democrats had lost and a Labour council had been elected. He informed me that we were now living in a self-styled Socialist Republic of Islington.

He went on to read from his paperwork that at a council meeting it was voted that the employee financial incentives had been withdrawn and he quoted, "We're not giving money to bloated plutocrats!"

I said, "Bloated plutocrats! I mortgaged my home to move into this factory!"

His attitude changed, and he became very sympathetic and apologised on behalf of the council, but there was nothing he could do, it was Labour council's policy. I learned years later that the leading activist on the Islington Labour Council at that time was a young Jeremy Corbyn!

Fortunately, we were getting busier and busier at work. This was in no small way due to a series of serendipitous introductions which led me to meeting the dynamic, Indian salesman, Manab Majumder. Manab, or as he was affectionately known, Manny, was a delightful man. He had been working with a large repro company in East London which had recently relocated to Kent. Manny's clients were all based around Central London, so he was looking for a repro company that could service them locally.

I was extremely eager for Manny to join us. If he could bring the quality of clients that he said he represented, I would appoint him as our sales director. He accepted this challenge and within a few weeks he had introduced three major magazine titles, all from nationally known publishing houses. I was soon to recognize the benefits of specializing in magazine repro. While the prices that we could charge were significantly lower than for advertising or book publishing work, the great advantage was the regularity and consistent dependability of the workflow.

Manny went on to win more and more titles for us, he earned his directorship and I owe a huge debt of gratitude to him. He often joked that he would make me a millionaire, albeit a "rupee millionaire!" he added.

We were still getting a lot of scanning work from John Young at Capricorn and during the summer we had also won four considerable tour programmes from Mel Bush, including one for the mega-star Elton John. We had employed another planner, the experienced and very accomplished John Droy and were looking to take on another scanner operator.

By winter of that year I felt in desperate need of a holiday. A local travel agent was offering a 'three weeks for the price of two' deal on the Caribbean island of Antigua and I snapped it up. Neither Birgitta nor I had ever experienced a tropical island, and we both fell instantly in love with it. Escaping from an English winter to enjoying blue skies, white beaches and turquoise waters – not to mention delicious food eaten to a background of reggae and calypso music – we had a ball, although one early experience might have put a sudden end to everything.

Never having seen such glorious, tall, swaying palm trees before, and right outside our hotel room, I lay down on the grass in the shade of one of the tallest. Within seconds an almighty crash right next to my head had me jumping up in alarm. A coconut in its husk is about the size of a large beach ball and weighs several kilos. One had fallen out of the tree landing inches from my head, a foot to the left would have splattered my skull. I couldn't help musing that you can spend your life worrying about a nuclear bomb falling, but then get dispatched by a bloody coconut!

In the spring of 1983, the prime minister, Margaret Thatcher, had been in office for four years. The first three years of her tenure had been marked by a poor economy and high unemployment. However, the previous year had seen economic growth and improvement in employment figures. On the back of this and her victory in the Falklands War, she called a general election.

Since Labour's Jim Callaghan had resigned in 1980, the opposition party had been led by the left-wing Michael Foot. Labour had swung so far left that several moderate MPs had quit the party to form the Social Democrat Party. Labour's manifesto for the election included such radical measures as abolishing the House of Lords, leaving the European Economic Community and abandoning Britain's nuclear deterrent by cancelling the Trident submarine programme and cruise missiles.

Thatcher's Conservative party won by a landslide, causing Labour MP Gerald Kaufman to famously say that the Labour Party's manifesto was "the longest suicide note in history"!

On the home front, Birgitta's ex-husband, David, had paid the deposit on a house for Daniel and Bobby who were only in their late teens. It was a large four-storey, terraced property in Finsbury, North London. He reasoned that they could fill the house with young "rooming" tenants, using those rents to pay off the mortgage. They would eventually own the house, giving them both a good financial start in life.

The boys told me that their dad had done a deal with his brother, their Uncle Yusuf. Apparently, since forsaking his musical talents, he had also neglected to pursue the international royalties on his recordings that were due to him. David offered to recover these monies for a commission. It was whispered that the first cheque to arrive was well into seven figures!

I had a different financial situation of my own at the time. Out of the blue, my old friend and business partner, John Young, of Capricorn Repro, had not only stopped sending work to us, he was refusing to pay the outstanding debt for the work that we'd been producing for him. It was a significant amount of money, around £8,000 – over £26,000 in today's money – and I wondered what the problem was.

When I confronted him about the debt, he simply said that he didn't have any money to pay me what was owed. When I suggested a repayment plan over a period, he told me that he couldn't afford anything. My only resort was to see a solicitor to threaten him with legal action. This cut no ice at all. He instructed his own solicitor who waged a war of attrition on us, constantly demanding "further and better particulars" on each of the jobs that we'd invoiced, a process that took many months.

As we were finally edging towards a court hearing I heard news that came as a bombshell. John had sold his company and had shipped out to somewhere in America!

The new owners of his company, a small publishing outfit, informed me that they had only bought the company name, equipment and the client list, they were not responsible for any debts; I would have to pursue John personally for any indebtedness. His staff were as shocked as I was at his sudden departure.

I discovered that he had freighted his flashy sports car, an Aston Martin DB5, over to the States, and as his wife was American, the move looked to be permanent. Nobody knew his whereabouts as he had left no forwarding address, he had just disappeared. My solicitor was no help at all. He had no experience at collecting a debt from a foreign country. He admitted that he could only blindly pluck a firm of lawyers from a Yellow Pages directory.

I couldn't get over this despicable act of betrayal of our friendship. I had been close to John for years. We had eaten at each other's houses. Earlier in the year I had taken him to stay with friends of mine in Germany to take part in their annual 'Gruen Kohl und Pinkel' festival. We had been drinking buddies. I was hurt and angry and determined to get the money that was owed to me.

Within hours of hearing of his moonlight flit, I telephoned several businesses who I knew had dealt with John. They were all equally shocked and dismayed, all having outstanding debts that were owed by him. Even the local mini-cab company that we all used for couriering parcels was owed money.

That same evening, I was grumbling to Birgitta about John's deceit and disappearance when she came up with an idea. It was a long shot but she remembered that John had a brother-in-law, an electrician, who had done some rewiring work on our house. Maybe he would know John's whereabouts in America?

I telephoned him saying that I owed John some money, did he have his address in America where I could send it? He told me that John and his wife were staying at John's mother-in-law until they found somewhere of their own. He then gave me their address; it was in a suburb of Milwaukee. Bingo!

The next morning I phoned all the companies that John had swindled, suggesting that we fly over together and confront him. No one was interested. I calculated that John had amassed over £100,000 in unpaid commitments, plus the sale of his business, so I knew that he had the money to repay us. I still couldn't get any of my fellow creditors interested in joining with me to accost him in person.

I knew that if I challenged John on my own it was extremely unlikely that he would hand over the money that he owed me.

A Bad Debt and a Good Deal?

I sought advice from my client, Harvey Goldsmith, the concert promoter. I thought that with his international business interests he would know the best way forward, he didn't. He could only suggest an expensive firm of New York lawyers who may or may not be able to assist me.

He conceded that they would probably follow the same protracted and costly route that my London solicitor had been obliged to take. It occurred to me that we were living in a debtor's paradise! Out of the blue I received help from an unexpected source.

Artistes Security Services had been a client of mine for some time. The company, as its name suggests, provided security for all the major rock stars and their bands. They supplied the limousines to ferry these guys from their hotels to the concert venues and the 'heavies' to protect them from exuberant fans. The company also owned rehearsal studios and a musical equipment hire service. Their offices and warehouse lay directly behind my factory. I produced all their corporate brochures, stationery, business cards and backstage passes.

The firm was owned by a colourful and somewhat nefarious character, Don Murfet. Don had spent time in prison and some years later warranted a complete chapter in Robin Barratt's *Mammoth Book of Hard Bastards*. I liked Don and had enjoyed many drinking sessions with him, listening to his tales of the recalcitrant rock stars that he looked after.

He always got me into the side door of musical events, allowing me to take our older children to see the likes of Pink Floyd performing *The Wall* at Earls Court, Rod Stewart at Wembley Arena and Elton John at the Rainbow Theatre.

I happened to mention to him my difficulties with John Young. He was instantly sympathetic and offered his help, saying that he hated when "regular tradespeople get stitched up". He told me that he had 'associates' in America that could get me my money. I would need to meet them and explain the situation. The next day I flew to New York.

Don had given me a telephone number of a contact based in South Bronx, at that time, the poorest and toughest neighbourhood in New York City. I arrived in Manhattan and checked into a Sheraton hotel on 7th Avenue, opposite Carnegie Hall.

Being in New York again rekindled memories of my business attempts eight years earlier, only this trip I had no time for sentiment or nostalgia. I rang the number Don had given me. The voice that answered had a strong New York accent with a slight Italian inflection.

I explained that Don Murfet had given me his number and that he may be able to help me with a debt collection. He asked me where I was calling from, then said he would call me back in my hotel room later. I presumed he was verifying my story with Don. A short time later he called me back and said that he would meet me in the hotel's coffee shop next morning.

At 10 a.m. the following day I had taken a solitary corner booth in the coffee shop and was nursing a mug of cappuccino. I was flicking through the thick file of legal letters that made up the Capricorn file, when a short, stocky, tough-looking guy approached me.

"Colin? Don's friend?" I nodded, and he eased his beefy frame into the booth to sit opposite me. He introduced himself as 'Howie'. I must admit that I was feeling extremely nervous – even now, recalling this event nearly thirty-five years later, I am reliving the anxieties that I felt at the time, and it was to get much worse.

I explained to Howie my relationship with John and the history of the debt. I offered to show him the file containing all the letters to and from the solicitors. He pushed the thick file away to one side of the table. His voice lowered and became quite menacing, "Forget the lawyers," he said, "He's in *my* country now, he'll play the rules *my* way."

He then asked me a question which I didn't quite understand. It sounded like, "Is he metal?" I obviously looked baffled.

"Does he carry a gun?" he asked.

"Oh no!" I shot back.

"Does he carry a knife?"

"No, no." I responded.

"So if I put a gun in his face it'll frighten him?"

Oh shit, I thought, this is getting too heavy. I knew that John would have to be frightened into paying me my money, but I absolutely didn't want him physically harmed. I explained this to Howie who seemed to take it on board.

"What happens next?" I asked.

Howie said that he'd fly up to Milwaukee, meet John, tell him that he represented me, and demand the money that was owed.

"What if he refuses to meet you?"

"I'll sit outside his house until he has to come out. If he keeps me waiting too long, my boys start getting mean, they'll throw rocks at the house until he does come out!"

With that unsettling vision in my head we left the coffee shop and walked up to Broadway to a travel agency. I bought Howie a return flight to Milwaukee. He told me to go back to my hotel room and wait for his call. We shook hands and he disappeared among the sidewalk crowds. I loaded up with pretzels and bagels from a street vendor, returned to my hotel room and waited.

Not knowing what was happening I imagined all sorts of scenarios, none of them pleasant. I had always reckoned on John not calling the law. I reasoned that he wouldn't want the authorities to know that he'd migrated to America as an embezzling larcenist. But suppose I was wrong? Heavies at his doorstep might cause him to panic and phone the police. They could come knocking on my door at any moment. I couldn't leave the room; how would Howie get in touch? Then the phone rang.

It was the middle of the night in London, and it was Birgitta calling me. She'd just had a phone call from John desperate to speak to me. She told him that I was in New York. She said that he sounded terrified. There were 'thugs' at his mother-in-law's house where he was staying.

Birgitta said that he could hardly speak, his voice was 'clucking'. She told me that I had to call them off, it had gone too far. I resisted, telling her that I hadn't heard from Howie yet. I still hadn't got my money; we'd have to sit tight and wait. The phone rang again. It was Pete, he'd had a call from John. He also said that I should back off. I told him that I'd come this far, and I wasn't returning until I had got my money.

I had a restless night's sleep and was woken very early the next morning with another call. This time it was Ron, our scanner operator who'd bought John's share of our scanning company, Kindpoint. He had been discussing the situation with Pete and was extremely concerned for me.

He said that I could be out of my depth associating with these 'gangsters'. He wondered what they'd expect in return. I must admit that these concerns had also occurred to me, but I was already in too deep and was determined to keep tightening the screw. If Birgitta, Pete and Ron didn't have the stomach for it, so be it.

Then Howie rang. He was in the lobby downstairs and wanted to come up to update me. In the room he told me that he'd spoken to John, albeit through his locked front door, and had 'persuaded' him to agree to paying me what was owed.

I wanted John to come to New York with the money. Howie had John's phone number and called him. In an icy voice he told John that if he didn't bring the money to New York he would buy the debt from me, "Colin will fly back to London," then slowly added with chilling menace, "and then you are mine!"

Those last ominous words had *me* petrified, and Howie was on *my* side.

He passed the phone over to me. John sounded panic-stricken. He pleaded with me not to have to come to New York. He was convinced that he'd be "jumped at the airport". He begged me to come alone to Milwaukee, promising he'd have the money in cash and he'd meet me off the plane with it. I agreed to go.

There was a flight around midday arriving about two in the afternoon, then returning half an hour later. I thanked Howie and took a cab to La Guardia.

During the flight I had many fearful forebodings. Suppose John was waiting with the police? Could I be indicted for being an accessory to demanding money with menaces? Would John risk involving the police? Would he be at the airport? Maybe he was buying time to do another disappearing act? These and many more concerns were circling in my head throughout the journey.

The plane landed at Milwaukee airport and taxied up to its designated gate number. Along with a hundred other passengers I made my way through the gangway and into the arrivals lounge. John was nowhere to be seen, nor, thankfully were a posse of awaiting policemen.

The final passengers had disembarked and had all walked passed me, I stood there alone. A minute or two went by, then, from behind a large pillar, appeared John. I didn't recognise him at first as he had always worn a beard. He had shaved it off. He looked pale and shaken. He walked towards me with arm outstretched for a handshake! I ignored it.

"Have you got my money?"

He nodded, indicating a bag in his other hand. We sat down at a table by a cafeteria. I was quite taken aback as he went into a long stream of apologies. He said that it had all been a big misunderstanding, he had always intended to pay me the money. He said that he was wrong to have listened to his solicitors while they dragged out the lawsuit.

I knew that this was all bullshit. I took the bag containing the cash. Only half the full amount was there, but the balance was written on a banker's cheque, I had my money. I told him that he had left a lot of angry creditors behind in London.

He acknowledged this and asked for assurance that I wouldn't give away his whereabouts. I said that I wouldn't. They'd had their chance to come with me but had declined my offer. To me it was all history now. He wanted to know who the heavies were that I had employed, and where had I found them. I didn't respond.

My flight back to New York was due to leave, I said goodbye and boarded the plane. The return journey was a nightmare! One of the most turbulent flights I'd ever endured. Typical! I thought to myself. All this cash and I may not live to enjoy it. In the event, of course we landed safely back at La Guardia and I was out on the town. I needed a beer!

The next day I phoned Don to thank him for his introduction to Howie. I also wanted to ask him how much I needed to pay Howie for his 'services'. Don surprised me by saying that I owed Howie nothing, he helped me as a favour to Don.

He said that if I felt that I should pay him something, then that was up to me. I'd also phoned Birgitta and Pete to let them know that all was well. I decided to treat myself to a couple of days in New York, maybe looking up old contacts, but first I wanted to meet with Howie.

This was midwinter and the biggest snowflakes I'd ever seen were falling on Manhattan, instantly covering its grime with a temporary sheen of pristine white beauty. I made my slippery way to Times Square where I was meeting Howie at a Dunkin' Donut diner. He was already seated when I arrived. We ordered coffees and I relayed my trip to Milwaukee.

He seemed really pleased for me, but was surprised when I handed him a packet, telling him it contained a thousand dollars as a thank you. He said that he hadn't expected payment, he was "just helping a friend out". He then took me by surprise saying that maybe I could help *him* out. In the back of my mind there had always been a gnawing apprehension that Howie might expect something in return for his efforts. I had hoped a payment might cancel out any obligations, apparently not!

Leaning forward and lowering his voice to a level hardly above a rasping whisper, he asked me if I knew that the Olympic Games were being held in Los Angeles at the end of July that year. Of course, I knew this, so nodded in assent. He then pulled a piece of paper from his pocket and slid it carefully across the table to me. It was a high value ticket for one of the Olympic track events. He stared at me waiting for my reaction. I didn't think he was offering me a free trip to the Olympics!

"It's a forgery," he said in a matter-of-fact tone. He went on to ask me if I, being in the printing game, could produce something as good?

I was horrified. I explained that my business was colour repro, the stage *before* printing. Any actual printing requirements that I needed would have to be outsourced.

I went on to tell him that I never got involved in anything criminal. Pursuing John for my money was the nearest I'd ever come to lawlessness. My heart was thumping. Visions of Coppola's *The Godfather*, where favours were expected to be repaid, were racing across my mind.

Howie pursed his lips, pocketed the forged ticket, leaned back in his chair, then smiled!

"OK," he said, "no problem, I just had to ask," he patted my shoulder, "and thanks for the money, any time you need help, you've got my number."

We stood up and shook hands and I thanked him again. He left the diner and disappeared into the crowds outside. I'd often wondered what 'Howie' was short for. It could have been 'Howard' or, more appropriately 'Howitzer'! I'd never been game enough to ask him.

Over the next couple of days, I rang a few of the business contacts that I'd made when I was working in New York with Color Precision. Several had moved on, and those that hadn't weren't too interested in meeting up. I was delighted though, when one contact was pleased to hear from me and agreed to see me.

I had first met Tricia Newell when she worked for a firm of lawyers on Wall Street. She had since set up a colour matching company targeting the fashion market. She was tall with dark hair and brown eyes, extremely attractive and very bright.

Over lunch at the fashionable Sardi's on 44th Street, just up from Time Square, she told me that she had taken on a partner, Joan, but the business was struggling. I still had a wish to do business in New York, the city I loved. I put it to Tricia that maybe she could be our agent in the States. She showed immediate interest but said that she'd have to put it to her partner.

Next day she phoned me with good news. Joan and she were keen to explore the idea further. After a successful meeting with Joan and Tricia, I arranged for them to fly to London to spend a week's induction and training at our factory.

We launched a new company, Latent Image US Inc. and produced a large format glossy brochure targeting the American market. The girls ran the office from Tricia's apartment on East 22nd Street in the Gramercy Park area of Manhattan.

There was one other contact I wished to get in touch with. While it didn't win any work, due to time sensitive deadlines, it did lead to a very interesting evening.

Before renaming his magazine publishing empire Dennis Publishing, Felix Dennis called his fledgling business in London, 'Bunch Books'. We had been dealing with Bunch for a while at Latent Image, producing the colour repro for his early computer games titles, *Your Spectrum* and *Your 64*.

Felix was a true maverick. A couple of years younger than me, he was stocky, bearded and extremely opinionated. He was working in New York launching *Star Hits*, a pop magazine he'd licensed from *Smash Hits*, the fortnightly teen pop title published by the giant media group EMAP, another client of ours.

I rang Felix and invited him out to dinner. After showing me around his premises on the Upper West Side where his designers were busy putting the finishing touches to the *Star Hits* launch issue, he suggested we eat at a favourite restaurant of his nearby.

In typical New York style, the restaurant had a small bar near the entrance. There were tall wooden barstools with padded swivel seats and relaxing back rests. Before dinner we made ourselves comfortable at the bar and ordered drinks.

A Bad Debt and a Good Deal?

I'd first met Felix some months before in his office in London. It was in the basement of his building just off Oxford Street. Hanging on the wall of the stairwell approaching his office, was a large drawing of a naked Felix. He was pictured standing between his two partners from the notorious underground magazine, *Oz*, who were also naked.

The drawing had some respectability as it had been done by the influential British artist, David Hockney. Felix was quite proud of the work, not least, because it portrayed his organ as the largest of the three!

Sitting at the bar, Felix recounted his time spent in Wormwood Scrubs prison back in early 1970, when he was convicted, along with his two partners, of publishing an obscene issue of their *Oz* magazine. They were subsequently released following a successful appeal led by the famous human rights barrister, Geoffrey Robertson QC.

Oz had always been a thorn in the side of the British Establishment. It was very left wing, heavily critical of the Vietnam War and full of articles on sex, drugs and alternative lifestyles.

The government's Obscene Publications Squad, a division of the Metropolitan Police, were determined to shut it down. It is worth reading Geoffrey Robertson's book, *Rough Justice*, in which he devotes an entire hilarious chapter to the Oz trial.

Following a lengthy drinking session at the restaurant's bar, we sat down to eat and Felix continued his rant on anti-establishment stories. The restaurant itself was nothing special; red gingham tablecloths and walls decorated with murals of the Italian coastline.

After a while Felix asked me what I was going to order to eat. I said that I hadn't yet seen a menu.

"They don't have one," he replied, "they can cook anything you want!"

Forgoing the facetious temptation to order grilled rhinoceros's testicles, I realised that without a menu it's not easy to decide. Choosing a meal is a process of selection and elimination. With nothing to select from, it's quite difficult to decide on something. I can't remember what I ended up ordering, but I do remember a very entertaining evening with Felix.

Felix subsequently went on to become the incredibly wealthy publisher of dozens of successful titles, including *Mac User*, *Maxim*, *Auto Express* and *The Week*. I enjoyed many memorable evenings with Felix over the ensuing years, but sadly he died of throat cancer in 2014.

He was a generous philanthropist, leaving the bulk of his vast fortune to the planting of Britain's largest broadleaf forest. I never got to know him that well, I don't think anyone did. He was very much a loner, a one-off, and I'll never forget him.

Unfortunately, despite Tricia and Joan's enthusiasm and the many trips I made backwards and forwards to New York, the business never succeeded. The industry was changing. Publishers were no longer buying individual sets of colour separations, preferring to purchase complete made-up pages of final films, which combined the pictures with the text and colour tints. Tricia said that although she enjoyed the sales aspect to her job, she was disheartened by the lack of results. She left to start a very successful real estate brokerage in downtown Manhattan, and I wound up Latent Image US Inc.

Pete was convinced that the future of our business lay in the computerized production of assembled page films. I agreed that he should explore the available technologies that were on the market. After a lengthy investigation he reported that there were only three manufacturers of interest, but they were all frighteningly expensive. Out of the three he favoured an Israeli company, Scitex, who had their European headquarters and demonstration suites in Brussels.

We flew over to evaluate it. By coincidence, the Scitex salesman, Pat Mulvaney, who accompanied us to Brussels, was one of the graduate students that I had instructed on the Magnascan, ten years earlier.

We took a large batch of our work and the operators at Scitex gave us a very impressive demonstration. We were told that work could be produced ten times faster than our manual methods using a fraction of the materials. We calculated that the staggering cost of the equipment, £500,000 – over £1.5m in 2019 – could be justified with the savings on labour. This was still a titanic commitment for us and a huge gamble, not least as the cost exceeded our entire current revenues.

This would be one of the first installations of its kind in London. It would lift our profile to a new level and should be an enormous sales aid to the company.

Once I had made my decision, Scitex were eager for me to sign for the deal on their stand at the forthcoming International Printing Exhibition, IPEX, to gain maximum publicity for themselves. They were obviously extremely keen for this sale to happen, so I used their excitement to negotiate a better settlement.

I got them to agree to a 12-month repayment holiday – with no rollover interest – a free Hell DC 300 scanner for inputting line artwork – worth about £50,000 – and a commitment to repeat the Brussels demonstration on *our* equipment, in *our* factory, twelve months after its installation.

Friday 18th May 1984 saw my fortieth birthday, and Birgitta had planned a surprise party at a favourite venue of mine. I had been a member of Richard Branson's Roof Gardens restaurant and nightclub for over five years. The club was situated on the sixth floor above a department store which had once housed Barbara Hulanicki's BIBA, the famous 60s Kensington fashion emporium.

It was a fantastic place, with an astonishing two acres of gardens, complete with mature trees, a lake and flamingos, plus a world class restaurant and discotheque, all high above the London skyline. The interior of the club was still decorated in its original art deco designs from its construction back in the 1930s.

I used the club frequently for entertaining important clients who were always impressed with its glamorous appeal. Unbeknown to me, Birgitta had organized for my mum, my brother Pat, and my girls to be there. Pete had arranged for all our staff to have the Friday afternoon off so that they could join in. Plus, he'd invited a few of our clients to participate. It was a wonderful afternoon.

Our staff had chipped together and presented me with an expensive Dunhill cigarette lighter onto which they'd had my initials engraved. I still treasure it today even though I no longer use it to light cigarettes.

At 6 p.m. I discovered that the surprises weren't over. Birgitta ordered a taxi which drove us to the airport and we flew to Paris where she'd booked us into the luxurious George V hotel.

The weekend was topped off with dinner at the historic art nouveau restaurant, Maxims. All in all, a fabulous way to celebrate a significant milestone in my life.

In early September, Pete and I attended the impressive Scitex stand at the large printing exhibition, IPEX. Amongst a fanfare of photographers and film crews, I signed the contract for our new equipment.

No sooner were the formalities completed when alarm sirens started blaring in the exhibition halls. Police cleared the building as there had been terrorist bomb threats on the Israeli company. In the event there was no explosion, but it was an ominous portent of the tribulations that lay ahead.

There was less tribulation on the home front now that Daniel and Bobby had moved out of the house. Birgitta and I had a lot more time to ourselves although the boys continued to bring their washing every week for their mum to do.

Having more space in the house we were able to invite Dad and Flo to stay with us for a short holiday. Dad put himself to work painting the entire front of the house, which was brilliant having it done so professionally.

During the year, Rachel had applied successfully for a transfer from the Civil Service office in Gloucester where she was working to their offices in Westminster, so she came and lived with us. As it turned out she was not happy with the transfer. She felt she was underemployed and told us some horror stories of over-staffing and waste in the Civil Service.

A Bad Debt and a Good Deal?

Rachel was an extremely capable girl so I suggested that she should try to find a job in magazine production. The publisher, Northern and Shell, owned by Richard Desmond, the self-titled 'Britain's most controversial media mogul', were advertising for a production assistant. They were looking for a school leaver so were only offering a minimal wage.

Rachel was twenty years old but took the large drop in income to gain the experience. She worked for that company for about three years learning all aspects of magazine production. She then joined me at Latent Image, successfully running our production department.

Meanwhile we were winning more and more magazine contracts, thanks mainly to our dynamic sales director, Manny. There were a flood of new launches hitting the newsstands, predominately personal computer titles. It's hard to imagine nowadays that as recent as the early 1980s the internet, as we know it, was still ten years away from development and the micro-computer was in its infancy.

At Latent Image we were on the threshold of trailblazing this new technology. In retrospect, we were less like pioneers and more like blindfolded lambs to the slaughter!

Chapter 16

The Saddest Loss

Immediately after the 1985 New Year celebrations we began preparing for the Scitex System's installation. It was a mammoth task. This was long before the miniaturization of computer processors. A specialized area to house the equipment had to be built.

The regional electricity company had to dig trenches outside the factory to feed more power into the building. The regulated control of the environmental systems was paramount. A raised floor to allow for the miles of cabling, and air conditioning and humidity controls had to be installed.

All this for a mere 300 megabytes of storage and memory; putting this in context, today's iPhone X is over *700 times* more powerful!

I employed an architect to design a huge 20-foot high tinted glass structure to showcase the bank of computers that were needed to process the digital information. While we were having to go to these lengths, I thought it timely to completely redecorate the factory.

We hung a suspended ceiling above the entire area creating a more studio-like appearance. At one stage I counted eighteen workmen, including carpenters, plumbers and electricians all busy preparing the site.

Finally, we were ready to accept the new equipment. At 6 a.m. on the 26th March 1986, we took delivery. Then it was the turn of the Scitex engineers, technicians and instructors to assemble the hardware and train our staff to operate it.

It Was The Best Of Times...

I had worked 14-hour days continually since the 2nd January organizing and supervising the project. I needed a break and some time to myself. Remembering the stunning beauty of the Catalina mountains and the Sonoran Desert around Tucson from my trip nine years earlier, I headed for the wide-open spaces of Arizona.

Arriving at Tucson airport I asked a taxi driver to take me to a hotel away from the town centre. He couldn't have chosen better. El Conquistador hotel and golf resort lay in the shadow of the Catalina foothills about twenty kilometres from the centre of Tucson. Surrounded by towering palm trees and the gigantic Saguaro Cacti, so indelibly linked to western cowboy films, and set in the expanses of the Sonoran Desert, I'd found my perfect sanctuary.

After sleeping off the jetlag and the exhaustion of the previous three months, I finally left my room to explore the hotel and its surrounds. The place seemed to be overrun by single men drifting around aimlessly. Several would nod towards me asking what sounded like "Arenare?". Clearly, I must have looked perplexed, so they would wander on by leaving me alone.

Eventually I discovered that the hotel was popular with large American corporations, not only for seminars and conferences, but also as a destination to send their burnt-out executives and salesmen for "Rest and Recuperation". The puzzling greetings I'd been receiving from the wandering guests had been the abbreviated question "R&R?"

Even more befitting, the hotel was conveniently hosting the annual conference for the American Psychiatric Association. I'm sure the delegates would have felt surrounded by enough subject matter to keep them busy for years!

I was feeling much recovered and the hotel arranged for a local wrangler Bill, a Vietnam war veteran, to take me out horse riding. We saddled up a pair of beautiful Palominos. With their pale golden coats, pure white manes, tails and fetlocks, I felt like Roy Rogers!

Bill had a rough, outdoor, weathered complexion and a dry sense of humour. As we were picking our way up the foothills, he looked up to the clear, cyan-blue sky, and pointed to the one solitary, fluffy, white cloud. He turned and drawled, "Y' know, the weatherman said there'd be clear skies today, guess you can't trust anyone these days!"

Later in the week I decided to pay a visit to Rodger Ford at his workplace in Tucson. I'd met Rodger when he was printing the Black Sabbath programme back in 1976. He had since sold out of his large printing company and was now busy expanding his AlphaGraphics instant print shops.

He invited me to lunch at his franchise training school. It was inspiring watching a true entrepreneur at work. There were around a dozen franchisees just finishing their morning's training session. Rodger suggested I sit in with them at their workshop. Each sat behind a new small computer which they were being instructed how to operate. It was called an Apple Macintosh.

Rodger flatteringly introduced me to the class as "an old friend from London who's just invested in a high-end colour system". He was almost apologetic that they were working with a more rudimentary system. That was not how I saw it.

I sat at one of the desks and marvelled at this little device in front of me. It was the first machine to use a 'mouse' to guide a cursor that could 'lasso' a line of type displayed on a tiny nine-inch screen and move it or enlarge it. There were several typefaces available, and I could see that this was a unique application for the developing desktop publishing market.

Over lunch, Rodger told me that he was looking for a master licensee to expand the franchise in the UK. He asked me if I would be interested in investing. I told him that it was a market about which I knew very little and that I already had enough on my plate.

If I could have foreseen the problems that I would be encountering, I might have given him a different answer. As it was, I travelled back to London refreshed and invigorated, looking forward to promoting our new equipment and expanding our sales.

From the outset our new page make-up system did not perform to our expectations. Its output was much slower than we had been led to believe. This was a huge disappointment and not a little concerning. At that time, Pete and I were unsure whether its slow performance was due to our initial inexperience of the system or, more worryingly, if during the demonstration in Brussels, Scitex had used additional, hidden, processing power, to exaggerate the speed of the equipment that *we* were buying.

However, as a sales aid it was superb. It looked fantastic and generated enormous interest from potential clients, which we generally managed to convert into more sales. Unfortunately, it wasn't fast enough to cope with the increase in these sales. We had to employ more scanner operators and planners to produce the extra work manually.

Another factory unit opposite ours had become vacant, so I took a lease on it. We installed a mezzanine floor and filled it with the additional staff. We continued to win more magazine titles and somehow managing to meet their deadlines.

It was over this period that I decided to indulge myself with the money that I had recovered from John Young in America. As it had been written out of our accounts two years earlier as a bad debt, I had it in my personal account to spend as I wished. I decided to treat myself.

I bought a second-hand Rolls Royce Silver Shadow, and booked a holiday in Antigua for myself, Birgitta and our two youngest, my Louise and Birgitta's Rebecca. Midsummer was the 'off' season in the Caribbean, so we enjoyed practically empty beaches and uncrowded restaurants.

Louise was very small for a twelve-year-old, but as a good swimmer she wanted to try waterskiing. The resort didn't have a lifejacket small enough to fit her, so she looked lost inside the adult jacket that they provided.

I stood on the beach at the water's edge watching her attempts to stand and keep her balance on the ski board. Time and again she lasted a few yards before somersaulting into the sea. She just wouldn't give up. By now the twenty or so holidaymakers on the beach had joined alongside me, willing her on. Finally, after at least a dozen attempts, she made it, lasting a complete circle of the bay.

As she returned and was wading up through the low surf to the beach, all those who'd been following her efforts stood and applauded. The loudest and most enthusiastic clapping came from her very proud dad.

It was on this holiday that Louise taught me to swim. I had always been frightened of water since being thrown into the deep end at the local swimming pool as a nervous nine-year-old. But in those clear, shallow, warm waters, with Louise at my side encouraging me, I managed to keep myself afloat for a few metres. She found a 'first five metres' swimming badge, which I proudly pinned to my swimming trunks.

The night-time flight home crossed into Louise's thirteenth birthday. We mentioned it to the cabin crew who arrived a little later with a magnum of champagne! Rather inappropriate for a thirteen-year-old, but Birgitta and I enjoyed it.

Later in the summer, two musical events coincided, bringing us additional work. The pop star, David Essex, had written and was performing in a musical show based on the infamous mutiny on the ship, *The Bounty*. It premiered in mid-July at the Piccadilly Theatre in London's West End, and we were producing the souvenir programmes.

The show was quite a spectacle. Critics joked that the 'star' of the show was the massive wooden replica of *The Bounty*, which was built on a series of hydraulics, allowing the boat to traverse the stage and pitch and roll. They unkindly reported that David Essex's acting was like the boat, wooden!

Mel Bush, the promoter, told me that they'd had to excavate deep underneath the stage to install the necessary engineering. He said that they went so deep that they were worried that they would hit the Piccadilly underground tunnel that ran beneath it! I took my girls to see the show, and despite the poor reviews, we all enjoyed it.

It Was The Best Of Times...

The week before *The Bounty* premiere, the indefatigable Bob Geldof of the Boomtown Rats band, had teamed up with my old client, Harvey Goldsmith, to present the incredible, day-long musical event, *Live Aid*.

The previous autumn, the BBC reporter Michael Buerk, had produced footage of a catastrophic famine 'of biblical proportion' in Ethiopia. This had inspired Geldof to organize his many friends in the music business to record a song, *Do they Know it's Christmas* to raise money for the famine relief. The song became a Number One hit over Christmas and raised £8 million.

This motivated the persuasive Geldof to organize an array of rock bands and superstars to perform in this unparalleled event at Wembley Stadium. It was synchronized with a similar event over in Philadelphia in the USA.

Birgitta's ex-husband, David, took Daniel and Bobby for the day as their Uncle Yusuf was supposed to be making an appearance – in the end he didn't. They returned to tell us excitedly how they'd been lucky enough to mingle backstage with such legends as David Bowie, Paul McCartney and Freddy Mercury.

The day of the event I was stuck at work with most of my staff working overtime to complete *The Bounty* souvenir programmes. Luckily my youngest, Louise, was living with us at the time, and tape-recorded the entire show for me. It ran to five, four-hour video tapes. I still have them, each with her neat, handwritten lists of performers tucked inside.

During the summer Dad and Flo came to stay with Birgitta and I for another short holiday. One afternoon Dad offered to mow our lawn in the back garden. He hadn't brought any suitable gardening clothes with him, so I lent him a pair of my old jeans as we'd always been a similar size to each other.

While he was mowing, I noticed that my jeans seemed to hang baggy on him. When I joked to him about it, he confided that he'd lost considerable weight recently; he reckoned around "two stone" – nearly fourteen kilos! I said that he should see a doctor and get this checked out.

He replied that he was worried that a doctor might tell him that he had cancer, particularly as he'd been a heavy smoker all his life. I argued that even if he did have a cancer, it should be attended to immediately rather than leave it. I added that the American President, Ronald Reagan, had just been diagnosed with bowel cancer, been operated on, and had a successful outcome. Dad's response was typical.

"Tch, Ronald Reagan! He's never done a day's work in his life!" Wonderful!

Without Dad's knowledge, I telephoned the Gloucestershire Royal Hospital and found the name of a senior respiratory physician who would see patients on a private fee-paying basis. After much persuasion I got Dad to agree to an appointment with him and said I would take care of his bill.

A week or so later I received a phone call from the doctor. He told me that Dad was fine as none of the X-rays showed any sign of cancer. I cannot tell you my relief. I loved my dad so much. Knowing what he'd endured throughout his life, to have had it cut short, as he was only sixty-nine at the time, would have been unbearable. I was overjoyed.

Three weeks later, I received a call from Flo. Dad was very poorly, so bad that he had taken to his bed. I had always seen Dad as a tall, lean, strong man, whose attitude to ailments had always been, "You work them off with hard graft."

For him to be confined to his bed I realized that he must be very sick. Flo went on to tell me that the specialist who had examined him had gone on holiday for three weeks. Dad's own GP had said that as Dad had been a private patient, no other specialist would attend to him! I was outraged. I raced to Gloucester, saw his GP and tore a strip off him. He was very apologetic.

Dad was admitted to hospital where it was discovered that his X-rays had been misread. He underwent a bronchoscopy which confirmed that he was suffering from advanced lung cancer. He was transferred to the Cheltenham General Hospital's Cobalt Unit for an intensive course of radiation therapy.

He seemed to respond well to the treatment, and after ten days was able to leave his bed and was discharged from the hospital. But the doctors told me that the prognosis was not good. They gave me the crushing news that they did not expect Dad to live much longer than three months. I was devastated.

Ignoring my business commitments, I took up residence in a hotel in Gloucester so that I could spend time with Dad. Even though his illness was weakening him, he still managed to walk with me to his favourite local pubs.

Prior to his illness, Dad's gait had been a purposeful stride, almost military. I noticed now that he was walking with his hands in his pockets. He explained apologetically that he was keeping his hands in his pockets to hold his trousers up as he was losing so much weight!

It is strange, but neither of us ever mentioned his malignancy. This was a bittersweet time. We enjoyed many long conversations. He reminisced a lot, and I especially enjoyed listening to his wartime Royal Navy stories.

He told me that his first sinking occurred early in the war during the Norwegian campaign. He was serving on an anti-aircraft cruiser, HMS *Curlew*. The ship sustained five days of aerial bombardment from German warplanes until she was finally hit and foundered in a Norwegian fjord.

He was picked up soon after by a relief ship. Incredibly, only nine crew members perished. This was only two more than lost their lives in an onboard accident that had occurred a few weeks previously.

The vessel was fitted with two large-bore anti-aircraft guns, nicknamed Chicago Pianos, so called due to their shape and the booming beat they made when firing. The gun crew were performing their maintenance and cleaning duties, clambering all over it, when a fault triggered a round of shells.

The Saddest Loss

Dad said that it was horrific, with body parts blasted all over the ship. The captain asked for volunteers to clean up the sickening mess. Dad put his hand up with a few others. They were awarded an extra rum ration that evening. Dad said they needed it!

Shortly after, when stationed in Scapa Flow, the sheltered body of water in the Orkney Islands, north of Scotland, he witnessed the damaged HMS *Prince of Wales* come listing into port. It was the sister ship to HMS *Hood*, 'the pride of the fleet', which had just been sunk by the German battleship *Bismarck*.

He said that a call went out for all hands to be on deck to welcome a brave ship home. Hardly anyone was alongside to cheer her, he said. They were all so disgusted at the loss, having no idea at the time of the power of the Bismarck. A fleet of eleven ships was then assembled to intercept *Bismarck* and her sister ship *Prinz Eugen*. Dad sailed on a cruiser scouting for the battleship HMS *King George V*.

It was in the middle of the night late in May 1941, when the sirens blared out and over the tannoy 'action stations' were called. The crew were told that they should be engaging *Bismarck* within the half hour!

Completely enthralled, I asked Dad how he was feeling then?

"How d' you think?" he replied, "I was shitting myself!"

Fortunately for Dad, thick fog suddenly descended and they lost contact with *Bismarck*. It was sunk soon after by other ships of the fleet.

Those days with Dad were precious. As he became less able to get out and about, I bought him Philip Zeigler's wonderful biography of the Admiral of the Fleet, Earl Mountbatten. He surprised me by saying that he'd not only served under Mountbatten on one of his ships, but he'd spoken with him! I was astonished, "Wow, really? Gosh Dad, what did you say?"

Dad got out of his chair, sprang to attention, saluted and said, "Paint shop ready for inspection Sir"! Despite his affliction, Dad never lost his wry sense of humour, and could still see the funny side of things.

It Was The Best Of Times...

Sitting with Dad, looking through his old navy photographs, I commented on some of the early ones showing him sporting a beard. He told me that in the Royal Navy those wishing to grow a beard had to apply for permission.

If you were successful you were instructed to stop shaving for six weeks, whereupon your beard was inspected and assessed. He said that if there were no 'bird's nests' in it, you could keep it. If it didn't come up to scratch, you were ordered to shave it off.

I reminded Dad of the time when I was about fourteen or fifteen years old, and I wanted to borrow his razor blade shaver as I felt I was beginning to grow a moustache. He had peered closely at my upper lip, then suggested I smear some butter on it and let the cat lick it off!

Getting Dad to talk about the third time that he was sunk was the most difficult as it was the most tragic. It was barely five months since he'd been on the ship HMS *Hermione* which had been sunk in the Mediterranean, when he was serving on HMS *Hecla*, a destroyer depot ship.

Apart from the normal ship's complement, a depot ship carried hundreds of marine artisans; engineers, welders, electricians, etc. On board *Hecla* were nearly 900 men. Most were there to repair and maintain the fleet at sea. She was steaming northward in the Atlantic off the coast of Africa on her way to join the fleet that was assembling for 'Operation Torch' the invasion of North Africa, when she was intercepted by a German submarine.

It was in the middle of the night, ironically on Armistice Day, 11th November 1942, when she was hit by five torpedoes. It is impossible to imagine the chaos and carnage that ensued as its escort ships, HMS *Venomous* and HMS *Marne*, fired depth charges to destroy the submarine.

HMS *Marne* heaved to, to pick up survivors of Dad's ship, *Hecla*. Netting and ropes were thrown over her side for the men to clamber up on. Many were so covered in oil that they couldn't be helped onto the nets. As men were attempting to cling on, the ship's sonar picked up a signal from the submarine. The *Marne* then steamed off at speed in pursuit, hurling the clambering men off. Two hundred and seventy-two men from Dad's ship perished!

Dad was eventually picked up by an American Navy vessel. He said that it was amazing the difference on board a US ship.

"They had blankets and fed us steak!"

A vast difference to the meagre rations that Royal Navy sailors had to put up with.

After spending many weeks with Dad, I had to return to my business in London to attend to a few urgent problems that I had been neglecting. Pete had been managing the company superbly in my absence, but there were a few issues that needed my attention. I had only been back for a few days when I received a phone call from Dad's sister, my Aunty Molly – who my own sister was named after. She said that she didn't want to be an alarmist, but she thought that Dad had taken a turn for the worse. She had called his doctor and thought that I should be aware. I left for Gloucester immediately.

I was visibly shocked when I entered Dad's bedroom and saw him propped up in bed. He had obviously suffered a stroke. The left side of his face had dropped, his mouth drooped down on one side, and he had difficulty speaking.

As I stood at the end of his bed, I was finding it hard to conceal my distress. Dad could clearly see my emotions and tried to signal to me that he was okay. I disappeared to the bathroom to try to compose myself. It took me a while having burst into tears the moment I'd closed the door behind me. To see this brave, modest hero in such a state was heartbreaking.

I called my brother Pat and sister Molly who both came to be with Dad. Over the next few days Dad's GP came regularly to administer morphine. He arranged for a night nurse to be on call. In the early hours of 13th December, Pat and I were sitting either side of Dad's bed each holding his hand, when this lovely man, with his last laboured breath, slipped away from us.

A couple of evenings later, Pat and I effected our own personal reminiscences of Dad. We visited all the local pubs where we had enjoyed a pint or two with him, to toast to his memory. There were quite a few; pubs and memories! At every one the landlords were saddened to hear of the death of the quiet unassuming painter and decorator who was always popular and would be greatly missed. At Dad's funeral, his coffin was draped with the Union Jack colours, a tribute to his military service.

Even though he was christened Arthur, he was only known as Pat, a nickname given to him by his Irish father as he'd been born on St Patrick's day. Unfortunately, the vicar conducting the service was unaware of this and kept referring to him as Arthur, causing many of the packed congregation to wonder if they were at the correct funeral; this would have amused Dad. Any confusion was drowned out by the exuberant singing of the Navy Hymn, with its rousing line, "for those in peril on the sea".

Chapter 17

Country Life and City Strife

The year 1986 heralded major changes in our lives. Margaret Thatcher's trade union legislation was beginning to take effect. Despite three million unemployed the economy was starting to boom, and I was well positioned to take full advantage of it.

I was enjoying the profits being generated at Latent Image. I had never in my life felt so well off. I was driving around London in my Rolls Royce, wearing expensive Italian suits, delighting in membership of exclusive nightclubs and casinos, and dining in the finest restaurants.

Cocaine, or 'Charlie', as it was generally known, was easily obtainable. A temporary, mild euphoria seemed to be worth the going rate of £60 a gram, and everyone appeared to be using it. Casino car-jockeys jostled to park my Rolls, as I was known to tip handsomely, and nightclub bartenders were calling me 'Mr Champagne'.

Birgitta and I had just returned from another holiday in the Caribbean, this time on the island of Barbados before flying over to the private island Mustique.

We stayed at the exclusive Cotton House Hotel, enjoying drinks at the legendary Basil's Bar, the popular hangout for Princess Margaret, Mick Jagger, Kate Moss and all the members of the jet-set. I felt that I was financially invincible. Oh, how it was all to change! But that was still a little while in the future.

Business was forging ahead. Due to the slow performance of our new Scitex equipment, I had negotiated a further six-month repayment holiday. The newspaper mogul, Rupert Murdoch, was indirectly helping me keep excessive wage demands to a minimum.

He had recently sacked his entire workforce of printers at *The Times* newspaper for illegal strike action. He had secretly constructed a massive new printing works at Wapping in East London and had done a deal with the electrical trade union to man the plant. This action, coupled with the defeat of the mineworkers strike the previous year, all helped to significantly reduce the power and influence of the trade unions.

I no longer had to accommodate regular demands for salary increases, longer holidays and ever shorter working weeks. We were now operating on a three-shift basis, keeping the factory operational twenty-four hours a day, seven days a week.

On the home front, my middle daughter, Claire, had recently married. Sadly, I wasn't allowed to be at the ceremony. Claire's mother, Jan, had insisted that if I attended with Birgitta, 'that woman', then she would boycott the wedding. In deference to Birgitta I felt that if she was excluded then I should withdraw.

I was very upset, but at least Claire had chosen not to have a church service, so I wasn't forgoing walking my daughter down the aisle. We made up for it that evening, when I hosted a large group of the wedding party, minus Jan, for a family dinner at the hotel where Claire and her new husband, Paul, were spending their wedding night. We had a wonderful evening, with Claire arriving still wearing her beautiful wedding dress – she looked sensational.

The months that I had spent in Gloucester with Dad when he was sick, had given me a hankering to move back to the area, albeit I was looking for something pretty grand. By the spring I had found exactly the historic mansion that I'd been envisaging.

I had received a brochure from an estate agent in Stroud, illustrating a glorious seventeenth century Cotswold stone manor house in picturesque Painswick. It was on the market for a quarter of a million pounds. The average house price at the time was about £40,000, but I persuaded Birgitta that we should drive down to view it.

Greenhouse Court stood in almost thirty acres of rolling pasture overlooking the Painswick valley with views directly across to the medieval Cotswold village of Painswick.

Built in the 1640s it was now listed as an historic building of interest. Several extensions had been added over the centuries; the most recent was a large Victorian addition which housed a full-sized billiard room on the first floor. The property also included a row of three cottages, now derelict, and a bank of stables and outhouses. I fell in love with it.

Behind its numerous stone-mullioned windows were over twenty rooms, many with oak-beamed ceilings and large inglenook open fireplaces. The owner, a local solicitor, had divided the house into two separate dwellings to accommodate his in-laws who also lived there. I could see the potential to open the house up again, creating a wonderful home for us, and a fabulous venue to entertain our large hybrid family and my expanding client list.

In the preceding couple of years, Birgitta and I had a few marital ups and downs. Most of our arguments had centred around my stepchildren, particularly Daniel and Rebecca. I was concerned for them to grow into independent, responsible adults with a healthy work ethic.

My opinions were rarely heeded, so I often bit my tongue and consoled myself that things would improve once they had all left home. I had every hope that moving to the country would give us a new start with a change in lifestyle that would be just the fillip that our marriage and domestic life needed.

With Birgitta's agreement, though slightly less enthusiastic than mine, we purchased the property. During the previous year, the housing market had started to boom in the UK, so we had no difficulty selling our house in Hampstead Garden Suburb. On a beautiful sunny mid-August day, in a convoy with two large removal lorries, we drove to Painswick to begin life in our new home.

From the outset, Birgitta was not happy with the move. One of her early complaints was that her favourite supermarket, Waitrose, which was just around the corner from us in London, was now a 20-

mile drive away. She also imagined, wrongly, that although we were only a hundred miles due west of London, the weather was worse in Gloucestershire than it was in London!

I felt that she would soon adapt to our new environment, particularly as both Bobby and Daniel loved the property and came to stay every weekend, often bringing friends with them. I could not have been happier with the house and set to immediately on a massive renovation plan.

As the house was partitioned into two dwellings, it was an absolute warren of passageways, staircases and vestibules. I called upon my architect friend Ian to draw up plans of the property, with his suggestions for opening it out.

The renovations were going to be an enormous task, not least as the stone walls were two feet thick, and in some areas three feet! Plus, we were removing the centre spine of the building, which went up two stories, a job that required no less than twenty-eight acrow-props to hold the rest of the house up!

I had chosen a local Painswick builder to do the main constructional work. I discovered halfway through the work that his firm also doubled as the local undertakers and funeral directors. I kept my fingers crossed that those services would not be required during the rather dangerous work with which his tradesmen were grappling.

Once the major construction work was completed, I was able to start decorating. I was happy and fairly competent at painting and paperhanging, as Dad had taught me very well. I completed the first sitting room, and Birgitta had selected the soft furnishings, curtains and carpeting, so at least we had one room as a refuge from what had become a building site.

One evening, soon after this small achievement, Birgitta and I had just gone to bed, when we heard the sound of breaking glass downstairs. As I crept out of our bedroom to investigate, it was a tad disconcerting hearing Birgitta locking the bedroom door behind me! I made my way apprehensively along the dark passageways and down the staircase, expecting at any moment to be confronted by burglars.

Reaching the front hallway, I saw the cause of the disturbance. A painting had fallen from its hook on the wall, landing on a large glass bowl on the sideboard beneath it, smashing it to pieces. Relieved beyond belief, I turned to open the door of our newly decorated sitting room. As I pushed the door open, an enormous, panicked, flapping, black jackdaw, flew into my face. I nearly shat myself!

It's not uncommon in country houses for jackdaws, which are part of the crow family of birds, to descend the chimneys, then get trapped inside a room. You'll often see wire mesh over the tops of the chimney pots to prevent this from happening. Once trapped inside they can do enormous damage, tearing at curtains and scratching furniture, not to mention bird shit everywhere. This jackdaw must have arrived only moments after we had gone to bed.

After I had recovered from the initial fright, I managed to calm the bird, grab it, and escort it back to freedom outside. I examined the fallen painting. Apart from the shattered glass bowl, there was no damage but also no explanation for its falling from a very well secured hook on the wall. Many people will laugh at this, but I am convinced that somehow, it was the house letting us know that there was a destructive jackdaw trapped inside our newly refurbished sitting room.

I have always been a firm believer that if you take care of your house, your *home*, then it will take care of you. It saddens me that houses have become commodities to be bought and sold just to generate a profit. Houses should always be appreciated as homes, sanctuaries where families are nurtured, friends are entertained, a natural base to comfort and kindle the human spirit.

Birgitta was beginning to settle into our new life. She not only had her boys staying over regularly, she also invited her parents from Sweden to stay. I got on well with my in-laws, possibly because neither spoke a word of English and I couldn't speak Swedish. But with hand signals and exaggerated miming we all managed to understand each other.

She had also discovered the nearby town of Cheltenham Spa. The beautiful Regency buildings, tree-lined promenade and open parklands, not to mention its elegant shopping centre, provided her with hours of pleasant distraction. One shop in particular had taken her fancy.

Alongside the fashionable cafés and bars in the expensive Montpellier district of the town, was a chic interior design boutique, owned and run by its eponymous owner, Maggie. Maggie's Interiors specialized in high cost, up-market fabrics and wallcoverings. Birgitta considered the contemporary and popular Laura Ashley prints too common. This chichi emporium introduced her to the more exclusive and costly fabrics of Osborne & Little, Colefax & Fowler, and Designers Guild. An introduction that was to cause us considerable discord in the near future.

Meanwhile I was enjoying myself playing at being the country farmer. I decided to purchase a dozen hens so that we could enjoy freshly laid eggs every day. There was an advert in the farming section of the local newspaper for 'Pullets'. I was told that these were young hens, generally less than a year old, and prior to the age when they would start laying. The advert had been placed by a farmer in Newent, a small town some twenty miles away. I took my stepson Daniel in my Rolls Royce to collect them. Being a total innocent, I imagined that they would be tiny, yellow feathered, fluffy little chicks which could be contained in the small cardboard box I'd taken to collect them in.

We arrived at the farm and the owner disappeared around the back of the farmhouse to collect them. I was stunned when he returned grasping six in in each hand, held upside down by their legs, fully grown, flapping fowls! We had no option but to release them inside the car, with Daniel on the back seat attempting to prevent them flying and fluttering all around us!

We got home covered in feathers and bird shit. Luckily Mum was visiting with a friend who was a butcher who knew how to trim their wings to stop them flying off.

****

The land on the property had been neglected. The grass in the meadows was nearly two feet high. I had purchased a flock of fifty sheep, foolishly believing that they would graze it down.

While buying some provisions in the local village, I bumped into a neighbouring farmer, Arthur Saunders who was driving along on his tractor. He cheerfully doffed his weather-beaten straw hat and gave me a wide grin. In his thick, gravelly voice with its broad Gloucester accent he called out to me.

"'Ere Col, I 'yerd you bought some sheep?"

"Yes Arthur," I replied, pointing over the valley to my land where the backs of the flock were just visible in the long grass. He feigned a puzzled searching stare.

"Well, oi can't see 'em, what colour be they?" he teased.

Arthur Saunders was typical of the local, rural farming community; hardworking, jovial and honest. I invited him over to inspect the pasture where I was keeping the sheep; I obviously needed his advice. He drove over to my fields and knelt in the long grass. His fingers probing the soil at the base of the pasture.

"'Ere Col, you've got some good 'erbage in 'yer. You've got cowslips and good clover." He went on to tell me that my meadows needed "'arvesting for winter fodder". He offered to come over with his "'arvester" and bale the grass up for me.

A few months later I called on Arthur to help me again. As well as the sheep, horses, a few young weaner calves and a dozen hens, I'd also acquired a Friesian cow. Arthur owned a couple of bulls, so I arranged with him to bring a bull over to 'service' my cow.

The moment the bull stepped out from his trailer, his ears pricked up and he snorted excitedly as he trotted over towards my cow. She was not interested. He followed her round and round the field until finally she ran down to where a small stream flowed. Temporarily getting her front legs bogged down in the muddy bank, the bull took advantage and stepped up onto her.

I turned to Arthur and said how lucky that the mud had stopped her in her tracks. Arthur just looked at me and said, "Don't worry Col, my bull would've followed 'er up a tree if er'd gone up one!"

****

Periodically sheep need dipping to protect them against parasites such as blow flies, ticks and lice. Not having my own dip I gratefully accepted the offer from a neighbour from whom I'd bought the sheep to use his dipping facility.

I rounded up about a dozen at a time and herded them into a horsebox trailer, then drove them over to my neighbour's farm. After several journeys to and fro I'd almost completed the flock. But there was one stubborn ewe who just wouldn't join the final group. No matter how much I coaxed her, she refused to join the others.

I was determined not to be outwitted by a sheep! I chased her round and round the field until finally I had her cornered. I threw myself forward landing on top of her where we both lay panting and exhausted. Just at that untimely moment, Johnny Griffiths, a local larrikin, happened to be walking along the lane on the other side of the hedge where I had my ewe pinned down. Peering over the hedgerow he stared down at us.

Tut-tutting, he said, "Col, I could destroy you in the village if this ever got out!"

****

There were so many amusing and engaging characters around us. The village pub, The Royal Oak, was now owned by my old friend from my apprenticeship days, Dave Morris. Dave had been the chef at his father's pub, The Royal William at Cranham village. That was the pub where Jan and I had our first 'fine dining' experience back in 1967 almost twenty years previously.

The Royal Oak was the social centre for the local community. Each evening it filled with neighbourhood farmers, tradesmen and professionals, all enjoying its bonhomie and smoky comfort. I was so happy during this period. Mucking out stables, planting my kitchen garden, looking after the livestock and renovating the house. But business matters were calling me back to London.

The extended six-month repayment holiday on the new equipment had expired and the Israeli Scitex corporation were demanding their money. I still wasn't happy with the performance of the equipment. Had its productivity been closer to the levels that Scitex had promised us, the repayments would not have been a problem.

This had been weighing heavily on me since the system's installation. I felt that I was being railroaded into signing the financial contract, committing my company to a mountainous debt. Scitex had arranged for the debt to be underwritten by an American bank, the Bank of Boston. Representatives of that bank were to meet me at my accountant's offices in London to sign the contract. With prevailing interest rates still above ten per cent, the repayments would be around £14,000 per month! I knew that this was unsustainable given the poor output from the equipment.

On the morning of the signing I took the train to London. During the two-hour journey I became so nervous about the impending meeting that I even ordered a large brandy from the buffet bar despite it being only nine o'clock in the morning! Having gained a little Dutch courage, I arrived at the accountant's offices just off Regent Street, feeling a little bolder.

I explained my reservations to Joe, my accountant. Like most members of his profession, Joe was a pragmatist. He agreed that committing to the excessive repayments would jeopardize my company but didn't volunteer any solution to the problem. We sat and waited the forthcoming confrontation.

I was expecting there to be only one or two agents from the bank, so I was taken aback when no less than *five* representatives were shown into the office! They all cheerfully trooped in and introduced themselves. This was a delegation of all the most senior managers of the London branch of the bank. They justified their number by explaining that as it was such a large transaction, they wished to celebrate the event, and take my accountant and I for a 'slap-up lunch' after the signing.

Sitting across from me, their main spokesman, the chief executive of the bank, took a large, bound agreement from his briefcase and passed it over to me. There was a palpable sense of anticipation in the air. I flicked through the pages of legalese before coming to the page that required my signature. Below the figure of £500,000 as the amount of the loan were the monthly repayments of £14,000!

I knew that by reneging on the deal, Scitex would unleash their legal department to instigate winding-up procedures on my business. I felt cornered. I seemed to be staring down the barrels of corporate suicide whichever way I looked.

Taking a deep breath, I told him that unfortunately I was still unhappy with the poor output of the system. I went on to say that I couldn't possibly justify the price tag that Scitex had placed on it, and therefore would not be signing the contract.

As I handed the document back to him there was a collective dropping of jaws and an audible gasp from the contingent. After much floor staring and shuffling of feet from the crew and an uncomprehending stare from the CEO, he placed the paperwork back in his briefcase and they all silently filed out again.

Over a subdued lunch with Joe, I pondered the quandary that I found myself in. I didn't know which way to turn, or who to turn to. On an impulse I phoned my old boss from Colour Precision, Tad Laskowski. I had remained in touch with Tad over the years, and we had often helped each other out with work. He was aware of the equipment that I'd bought and understood the difficulties that I'd experienced with it. When I told Tad what had just occurred in Joe's office, he was very bullish.

"You can't just roll over and let them trample you," he said, "you've got to fight them!"

He offered to meet me that afternoon to introduce me to a lawyer friend of his who he was confident could help me.

Beneath Dennis Cooper's bespectacled, mild-mannered exterior, lurked a carnivorous appetite for a legal brawl. After listening to my grievances about the equipment, Dennis fired off a four-page letter to

Scitex, detailing my complaints and demanding reparations. I left his office with Tad, feeling buoyed-up and more positive.

There followed several months of threats backwards and forwards, with Dennis even enlisting the help of an Israeli legal colleague, "to better understand the mindset of the Israeli opposition"! Finally, Scitex accepted an offer of *half* the original sum demanded! I happily signed a new financial agreement and now felt much more optimistic about the future of my company.

Chapter 18

New Arrivals and a Departure

At Greenhouse Court I continued to enjoy 'the good life'. Our first Christmas there we entertained all our children with several of their partners and friends. My mum also came and stayed over for a while; she was a lot of fun. She was quite witty and could be very entertaining, although I could never be too sure whether she was joking or being serious.

On a particularly windy day, she remarked how much she hated the wind. She said that she could cope with ice or snow but felt that windy days were getting more frequent and were blowing harder. She believed that it was due to the recently discovered hole in the ozone layer! When I expressed surprise and doubt at this deduction, she replied, "Oh yes, I reckon it's letting a draught in!"

That winter there was heavy snow in the area and we were due to start lambing. Back in October, a neighbouring farmer had lent me his ram – called a 'tup' in that part of the world – to 'cover' my flock of ewes.

They were all about to start dropping their lambs while there was still thick snow on the ground. We used a couple of empty stables to provide shelter for the mothers and their lambs for the first twenty-four hours after being born. Nearly all the ewes gave birth to twins and started nursing their offspring with their milk immediately.

There were two lambs from the flock that were rejected by their mothers. No amount of coaxing by smothering the newborn in a surrogate's scent, could induce one to foster these orphans. We ended up bottle-feeding these two mites and keeping them warm in our kitchen next to the Aga cooker.

Eventually I made a kennel from hay bales outside the kitchen door. As they grew older, they wandered inside and played around the house, mixing easily with the dogs and the cat until they were able to graze in the paddocks with the rest of the flock.

One ewe was having a difficult birth. My sheep-farming neighbour's wife, Sarah, came over to help me. A baby lamb should have both its front legs and its head forward, ready for its birth. This one had turned sideways and was struggling, as was its mother.

Sarah knelt behind it and slid her arm up inside the ewe. Confirming what she suspected she then allowed me to feel the position of the lamb. In the freezing cold air of the winter morning, it came as quite a shock to feel the piping hot temperature inside the sheep.

Having managed to turn the lamb to its correct birthing position, it slipped out naturally. I felt quite triumphant and celebratory. Having not seen the birth of any of my daughters, I realized, regretfully, just what I had missed out on!

Over the Easter holiday, our Doberman house dog, Natasha, who I'd had mated with a friend's Doberman, gave birth to *eleven* pups! I'd bought a special whelping pen for her which was just as well, given her multiple births.

For the first few days following the births, we had to manually alternate the pups every twenty minutes to allow them all to feed sufficiently from their mother's milk. Luckily, all our children were staying for the Easter holidays, so we all took shifts in the feeding routine throughout the days and nights until the pups were able to sort themselves out.

The hens were all laying regularly, so we were kept well stocked with fresh, free range eggs, and having the occasional 'hack' out with the horses, life could not have been sweeter.

My clients needed little persuasion to spend weekends with us sharing our bucolic lifestyle. One client was always welcome and paid several visits especially when she was launching her new glossy magazine, *Period Living*.

Louise Matthews was a publisher with whom I had been friendly for a few years. She had offered to feature Greenhouse Court in an early issue of the magazine. I was very excited with this opportunity to showcase our home in a prestigious glossy, thinking of the extra value it would add to the property should we ever have to sell it. Birgitta wasn't interested and vetoed the idea, which really upset me. I put it down to her still protesting her dislike of our new home.

I have maintained contact with Louise and her husband, Richard, and we are still friends some thirty years later. The CEO of Louise's company, Tom Moloney, also became a close friend and enjoyed visiting. Tom loved taking the horses out riding.

I'd re-established friendship with Tony Elliot, the owner of *Time Out*, so we were again producing the colour images for it. His production director, Dan Sargent, became a good friend and regular guest with us. He always arrived with armfuls of Moët & Chandon champagne.

Other good friends, also clients, Tricia and Terry Jones, the founders and owners of the style magazine *i-D*, were occasional visitors, generally on their way either to or from their country house in Wales. My bank manager, Fred Tongue, was a regular visitor; even the lawyer, Dennis Cooper, who'd helped me fight Scitex, jumped at an invitation.

****

It was the perfect venue for entertaining, living up to all my hopes and expectations. Nearly all my clients had become close friends making for happy occasions when they came to stay.

A weekend visit would always include a country walk as the house backed onto a natural beech woodland. There were winding tracks up through the woods and over to the neighbouring valley with its tranquil Cotswold village of Slad, the area made famous by the author, Laurie Lee, who still lived next door to the village pub, The Woolpack.

Laurie was often in the pub and ever happy to entertain us with his local stories and gossip. My visitors always left with a signed copy of his classic book, *Cider with Rosie*, the celebrated story of his growing up in the village.

In the summer of that year, 1988, Claire, my middle daughter gave birth to a baby girl, Emme, giving me my first grandchild. Due to some prenatal concerns, she had spent the previous four weeks under observation in Cheltenham hospital.

It was fortunate that I now lived nearby and could visit most days to relieve her boredom. I'd pick a bucketful of strawberries from my kitchen garden and armed with a few boxes of small jigsaw puzzles we'd spend the afternoons scoffing berries and competing with the puzzles.

Later that year when Christmas came around, we had a huge family gathering. As well as our new baby granddaughter, we'd also invited Birgitta's ex-brother-in-law, Alex and his wife Anita. I'd also invited a chef friend who'd arranged a large commercial-sized oven to cook the enormous turkey that we needed to feed everyone. I couldn't imagine myself being any happier. However, ominous storm clouds were gathering on the horizon.

Computerized technology was advancing at a startling pace. A visionary American physicist Robert Noyce, and his gifted engineer partner Gordon Moore, were developing microchips at their company, Intel, which was to have a profound effect on our industry.

Gordon Moore had given his name to Moore's Law, which states that micro-processors would double in speed every two years. They would also halve in size *and* price over the next ten years. This meant that companies employing their technology inside their equipment would always be playing catch up. It was impossible to depreciate assets fast enough on a company's balance sheet. As the New Year 1989 began, this problem was just around the corner and would require my wholehearted attention.

Meanwhile Pete was still managing the company in my prolonged absences. He was now getting considerable help from my eldest daughter, Rachel, who had joined the company the previous summer.

New Arrivals and a Departure

Having worked for the magazine publishing company, Northern and Shell, for three years, she had gained immense experience in their production area. She now embarked on reorganizing our production department. As a dedicated and very capable person, she quickly established an efficient system of work throughput, and became popular with our clients, suppliers and workforce.

In light of the technical developments, Pete was concerned that our equipment needed updating. There was a new generation of colour scanners and new software written for page make-up devices; we needed to re-invest. Selecting which direction we should take required me to spend more time back at work.

Often staying overnight in London did not go down well with Birgitta. Eventually, Pete and I opted to purchase new colour scanners and more computer processing power to cope with the changing technology and ever-increasing workload, plunging us into further and increased indebtedness.

Despite my new commitments at work, I was still trying to spend most of my time at Greenhouse Court. Louise, my youngest often came to stay, which was wonderful for me as it helped counter the difficulties that I was still experiencing with Birgitta's daughter, Rebecca.

I had never enjoyed a closeness with Rebecca, who had always harboured a slender resentment towards me. Now, as a stroppy teenager, I found her often confrontational attitude disruptive and hard to manage. As the adage 'blood is thicker than water' affirms, Birgitta regularly sided with Rebecca in any domestic disagreement.

After leaving high school, Louise had found herself a temporary job serving on the delicatessen counter at a supermarket in Gloucester. She also found a small bedsit in Cromwell Street in the city. Years later it came to light that she had been living just a few doors away from where the notorious serial killer Fred West and his wife, Rose, were committing their grisly homicides in the basement of their house.

Rachel was to tell me of an equally alarming incident when she was living in Pembroke Street with her mother. Walking to school one morning when she was about fifteen years old, she was aware that she was being followed. A man was approaching her from behind. As she quickened her step, he came right up behind her.

She said that he was so close he actually fell into step behind her and she could feel his breath on her neck. She broke into a run and crossed the road. She looked back to see him leering and laughing at her.

She saw him once more when she was in town with her sisters; she pointed him out to them. It wasn't until she saw his photograph plastered all over the front pages of every newspaper that she identified him as Fred West.

The street where he'd followed her was around the corner from Pembroke Street, Midland Road, where he'd originally lived and where he'd murdered his first victim, his own stepdaughter!

****

We'd lived at Greenhouse Court for over two years but Birgitta still hadn't settled. She never enjoyed it to the same extent that I did. If she wasn't away visiting her parents in Sweden, she would occupy her time shopping in Cheltenham, choosing expensive furniture and decorations for the house.

As I began to struggle financially with our huge mortgage repayments, plus the new liabilities at work, she showed no concern for our increasingly precarious situation and continued to spend money that we simply did not have.

During the soaring house prices boom in the late 1980s, Greenhouse Court's value had risen to almost £1 million and I made the foolhardy move of re-mortgaging the property. This temporarily took the pressure off but only delayed the inevitable calamity.

My self-imposed parsimony was negated as Birgitta continued with her reckless extravagance. Only the very best, the most luxurious fittings and soft furnishings would satisfy her and compensate for her disenchantment with our country living. It was destined to end in tears.

The final straw happened when I found her measuring the windows in the kitchen. She was holding bunches of expensive material pattern books. She told me that she was ordering new curtains and blinds, and they would *only* cost £20,000, – about £48,000 today. When I told her that there was no way that we could afford it, she just turned and said, "I don't want to know that, this is what I'm doing"!

Adding to these domestic woes, the business was suffering a downturn. We had lost a couple of magazine clients, and for the first time in our history, the monthly management accounts showed a loss. This was followed in the subsequent month by another set of figures in the red. Another month like this would put us in big trouble; I was staring at possible insolvency. I had to return to London and take the helm again.

Much as I loved our home in the Cotswolds, my main priority was my company in London and getting it back on track again. I booked into a cheap hotel in North London and threw myself back into business.

Pete was a fantastic, reliable, committed operations man, a 'safe pair of hands', but I realized the company needed a *driver* again. I attacked the challenge with gusto. After six weeks of relentless work, analysing every aspect of the business, making dramatic reductions in overheads, which unfortunately meant laying off some staff, and re-establishing contact with all our customers, we stemmed the flow of losses.

We picked up some new business and I discovered that I was enjoying the cut and thrust of it all again. I found that I was happier on my own away from Birgitta's constant demands and her total indifference to the stresses that I was under, not to mention Rebecca's snide asides.

Taking advantage of the prevailing property boom, Birgitta's boys, Daniel and Bobby, had sold the house that their father had bought for them, making a whopping profit to share. Instead of re-investing it into another home for themselves they went on lavish spending sprees.

Bobby bought a series of expensive motor cars, including a classic sports car which got written off, uninsured, by a drunken friend of his. As young men in their twenties they'd never had so much money, and it went to their heads. Predictably, the money soon ran out and the partying ended. I had little sympathy for them.

It may smack of hypocrisy, criticising my stepsons for their profligacy while I had been notorious for extravagant spending in the past. The difference was that I felt I could justify my occasional splurges as I had worked hard for my money, whereas the boys had their fortune handed to them on a plate.

During this time, I was still battling to save my business which was struggling and heavily in debt. I was forty-five years old and confident that I could rebuild it again. I then took one of the toughest decisions in my life. I had anguished over it for several months but I decided to separate from Birgitta.

Even though I still loved Birgitta and was so attached to my lifestyle in the country and it deeply saddened me, I felt that the situation there was never going to change, it was never going to be ideal. There would always be Birgitta's over-indulged children and her self-indulgent spending. I felt that I'd had enough and couldn't cope with them anymore. There was more than enough equity in the house for her to sell it and buy another for herself, though probably not as grand as Greenhouse Court. I thought that this would be a generous settlement.

When I told her of my intention, I don't think she fully believed me. We'd had spats before when I had threatened to leave, but never gone through with it. This time was different and I filed for a divorce. Little did I realize how totally uncomprehending of our financial situation Birgitta was, and how unrealistic her excessive monetary demands were to become.

Chapter 19

Lonely Garret and Lonely Hearts

Birgitta and I had been together for fifteen years; before then, I had been with Jan for eleven years. I was in my mid-forties and had effectively been married since I was a teenager. I was about to begin a whirlwind two years of bachelorhood which would witness such excesses that would see me bouncing between a health farm and a hospital.

Not wanting to spend Christmas on my own I bought a cheap flight to Kyrenia in Turkish occupied Northern Cyprus. My old friend, the chef Nick Karahasan, had invited me to stay with him at a hotel he was running for the now disgraced businessman, Asil Nadir.

In the get-rich-quick days of the late 1980s, Asil Nadir had been a shining star. Allegedly robbing the company he'd founded, Polly Peck, a FTSE 100 listed corporation, of many millions of pounds, he fled to his birthplace of Northern Cyprus, where there was no extradition treaty with Britain.

The Turkish Republic of Northern Cyprus was not recognized by the United Nations; it was a rogue state and thus didn't exist. Following the Turks' invasion of the island, hundreds of thousands of Greek Cypriot residents had fled to the south of the island; it was off the tourist's map.

Kyrenia still maintained a vibrant community of Turkish Cypriots and British ex-patriots. The bars and cafés were bustling, unlike the ancient harbour-city of Famagusta, where the Turkish army had landed.

On Boxing Day, I drove to Famagusta to see for myself the destruction and dereliction. On a hillside approaching the city, I pulled over and got out of the car to take some photographs of the picturesque bay below me. An army jeep appeared from nowhere, and I was surrounded by four soldiers all pointing their weapons at me. I was ordered back into my car and told that photographs were forbidden. Luckily, they didn't confiscate my camera.

There was an intimidating military presence everywhere. The once major tourist destination had been abandoned. The luxury hotels that lined the seafront all bore the scars of aerial bombardment and mortar shells and were deserted – it was a ghost town. I read recently that it remains empty and fenced off to this day.

Flying back from Kyrenia on New Year's Eve, I stopped over at Istanbul, the historic city that spans the cultures of East and West, Christianity and Islam, and separates Europe and Asia. My first impression was of a populace of heavy-set, scowling, surly moustached faces, and that was just the women!

I only spent a couple of days sightseeing, long enough to marvel at the Blue Mosque, shop at the Grand Bazaar, and eat the freshly caught fish on the Galata Bridge, but there were urgent matters to attend to back in England.

Birgitta was dithering over selling Greenhouse Court. She had engaged a divorce lawyer who was advising her to demand that, as well as the equity in the house, I also pay her a large slice of money from the business.

I had supplied her with our management figures showing our losses and the massive debt that we were carrying. This had cut no ice at all, and she continued, through her lawyer, with the ridiculous demand for £500,000 in cash! By the spring of 1990 house prices, particularly at the top end, had started to tumble. I decided to drive to Painswick to try to persuade her to temper her demands and sell the house urgently.

I had sold my Rolls Royce to put some cash back into the business and was now driving a tiny second-hand Fiat Panda. Rachel came with me on the drive down to give me some moral support.

When we arrived, I collected the remainder of my clothes and some books that I treasured. I stressed to Birgitta my fears of the falling house prices, but she was oblivious to my pleas which fell on deaf ears.

In London I was renting a small furnished flat overlooking a railway line in Camden Town. The block of units, which was built on pillars, rocked slightly when heavily laden goods trains crossed the bridge outside my bedroom window. My mum didn't believe this when I told her, accusing me of exaggerating until she visited me and experienced it for herself. It was quite a disturbing occurrence at first, but it's amazing what you get used to when needs must.

I was still paying the hefty mortgage repayments on Greenhouse Court until finally, in early June. Birgitta's lawyers accepted that there was no extra money available and the house was sold.

Ironically, despite Birgitta's constant complaints about missing London during our two years in the country, I was astonished to hear that with the proceeds of the sale of Greenhouse Court, she had purchased a coach house not ten miles from Painswick!

Relieved of the heavy financial burden of Greenhouse Court, plus the emotional stress of the acrimonious divorce settlement, I was able to really focus on my business again. Major changes were sweeping across the globe. The mighty Soviet Union was breaking apart, the Berlin Wall was being torn down, and Britain was sliding into another recession.

Germany's reunification presented an opportunity. Roger Waters, one of the original members of the band, Pink Floyd, was to produce his rock extravaganza, *The Wall*, at Berlin's Brandenburg Gate, previously a no-man's-land next to the Berlin Wall. Through my old contacts at Harvey Goldsmith Entertainment, I got the contract to produce the prestigious souvenir programme for the event.

Remembering this occasion, I can recall a terribly embarrassing meeting with Pink Floyd's lead guitarist, David Gilmour. Richard Branson had refurbished his Roof Gardens nightclub, and I was invited to the opening night party.

As Branson owned Virgin Records, I found myself surrounded by the who's who of the music business. Standing next to me was David Gilmour. Having been a huge fan of Floyd all my adult life and rating him as one of the best guitarists in the world, I couldn't resist approaching him to shake his hand.

After gushing a garbled praise and thanking him profusely for all the pleasure I had listening to him play, I expected him to nod acknowledgment and swiftly move further away from me. Instead, this incredibly polite gentleman seemed genuinely flattered.

He asked if I had a favourite Floyd album. I immediately unleashed a torrent of further praise on all his albums. Listing each one throughout his career, adding that as every new album was released, I thought it couldn't be bettered, until the next one arrived and topped it.

He was nodding enthusiastically as we reminisced on all the band's achievements. I told him that I had been to all their concerts, even going to all seven nights at Earls Court where they first performed *The Wall*. He listed intently, then asked me further questions.

I couldn't believe my good fortune; I was having a conversation with this living legend. I felt like an old friend. In the back of my mind I was imagining him calling me to help him while he struggled with some lyrics that he was writing.

The band had recently had a much publicised falling out and had split up. I thought that this was such a tragedy and wanted to commiserate and say what a shame it was that they'd broken up. Instead, for some inexplicable reason it came out as, "It's such a pity that you're all *washed up*"!

"Oh, I wouldn't say that!" he said, and abruptly turned and got into conversation with Pete Townsend, the lead guitarist of The Who, who was hovering nearby. It was too late; I was staring at his retreating back. I tried to attract his attention to say that I didn't mean "washed up", I meant "broken up" but my moment was gone. I made my way back to the bar feeling utterly stupid and regretful.

Throwing myself back into business kept my days fully occupied but living alone in my little flat was becoming boring and depressing. I was looking for social distractions. Many evenings were spent in restaurants and bars in the company of clients but I missed a female relationship.

Long before the internet and its many dating sites, newspaper's classified advertising pages carried columns of people seeking to attract the opposite sex. In London, *Time Out* had a famous 'lonely hearts' section. I placed an ad in it. The following week I received *fifty-seven* replies, it felt like it was my birthday!

Most of the replies were from women who were looking for a long-term relationship. I must confess, I wasn't, I just wanted some fun and laughter. This was certainly provided by a few of the encounters to which I was introduced.

By the early summer, no longer committed to a massive monthly mortgage, and with business back on an even keel, I could afford to splash out again. I was spending frequent weekends in my favourite city, New York.

I justified to myself the cost of the trips by topping up my wardrobe as clothes were half the price stateside than they were in London. On one visit I contacted Tricia, who'd worked with me when setting up Latent Image US Inc.

Tricia had set up a successful real estate brokerage in downtown Manhattan. I really enjoyed her company. She was tall, very attractive and still single. Our shared love of the theatre, cinema, concerts and dining out, made for ideal companionship.

On one occasion I took Rachel, my eldest daughter with me for the weekend. I introduced her to Tricia who was very accommodating, putting us up in her swish apartment on East 22nd Street, opposite the famous triangular-shaped, landmarked Flatiron Building.

We had a fabulous time, even taking a scenic helicopter trip over the sites of the city. As my finances continued to improve, I flew the supersonic Concorde, cutting four hours off the seven-hour flight time. It was amazing, and with a five-hour time difference,

I effectively landed in New York, two hours before I had taken off from London!

At work we were having some major staff changes. Joanne, who had been with us since I had set up the company in 1979, had sadly decided to move on. She had studied for and passed the exams for The Institute of Chartered Secretaries and had accepted a senior management position outside of our industry.

Before she left she had advertised and found us her replacement. Jacqui fitted in to our team from the moment she arrived and was to stay with us for over ten years. She was not only an extremely competent company secretary and my personal assistant; she was also great fun outside of work. With a lovely singing voice, her impersonation of Billie Holliday guaranteed that she was a hit at every one of our office parties. Jacqui was a wonderful addition to our management and became a very good friend.

Rachel was still managing our production department. As neither she nor I had permanent partners, we spent a lot of time together, socializing in London.

I think that a father and daughter relationship is quite unique and very special. As I was separated from my girls when they were young and had spent less time with them than I would have liked, it was wonderful to have the opportunity to enjoy their company now that they were growing into young women.

One Sunday Rachel and I were enjoying lunch in one of our favourite restaurants, Joe Allen's in Covent Garden. This basement American brassiere, was a great spot to while away a lazy Sunday afternoon, watching the antics of all the theatrical luvvies that frequented the place. We were probably finishing our second bottle of wine when I suggested we should try to get tickets for the Tchaikovsky concert at the Royal Albert Hall that evening.

On certain Sundays, the Royal Philharmonic Orchestra would combine with the Royal Choral Society to present a 'Classical Spectacular' featuring the works of Tchaikovsky. It would always finish with his rousing *1812 Overture* complete with cannons and bells!

Rachel needed no persuading so we finished our drinks and hopped a cab over to the Albert Hall. It was sold out! We hung around outside the magnificent building hoping to spot a tout selling tickets.

Out of the blue we were approached by two young women who asked if we were looking for tickets. It transpired that they were visiting from out of town. They had four tickets but two of their friends couldn't make the evening; I immediately offered to buy them.

The four of us sat together in one of the boxes that lined the auditorium. Rachel was sitting next to the girls and got into conversation with them. In an incredible coincidence, both had management jobs with one of our largest clients.

During the interval I bought a bottle of champagne for us all to share. The two girls really appreciated this; we all got chatting and they turned out to be a lot of fun. One of them, Jo, tall and vivacious with beautiful green eyes, had certainly caught my eye.

When the concert finished, we were all keen to carry on the party atmosphere. I suggested we continue at the Roof Gardens just up the road in Kensington. Arriving inside the club we were confronted with an unexpected sight. I hadn't realized that Sunday evenings were Gay nights!

The bar, lounge area and dance floors were a jostling crush of naked, sweating torsos. We joined the throng but I've never felt so out of place in my life. After a few drinks we decided to split. As we were saying our goodnights, Jo slipped me her phone number and invited me to call her. I felt that maybe my love life could finally be looking up.

Historians would record that month of August 1990 as when the infamous Saddam Hussein of Iraq invaded the tiny sovereignty of Kuwait. The consequences of that invasion are still being felt throughout the Middle East to this day.

On the sporting field, English soccer fans were licking their wounds having recently been knocked out of the World Cup semi-finals in a penalty shoot-out against Germany.

In the south of France, Madonna's controversial 'Blond Ambition World Tour' was reaching its sexually explicit conclusion. Madonna's current boyfriend was the actor, Warren Beatty, who was twenty-two years her senior, the same age difference as between Jo and me!

A few days after I had first met Jo at the Albert Hall, I rang her up and we met for dinner. I was completely smitten with her. She was intelligent, very amusing and extremely attractive. I visited her house which her very middle-class parents had helped her buy; it needed decorating. Over the following weekends I set to and redecorated it.

During this early flush of romance, I invited her to holiday with me in Barbados. We flew off together a few days later. The almost generational gap between us was brought brutally home to me as, dressed as Zulu warriors, Jo and I strutted and danced behind a slow-moving truck which was carrying loudspeakers the size of small houses. The ear-splitting music blaring out was a groin-grinding reggae number, popular at that time in the Caribbean. We were participating in the annual 'crop over' carnival on the island of Barbados. We had danced in the procession from early morning, the sun was now disappearing below the ocean's horizon, and I was absolutely knackered; Jo still wanted to party.

After a wild two weeks of sun, rum and a certain local herb, the difference in our ages was beginning to tell. We returned to England and I sensed a cooling off from Jo. We both had pressing work commitments and saw each other occasionally over the next few months until it finally fizzled out.

Towards the end of the year the political landscape was about to change dramatically. Sir Geoffrey Howe, one of Prime Minister Margaret Thatcher's strongest allies, resigned from the government over her attitude towards the European Community.

Days later he delivered a damning criticism of her in his resignation speech to parliament. Despite the cruel comment from a former Chancellor of the Exchequer Denis Healey, that criticism from Geoffrey Howe "was like being savaged by a dead sheep" the speech sparked a leadership challenge.

Michael Heseltine, a former Minister of Defence, nicknamed Tarzan for his long hair and swashbuckling manner, fancied himself as the next prime minister and issued a challenge. In the event, two other cabinet ministers threw their hats into the ring and the virtually unknown John Major emerged the final victor. From day one, Major struggled to maintain unity in his party, famously referring to a group of his dissenting backbenchers as 'The Bastards'!

Throughout this period of political upheaval, my private life was equally turbulent. A very good friend, Tom Moloney, who was the CEO of one of my largest clients, introduced me to an acquaintance of his who he'd met when visiting Australia.

Gabrielle was from Sydney and was working in London for the British cinema advertising company, Pearl and Dean. She was enormous fun and could always make me laugh. She was full of the bonhomie typical of Australians. I tried hard to secure her employment in our sales department but the restrictions placed on us by the immigration authorities made it impossible.

Nevertheless, we became very good mates and eventually she was to introduce me to a friend of hers who would change my life completely!

Chapter 20

Affliction and Affections

During the balmy autumn of 1990 I was enjoying dating a very smart young woman who I'd met in a nightclub. Simone was from Brazil and was involved in the fashion business. She imported women's stylish garments from her hometown of São Paolo for sale in the UK.

She had dark eyes and the classic beauty of an ancient Egyptian princess. She was regularly invited to parties, mixing with fashionistas such as John Galliano, Ozwald Boateng and the talented but ultimately tragic, Alexander McQueen. This was not my scene at all but I grew very fond of Simone and invited her to spend Christmas with me in Morocco.

We flew into Marrakech then drove to the small harbour town of Essaouira on the Atlantic coast. Essaouira was made famous by the film director, Orson Welles. He filmed his acclaimed *Othello* there. We actually stayed in the presidential 'Orson Welles suite' at the Hôtel des Iles near the gates of the old city, even sleeping in the four-poster bed that the great man himself allegedly used.

It was here on Boxing Day that I first experienced symptoms of an illness that I initially tried to dismiss but I became so weak with flu-like aching that we had to cut the holiday short and fly back home.

Once back in my flat I started to feel a bit better. This was just as well as I had arranged to spend New Year with Tricia in New Orleans. Two days later I flew into New York, met up with Tricia and we flew on down to New Orleans. Having spent my early teens listening to Dixieland jazz and collecting all the records of Chris Barber, Kenny Ball and even owning an old Bakelite 78 rpm disc of Louis Armstrong's classic, *Basin Street Blues*, I was so excited to be visiting the city where it all started.

We stayed in the Latin Quarter just off Bourbon Street. Sadly, this was my first disappointment. Instead of my imagined jazz bars and musical venues, Bourbon Street was mostly lined with striptease parlours, blue movie theatres and general burlesque!

Calling into one bar for a beer, Tricia ordered a decaffeinated coffee. Giving her a withering disdainful look, the barman just drawled, "We don't serve Yankee coffee down here." I felt that some elements were still fighting the civil war.

We spent a few days doing all the touristy things; the Garden District, plantation houses and a cruise on a Mississippi paddle steamer.

Throughout the holiday I continued to suffer with the unpleasant flu-like symptoms that I'd first experienced in Morocco. Determined to overcome them, I attempted to beat whatever it was that was ailing me by doubling down on my revelries, but it became disconcerting, not to say quite worrying, that apart from the constant aching in my back, I was occasionally losing my balance and kept stumbling over. Tricia and I returned to New York and I flew back to London.

I spoke to my GP about my symptoms and he immediately referred me to a neurologist in Harley Street. His examination of me did nothing to allay my fears. Inviting me to lay on his couch he said that he was concerned at the amount of muscle mass that I had lost from my limbs. When he weighed me, I was alarmed to discover that I had lost over two stone in weight.

He then proceeded with a feather in one hand and a pin in the other, to ask me which felt sharp and which didn't as he stroked and poked the soles of my feet. I could feel nothing at all! When he tried to get me to stand upright and still, placing the heel of my right foot in front of the toes of my left, I couldn't and fell over. He called an ambulance and booked me into the Royal Free Hospital in Hampstead.

As a child growing up in the 1940s and 50s I had escaped all the prevailing infectious diseases – polio, diphtheria, tetanus, whooping cough and scarlet fever – that were not uncommon prior to mass vaccinations. Apart from having my tonsils removed when I was four years old, I had avoided hospitals, maintaining an unhealthy fear of them.

Now, at forty-seven years old, displaying symptoms of any number of paralysing and incurable disabilities, I found myself surrounded by white-coated registrars and pin-striped consultants all eager to perform unpleasant tests on me.

I was kept in hospital for a month undergoing all manner of X-rays, CAT scans, MRI scans and EEGs. I had endoscope and colonoscope investigations, lumbar punctures and endless blood tests. I was examined by neurologists, gastroenterologists and cardiologists; all the while I was being administered with heavy opioid based medications to try to relieve the severe pain in my back and legs.

I could no longer stand up, let alone walk, so was confined to a bed or a wheelchair. I was being tested for all 'the nasties' as the doctors referred to them; the cancers, motor neurone disease, multiple sclerosis and the fatal – and endemic at the time – AIDS! It was a terrifying time.

After four weeks 'resting' in hospital, I slowly began to regain my balance and was able to walk a few wobbly steps. The pains in my body were gradually receding. I was eased off the pain-numbing medication, and mercifully the doctors ruled out all the nasties.

As I slowly began to recover, the best diagnosis that was offered was that I had suffered from a viral transverse myelitis. It is still unknown how transverse myelitis is contracted. The best explanation for my condition was that I had picked up a virus, possibly in Morocco over Christmas, and it had attacked the central nervous system in my spine.

Normally, one's immune system fights off a viral infection. My ignorance of this fact allowed me to abuse my immune system by continuing to overindulge in drinking, partying and jetting around the world, not letting my body rest and recover.

It took several months for me to fully recuperate. I took the opportunity to convalesce at my mum's home in Gloucester. Mum had recently moved into a small bungalow on the outskirts of town; she called it her 'Wendy House'. She lived alone now so welcomed the chance to have me there as company and 'fatten me up'. Despite my wasted appearance, she loved to show me off to all her friends and neighbours. One after another she invited them in to look at me!

"There he is," she'd say, pointing at this pale wizened figure curled up on her couch. The visitor would creep forward and peer at me.

"How are you love, you are getting better?"

"Getting there, getting there." was my stock reply.

The visitor would be shown out, only to make way for another a short while later. Two visitors who were a pleasure to catch up with were my two aunties; Aunty Molly, my dad's younger sister, and Aunty Mabel, Mum's younger sister.

Aunty Molly reminded me of Dad, she had the same eyes and some of his mannerisms. She had done quite well in life, marrying into a wealthy bakery family. Her husband had died quite young leaving her well provided for.

She married again, this time into a wealthy pharmacy family. Again, she outlived her husband who left her with a substantial inheritance. Even though Mum was very fond of Aunty Molly, having known each other since they were young girls, she used to irritate Mum with her constant pleadings of poverty.

"Ooh, I can't afford that!" she'd say, shaking her head and frowning. What it was that she couldn't afford might only have been the brand of butter that they were enjoying on the sandwiches that Mum was offering.

Mum's sister, Aunty Mabel was a completely different character. She was eight years younger than Mum and had been just a small child when Mum had left home as a young teenager in Birmingham.

When Aunty Mabel was fifteen years old, she had written to Mum in Gloucester, asking if she could join her there as she also wished to leave home. Mum was newly married with her own home and a husband away at war. She hadn't seen her little sister for eight years so readily agreed. Mum told me that she went to meet Mabel off her train at Gloucester Railway Station.

As Mabel stepped down onto the platform, Mum got quite a shock. Instead of the shy, restrained adolescent girl that Mum was expecting, she said that Mabel was not only wearing makeup and lipstick, she was also smoking a cigarette and surrounded by attentive young servicemen!

Before Aunty Mabel managed to turn her life around, she was a bit of a tearaway. As a young lad, I remember her riding her motorbike. I didn't know at the time, but the man that she became involved with, 'Uncle Geoff', was a petty criminal. He served time for a variety of burglary offences and even organized an attempted mass breakout from Gloucester Prison.

She had a daughter with the burgling Geoff, a girl about my age who I vaguely remember. Apparently, this daughter as an adult, together with a male partner, was involved in a murder!

Some years later, Mum told me that it was said the pair of them had only meant to rob their victim. They had knocked him unconscious and stuffed him into the boot of their car, intending to drive him some distance, then leave him.

Unfortunately, either the trauma of the attack or goodness knows what, when they came to release him, he had choked on his own vomit and died. I believe the charge was changed to manslaughter, and Mabel's daughter and her violent partner were both imprisoned.

I can't begin to imagine the distress this would have caused Aunty Mabel, let alone the victim's family. There is a much happier ending to Mabel's story.

After separating from Geoff, she became a bus-conductress – or 'Clippie' as they were nicknamed. In the days before driver-only buses, every bus had its own conductor. This person rode on the bus, wore an official uniform and sold passengers a ticket for their journey.

There's a lovely romantic story, as Mabel fell in love with the driver of her bus, a delightfully pleasant gentleman called Dennis. Her love was reciprocated and they married and lived 'happily ever after'.

Unlike Mum, who was a true-blue Tory, Aunty Mabel was very left wing and had a strong social conscience. Not having children of their own, she and her husband, Dennis, adopted a pair of young twin brothers. They had met the boys when visiting a local orphanage that they supported.

Both young boys had mental disabilities, not surprising considering that they had been deserted by their parents and spent their formative years being handed from one set of foster parents to another before ending up in an orphanage for unwanted children.

Mabel doted on her boys giving them a warm, loving home which set them on the path to becoming responsible, hardworking young men.

I loved Aunty Mabel. She was a strong trade unionist with a big heart. She was involved with local politics, sitting on the local council. As an elderly lady, she visited me in London, inviting me to the Houses of Parliament.

Standing beside her in that historic lobby, I was amazed when senior legends of the Labour Party, Michael Foot and Tony Benn, stopped by to say hello and pay their respects to her. She knew everybody and was popular with everyone. In her later years she suffered uncomplaining with crippling osteoporosis. At her funeral, her local member of parliament gave a moving tribute to her. I still miss Aunty Mabel very much.

After a couple of months recuperating at Mum's, I was fit enough to return to work in London. During my long absence Pete, with the assistance of Rachel in 'Production', had managed the company brilliantly. Britain was heading into another recession, unemployment was creeping up again, but Latent Image was flourishing.

Fortunately, consumer and business magazines, now the backbone of our turnover, seemed to be recession proof. The explanation for this phenomenon reasoned that while small luxuries such as theatre tickets or dining out might be forgone during hard times, a couple of pounds spent on a magazine represented good entertainment value. In fact, new magazines were being launched every month.

Most of our magazine customers were now designing their pages on Apple computers, which had become more versatile and powerful with the advent of desktop publishing. My youngest daughter, Louise, had successfully applied for a job operating an Apple Mac at one of our clients, the teenage magazine, *Just Seventeen*. After she'd worked there a while, I had persuaded her to come and work with us. It was fantastic having two daughters minding my business, although Louise has chided me ever since for acquiring her too cheap!

Now that I was feeling more like my old self, I contacted Tricia again, telling her about my recent illness and time in hospital. She sounded genuinely concerned and invited me to stay with her over Easter.

Since getting to know Tricia better during my recent trips to New York and really enjoying her company and friendship, I began to recognize that I was harbouring a secret passion for her. So I jumped at the invitation hoping that maybe our relationship might develop into something more intimate.

In the event, although we spent four fabulous days together, disappointingly, despite my amorous attempts, our friendship remained at the platonic level. I consoled myself that it had been an ambitious notion, not least considering the Atlantic Ocean that lay between our two homes. I did realize how fond I had become of Tricia, but any romantic thoughts appeared to have been thwarted.

Socially I was still spending most evenings with clients and enjoying the occasional date with my old friends, Simone or Gabrielle. On my birthday in May that year, I'd arranged to take Simone to dinner at the Roof Gardens nightclub.

That same evening, Gabrielle was having a dinner party with a girlfriend of hers and two guys from London. She asked me if I would sign them in as guests of mine at the club when they had finished their dinner. Simone had been invited to a party later that night at one of her fashion friend's house. I wasn't keen to go, so she left after dinner, and I waited at the club to sign in Gabrielle and her friends.

It was almost midnight when they arrived. I'd almost given them up and was about to leave. The two guys were wearing jeans, so the concierge was struggling to find them trousers to conform with the club's dress code.

I might have told him not to bother and apologetically refused them all entry had it not been for Gabrielle's girlfriend. She was quite a stunner; extremely attractive with long dark hair and vivacious looks.

I had planned to escort them into the club, then make my apologies and leave. Seeing Gabrielle's friend made me change my mind. I saw them all to a table and ordered a bottle of champagne. While Gabrielle was chatting to the two guys, I struck up a conversation with her gorgeous friend.

She was also from Australia and was a consultant physician working at the specialist cancer hospital, the Royal Marsden, in London. I found her totally engaging and chatted with her into the early hours.

Eventually, deciding that I'd hogged her company and conversation for too long, I regretfully said my goodnights. It had been an eventful birthday, topped off by meeting this fascinating and entertaining young doctor, whose name was the same as the beautiful musical instrument, Viola.

Chapter 21

Temporary Insanity

I could never have imagined the incredible changes to my personal and working life that the summer of 1991 would bring. The old joke that girlfriends are like buses, you wait for ages then two come along at once, could not have been truer in my case.

Just a couple of days after meeting Gabrielle's disarmingly attractive friend Viola, who I really felt that I had connected with, I received a phone call from Tricia in New York. She told me that she was taking a week's holiday and would like to come to England. The flat that I was renting had a small second bedroom, so I offered her to stay in London with me. I said that I'd be delighted to show her around, and if she wished, we could explore some of the English countryside together.

I met her at Heathrow airport and drove her to my little apartment. I was really pleased to see her and so happy to be in her company again. I'd known Tricia on and off for over twelve years, a large part of which I'd carried a romantic torch for her.

After showing her to her room to unpack her things, I was about to leave her to it, when the welcoming hug I'd offered became a reciprocated tender embrace. I was taken completely by surprise, but no less delighted when our long-term friendship suddenly transposed into that of lovers.

I could not have been happier. We spent an idyllic week travelling around the West Country, visiting picturesque villages and spending our nights together in quaint guesthouses. Like all special holidays it ended too soon. As we were saying our goodbyes at the airport, I was already making plans to visit Tricia in New York before the month was out.

Meanwhile there had been a wonderful event in the family. Claire, my middle daughter, had given birth to another beautiful girl. Emme now had a younger sister, Hayley. I was now the proud grandfather of two gorgeous granddaughters. I drove to Gloucester to visit the new arrival.

While carefully cradling the little bundle, smelling of talcum powder and baby oil, with her frowning, crumpled features peering up at me, it was hard to imagine that twenty years hence, she would transform into a stunningly elegant model. And her wriggling, mischievous sister at my knee, would become a partner in a successful law firm.

As one new arrival came into my life, another was leaving; my Australian friend Gabrielle was returning to Sydney. A posh friend of hers, Lady Iona something-or-other, was throwing a farewell party for Gabrielle at her swanky house in Chelsea, and Gabrielle invited me along.

I arrived at a party in full swing. The place was full of Sloane Rangers and Hooray Henrys, but also a smattering of Australian ex-pats. Among them the delightful doctor friend of Gabrielle's who I'd met at the Roof Gardens nightclub, Viola.

We immediately got into conversation. She was wearing a striking red gingham jacket. When I complimented her on it, she said that she'd bought it at Saks of 5th Avenue in midtown Manhattan. This set us off talking non-stop about our favourite city, New York.

Viola told me that she had recently returned from a five-year contract, working at the renowned Emory University Hospital in Atlanta, Georgia, and had spent many weekends sightseeing and shopping in New York. I could have spent the entire evening enjoying this fascinating woman's company and couldn't understand how such an attractive lady could still be unattached. Had I not embarked on a relationship with Tricia, I would certainly be dancing attendance on Viola.

Putting all selfish, lascivious reflections out of my mind, I did think that she might make the ideal partner for my single friend and drinking buddy from *Time Out*, Dan Sargent. A few days later I arranged to introduce them to each other. Having raved to Dan about this gorgeous single girl that I'd met, I told him that I was having an early evening cocktail with her, and would he like to join us? I suggested to him that if he 'hit it off' with Viola, I would split and leave them together.

Using a little subterfuge, I told Viola that I was having an early evening cocktail with a single friend, Dan, and would she care to join us? I also suggested to her that if she 'hit it off' with Dan, then I would split and leave them together!

The rendezvous I'd chosen was a trendy new bar in Soho. I arrived at the same time as Viola and we were immediately engrossed in lively conversation as though we'd known each other forever. Dan arrived shortly afterwards and I made the introductions.

By most standards Dan would be considered tall and not unattractive. He is urbane and engaged in an interesting and topical line of work. He has a self-confessed tendency towards arrogance but a lively sense of humour, if a little on the esoteric side. Sadly, we saw none of his humour on the evening of the get-together. Indeed, there was no 'spark' at all happening between him and Viola.

As the evening progressed, I felt less inclined to leave. This was partly because there appeared no simpatico between them, but mainly I was enjoying Viola's company and attention too much. We all agreed to have dinner together. Both Dan and Viola were aware of my commitment to Tricia in New York, so it all appeared quite innocent and platonic.

Following dinner, I suggested that we move on to see some live jazz performed at the famous Ronnie Scott's club, where I had recently become a member. Typical of jazz club venues, Ronnie Scott's interior is small, dark and intimate. Candlelit, red-clothed tables in tiers around a small stage which had seen such jazz legends as Ella Fitzgerald and Nina Simone.

It Was The Best Of Times...

A waiter showed us to a table and we ordered drinks. There was a modern-jazz quartet playing as we settled in to listen. Before long, Viola and I were back in animated conversation. Dan was more interested in listening to the music. Our chattering was obviously irritating him as he was continually 'shushing' us. We ignored him. Eventually, in the early hours we all left the club and said our goodnights. I had enjoyed another stimulating evening in the company of this extremely engaging young woman.

On the 28th June, less than four weeks since Tricia had flown back home, I flew to New York to see her. We had planned a short holiday around Cape Cod, then a drive to New Hampshire for a cousin of Tricia's wedding. Again, we had a wonderful few days together.

After taking the ferry to Martha's Vineyard, where the famous movie *Jaws* had been filmed, and whale watching off the coast of Nantucket, we drove to Boston to pick up Tricia's brother Michael and his wife and two daughters who were attending the wedding with us.

I'd been looking forward to meeting Tricia's brother as she spoke so highly of him. Tricia also confided that his eldest daughter was her favourite niece. After collecting the family, we took off on the long drive to New Hampshire.

It was initially hard for me to warm to her brother. When I asked him if he'd ever visited England, he seemed surprised at the question, saying "Nope" then adding that there were ten more places he'd rather visit before England, and they were all in the United States! He struck me as being a very parochial, mid-west American, completely the opposite to Tricia. I realized later that Michael was just being wary and cautious of me as he was very protective towards his sister.

Following the wedding and the drive back to New York, Tricia and I discussed ways that we might be able to spend more time together. As we both had the responsibilities of our own companies to manage it was not going to be easy.

Our week's holiday was over and I was about to head back to England again, our situation seemed impossible to resolve. Even though the real estate market was slowing down as the USA, like the

UK, was sliding into another recession, Tricia could still not leave her business for at least a couple of months. Pondering this conundrum, I flew back to London.

Reflecting on this period in my life, the only explanation that I can offer for the solution to our conundrum was 'temporary insanity'. I am not sure whether it was my love for New York or my lust for Tricia or both, that prompted me to embark on a venture which, looking back, was doomed from the start. I cannot remember whether it was my idea or Tricia's, but whoever it was, I must take responsibility for it.

Over the ensuing months, as the plan was being concocted, I flew over to New York several times, sometimes just for the weekend. Tricia flew over to England in September, when I introduced her to all my family. We drove to Yorkshire to visit my brother and to Gloucester to visit my sister and my mum.

It was during this time that my company was enjoying a period of relative prosperity. I was fortunate to have Pete and two of my daughters, Rachel and Louise 'minding the shop'. I felt the company was strong enough to again allow me to forgo my direct involvement and take off on another adventure.

At first sight the plan seemed simple. I would join Tricia over in New York selling real estate with her. To achieve this aim, I would first need to obtain the required real estate sales licence by attending a ten-day concentrated course at the Manhattan campus of New York University.

Not possessing a Green Card permitting me to work in the States, I needed to acquire the appropriate visa to allow me to work. To introduce me to my new career, Tricia said that she would help me find listings while I familiarized myself with the territory in which she'd chosen to work.

I gave notice on my flat in London and vacated it in late September. I flew to New York and moved in with Tricia. The first cracks in the plan appeared soon after. Having lived most of her adult life on her own, Tricia was having difficulty adapting to sharing her home. The problem was exacerbated by my occasional but apparently deafening night-time snoring!

On top of this Tricia was particularly stressed as due to the deepening recession, the residential property market had bombed, forcing her to lay off her two staff and close her office. She was now having to work from home, and I was left with the feeling that I was 'getting under her feet'.

As luck would have it, a rental apartment directly adjacent to Tricia's became vacant, so I snapped it up. We both agreed that in this initial stage of our relationship, neither of us wished to 'swamp' the other, consequently we should ease ourselves more gradually into it.

I was very happy with my new apartment and refurbished it immediately with all new furniture. From our 29th-floor level on East 22nd Street, my view faced downtown towards the ill-fated twin towers of the World Trade Center in the distance. Next door, Tricia's apartment looked uptown towards Central Park, with great views of the Empire State and Chrysler buildings. Billy Joel's recently released *Uptown Girl* could not have been more appropriate.

I completed the real estate salesperson's licence course and passed the exam. I had many meetings with a firm of immigration lawyers who didn't inspire me with much confidence especially when they suggested that I might be more successful applying for a Green Card lottery ticket!

The lottery had been established the previous year. Run by the United States government, it was issuing 50,000 permanent residencies annually. Apparently, there were over twenty million applicants; I wasn't one of the lucky ones. The system was made famous by the romantic comedy starring Gerard Depardieu and Andie MacDowell released that year, *Green Card*.

Up until I moved to New York that summer, I'd always thought that the Gold Coast was a small British colony in West Africa, now called Ghana. The Gold Coast in New York realtor-speak refers to a tiny district in Greenwich Village stretching either side of 5th Avenue from 14th Street in the north, down to Washington Square in the south. It is so called due to the staggeringly high prices of property there. It was also the area where Tricia specialized and did a lot of her business.

After 14th Street, the wide four-lane 5th Avenue narrows to two lanes. Both sides are lined with landmarked pre-war hotel buildings, now converted to chic apartments. Many retain their entrance marquees, lobby receptions and even porters.

The narrow tree-lined side streets off Fifth in this historic district have a unique character. Expensive loft conversions in 1960s' office blocks and small industrial units adjoin four-storey brownstone townhouses. This was the territory that I was to concentrate on.

The huge incentive for business was the massive eight per cent commission a real estate brokerage charges when accomplishing a sale. I was shocked when I learned the size of this commission, when compared to Britain's 2–3% charge.

Real estate was regarded as the bedrock of the American economy. According to Forbes, in 2016 the top ten real estate developers in New York alone, had a net worth between them in excess of US$ 43 billion; Donald Trump was near the top of the list.

My first work concerns in the autumn of 1991 were not only finding then persuading vendors to entrust me with the sale of their property, but also seeking out potential purchasers. Where does one start? The help in finding listings, which Tricia had initially offered, amounted to pointing me towards the classified section of the New York Times newspaper.

I would trawl through columns of properties for sale, searching for the private ones, with no realtor already instructed. I then telephoned the residence and attempted to charm them with my sales spiel. More often than not they slammed the phone down!

While Tricia and I still enjoyed the occasional evenings out together, I sensed a growing detachment in our relationship. The original ardour was gradually, but noticeably cooling. My *bon vivant* instincts were beginning to bother her, particularly when overindulging in smoking and red wine caused my snoring to rise to unacceptable levels.

Unsurprisingly I was finding myself with more time on my own. On these occasions there were several neighbourhood bars I enjoyed visiting. One of them, P. J. Clarke's on 55th and 3rd, I hadn't drunk in since I had first worked in New York back in the 1970s. Jostling my way to the front of the crowded bar, I caught the young bartender's attention, ordered my drink and said to him, "D' you know, I came into this bar nearly twenty years ago!"

He just looked at me, shrugged his shoulders and said, "Well, I'm serving as fast as I can!" I just loved that New York sense of humour.

One evening, out enjoying a couple of beers alone, I found myself standing next to a couple of guys who were in earnest conversation. I couldn't help overhearing that they were discussing Martin Scorsese's recently released film *Cape Fear*.

Tricia and I had just seen the film the night before. As a huge fan of Scorsese, I was disappointed in this remake, especially comparing it to the original 1962 version. I couldn't help myself interrupting their debate with my own critiques. They were extremely gracious and invited me to join them.

Ken shared a loft around the corner in 'the village', his friend, Tom, was visiting from out of town. They were similar ages to me and we were soon immersed in comparing the merits of Scorsese's films.

Towards the end of the evening after exhausting all movie talk and consuming countless numbers of beers, I had learned that Ken was a photographer and like myself, had two failed marriages behind him. Our conversation progressed through solving the world's problems before degenerating into sharing the rudest jokes.

With each new round of drinks, we toasted each other's health while collapsing into helpless laughter at the latest punchline. In the space of a few hours we had become best buddies.

If it hadn't been for Ken, my sojourn in New York would have been a lot more miserable. As my relationship with Tricia deteriorated further, I saw more and more of him. Whenever I felt

Temporary Insanity

alone and unhappy Ken made himself available to cheer me up over a few beers or a meal out.

The New York residential sales market was in a dire state as America slipped further into recession. I had been able to attract only a few listings and even fewer potential buyers. If it wasn't difficult enough finding properties and customers, I even found it hard wrestling with bunches of keys and struggling to open apartment doors for prospective purchasers. I came to realize that my heart wasn't really in my new line of work.

It was a bitterly cold Sunday morning early in the new year, 1992. Tricia was heavily engrossed on the telephone when I popped over to let her know that I was going out to meet Ken for a quick beer.

Not wishing to distract her, I wrote a short note on the back of a used envelope to let her know that I wouldn't be long and slid it next to her on her desk. I caught up with Ken and we trudged against a biting wind howling along 5th Avenue. We crossed Washington Square and headed towards our favourite bar, Berry's, on the corner of Spring and Thompson Street in Lower Manhattan's SoHo. Seating ourselves at the bar, I told Ken about my problems selling real estate and the difficulties I was experiencing with Tricia.

Ken originated from California. He had their laid-back attitude to life. He had served as an aerial photographer during the Vietnam War, flying numerous dangerous missions recording bombing attacks, even covering America's, then secret, invasion of Cambodia.

These experiences, coupled with his relaxed demeanour gave him a wonderfully carefree, easy-going view of life. So it came as a surprise when he leaned forward on his barstool, turned and asked me why I was continuing to struggle with work that I didn't like, and in a relationship that I wasn't happy in?

He went on to question why, if I had a successful business in London, I wasn't back there enjoying it? These were questions that I hadn't faced up to asking myself, but Ken was articulating my deepest disquiet.

After a couple of drinks, I left Ken at the bar and walked back to my apartment mulling over what he had said. It was early afternoon and I was about to get freshened up to see Tricia when she burst into my flat. Striding up to me with a face like thunder, she was waving a piece of paper in her outstretched hand.

"What's this?" she barked at me.

I looked closely and saw that it was the note that I'd left her earlier on.

"You've written on my property!" she snarled.

I was flabbergasted. I thought she was joking; she wasn't. I pointed out that it was a used envelope. Cutting me short, she ignored my protests that it was a piece of scrap paper and continue to berate me.

In the past I'd allowed her bullying outbursts to wash over me. Often when we'd had a disagreement, her admonishments could last several days until she could feel 'in harmony' with me. I'd always suffered her scolding and disapproval as I felt a tinge of guilt regarding my smoking – she had quit some years before – and my occasional intemperance.

This time was different. I told her that I'd had enough of her reprimands and lecturing and withdrew to my bedroom. I heard my front door slam shut. I have to confess, I sat on my bed and cried.

I felt overwhelmed with disappointment. I was disillusioned with Tricia and my real estate sales job. I concluded that Ken was right to question my reasons to remain in New York. I decided there and then to quit.

I rang Ken to say goodbye and to offer him my television set as I knew that his wasn't working. I packed my clothes and books that I'd bought from London. There was a flight early the next morning. As I left before dawn, I didn't want to wake Tricia and risk another scene.

Downstairs in the lobby, as I gave them my keys, I told the grateful porters that they could share my furniture between them to sell. I phoned Tricia as soon as I landed in England. She seemed neither surprised nor saddened. I guess you could have written all there was to say on the back of an envelope!

Chapter 22

True Romance

The adage, 'bad start, good ending' was again to prove itself correct. Unlike Her Majesty the Queen, when three of her four children's marriages were to end in heavily publicised, messy divorces, and her house, Windsor Castle, was to burn down that year, prompting her to label it her *'annus horribilis'*, 1992 turned out to be probably one of the best years of my life so far.

It was a pretty good year also for Prime Minister John Major who, against all polling predictions, took his Conservative government to an election success. This surprising victory caused the leader of the Labour opposition party, the Welshman Neil Kinnock to immediately resign, making way for his shadow treasurer, John Smith to take over.

The unfortunate Smith was soon to die of a heart attack paving the way for the then telegenic Tony Blair to become prime minister some five years hence.

None of these events could have been on the forefront of my mind when I arrived back in London licking my wounds and homeless. My first priority was to find somewhere to live. I checked into a hotel in Marylebone and on the off chance called the landlady of my old flat in Camden Town. It was still vacant!

Within a week I was established back in it so could now turn my attention back to my business. Technology was moving forward at a frightening pace and most of our equipment again needed upgrading.

Apple Macs were now the predominant tool our customers were using for their design work. The discs containing their work that they supplied to us did not interface simply with our Scitex equipment. Out of the blue we received a visit from an old work colleague from Pete's and my days at Crosfield Electronics back in the '70s.

Dick Tibbitts had gone to take charge of Crosfield's Far East office based in Singapore. He had been responsible for sales throughout Southeast Asia. On his business travels he had come across a small company in Australia which had developed a clever page make-up system that would interface seamlessly with Apple Macs.

Dick had left Crosfield's to represent this company and expand their sales in the UK. The system was called Jupiter and had been conceived by two young whizz kids who called their eponymous company Wright Technologies after its founder. After explaining the workings and benefits of the system to Pete and I, Pete quipped that if it was as good as Dick was saying, we should purchase two! It was, and we did!

Back in the bosom of my business which was now thriving, with sales increasing and employing over thirty staff, I felt confident enough to begin looking to purchase a permanent home for myself. It was an excellent time to buy. The country was in a deep recession and property prices had fallen to an all-time low.

Over the following months my evenings and weekends were spent flat hunting. There had also been one other unresolved question that had been lurking in the back of my mind. I wondered if the lovely young Australian doctor, Viola, whose company I had so enjoyed, was still working in London and was still unattached? I called the hospital where she worked and was put straight through to her.

She was surprised but seemed delighted to hear from me. I told her that things hadn't worked out for me in New York, that I was back in London now, and would she like to have dinner with me one evening?

She told me that she was joining a group of girlfriend nurses to attend a local Valentine Day, Policeman's Ball that Friday evening, and would I like to join them? She also offered that I could stay overnight afterwards at her hospital apartment. I could not have been more excited!

It was a black-tie occasion so I arrived at her apartment in my best 'bib and tucker'. Her girlfriends were all crowded inside enjoying glasses of champagne. Viola greeted me like an old friend, then showed me to her spare room where there was a single, blow-up, rubber mattress on the floor waiting to be inflated, this was to be my bed for the night. I must admit that it wasn't quite what I was hoping for, maybe I had fantasized too much and was definitely guilty of wishful thinking!

The 'Ball' was being held in a community hall inside a Territorial Army Centre some five miles away; it was raising money for local charities. We arrived at a cavernous room. There was a temporary bar set up at one end although not a great selection of drinks available. A few long tables were arranged around the perimeter of the room, leaving a dance area in the centre.

The high ceiling was festooned with a few dozen large red balloons. It wasn't exactly my sort of evening's entertainment, but it was more than made up for with Viola's sparkling company. In the end it was a fabulous evening. Viola was obviously an extremely popular girl among all her friends. It was delightful to witness this consultant physician's genuine egalitarian attitude to all the young nurses around her.

During the evening Viola told me that she had recently purchased a flat in Harrow-on-the-Hill. She had just finished having it renovated and was planning to move some of her things into it over the weekend. I offered to stay and help her which she gratefully accepted.

As the evening drew to a close, and after a combination of too many cheap bottled lagers and in an effort to impress her, I made generous bids at the charity auction. This culminated in me buying all the red balloons that were strung high up on the ceiling.

Viola and I then had enormous, if not perilous fun, climbing a tall stepladder to retrieve them, much to the amusement of the stragglers left in the hall. My night-time wasn't so much fun, laying alone in her spare room on the tiny, uncomfortable, inflatable mattress.

The following morning, feeling unpleasantly hungover, I helped Viola with her move. It took nearly all day to pack most of her clothes and her large collection of books into boxes, then load them into the car. She enlisted the help of a colleague, a young radiographer, Richard, to help and used his car too.

Finally, with both vehicles packed to the gunwales we set off for Harrow. The flat that Viola had bought was on the first floor of a converted Victorian terraced house. It had an averaged size living room, with natural light from a large bay window, an open fireplace and original, sanded and varnished wooden floorboards.

There was very little furniture and considerable builder's dust everywhere. The overall impression was quite uninviting. It was a cold February evening and we couldn't get the central heating nor the hot water to work.

We unloaded all the boxes and Richard left. I felt that the flat wasn't quite ready to be comfortably habitable. It needed a plumber to fix the problems and a thorough clean throughout. I suggested we call it a day and I take Viola back to my place for the night, where she could have my spare bedroom and could then arrange for the work to be completed the following week, she readily agreed.

To ensure the day ended on a pleasant note I proposed we enjoy a dinner out together. We found a welcoming French restaurant and settled in for some delicious food. In the middle of our meal I was surprised to hear "Hey Colin!" from another diner.

I looked up to see a smiling Tad Laskowski, my old boss from Colour Precision standing over us. After introducing him to Viola and exchanging a few pleasantries he left to re-join his guests. I have to say that I felt very proud to be able to show off my extremely attractive dinner date.

Next day I woke with another head-splitting hangover. I had discovered during the previous night's dinner that Viola didn't actually drink. While she often, to be sociable, held a glass of wine or champagne in her hand, she never really drank it. She just put it to her lips, took the smallest of sips, then left it. Consequently, I had drunk virtually the whole of the bottle of the fine French Burgundy that I had ordered on top of the four pints of beer, 'just for ballast', all topped off with several large brandies!

I'm ashamed to admit that on those occasions I sometimes used a little narcotic assistance to ease my suffering and perk myself up a bit. I was crouched over my coffee table snorting a small line of coke, when Viola suddenly walked into the room.

"What are you doing?" she exclaimed.

I sheepishly tried to justify myself, mumbling about my shocking hangover, etc. Before I could finish, she stunned me by bursting into tears.

"You're killing yourself!" she cried, "You are such a nice man, but you smoke, you drink, *and* you are doing drugs!"

I lamely tried to protest that it was only occasionally that I used 'Charlie'. She was having none of this. She sat me down and gave me a stern lecture on the perils of my way of life. She even drew small diagrams of the inner workings of my body and the damage that I was causing it.

As she was an oncology specialist, I sat meekly and attentively listening to all her admonishments. We did end on a slightly lighter note when she told me that persistent use of cigarettes, alcohol and drugs could cause my private parts to shrink. I protested that I had no problems in that area!

Following my ticking-off for my irresponsible ways, I was surprised when Viola agreed to join me for a Sunday lunch at my favourite restaurant, Joe Allan's in Covent Garden. Despite my nearly ruining it, a wonderful weekend ended on a high.

Over the next few weeks Viola and I saw a lot more of each other, culminating in her inviting me to join her on a trip to Edinburgh where she was accepting a cheque on behalf of the hospital for their cancer research programme.

The donation was organized by a young university student, who she had diagnosed and who had been treated for and overcome, testicular cancer. He had created a fashion show with his fellow students, and all the proceeds were going to the hospital.

The event was held in the historic eighteenth century Assembly Rooms. The grand ballroom was packed with several hundred enthusiastic fashionistas. After the show, Viola gave a very impressive and confident speech of thanks on receiving a very large cheque.

By now I realized that I was falling in love with this amazing woman. I had booked my favoured holiday destination, Morocco, for two weeks to include some horse trekking in the Atlas Mountains. I invited Viola to join me.

Before the holiday, which was still two months away, we continued to spend many evenings and weekends together, often with Viola staying over in my small flat. Eventually she no longer felt it necessary to make use of my spare bedroom!

It's often said that holidays, particularly ones involving a lot of travelling, can be quite stressful. Taxis and airline delays, disappointing accommodation, missing luggage, etc. can all be a good test for a relationship. Well, every day of our two-week holiday was magical. Viola's effervescent personality and our shared gregarious natures ensured that we were continually in tune with each other. She took everything in her stride.

From the moment we boarded the ageing Royal Air Maroc, Caravelle aircraft, she was befriending cabin crew and fellow travellers alike. We even got an invitation to dinner that evening at his home in Marrakech by a local passenger sitting next to us.

Horse trekking in the High Atlas can be very arduous, especially for a novice rider. Again, Viola threw herself wholeheartedly into the experience. With just our local guide, Abdul, and a mule carrying our provisions, we climbed to remote Berber villages, only accessible by horse or mule, enjoying the hospitality of the head of these communities.

Viola was equally at home, squatting in mud-brick adobes, sipping on ultra-sweet mint tea, as she was in the swanky La Mamounia luxury hotel where we ended our stay. We returned to England a committed and devoted 'item'.

Back in London I could focus on finding an apartment. Over the previous months I'd inspected dozens of flats, most of them were depressing. I finally found just what I wanted. It was in a new purpose-built five-storey, brick building in the centre of London's famous Covent Garden immediately opposite the world-renowned Royal Opera House.

Due to the current, dire economic situation, only one flat had been sold so I could take my pick. I settled on a large, bright, one-bedroom unit on the first floor, reasoning that in the event of a fire, I could jump from a window! The building was bordering on luxurious, with a large carpeted foyer, lifts and even a full-time porter.

The flat itself was finished to an extremely high standard, with solid, panelled, wooden doors, generous skirting boards and wide architraves. A large L-shaped living room could easily be divided to accommodate a second bedroom if needed. In August that year I finalized the purchase and moved in.

Apart from a bed and a television set, I had no furniture. Displaying her prudent side, Viola had suggested that I wait until the January sales before buying anything else. She said that she'd be happy helping me find bargains to complete the furnishing.

For the following six months, the large cardboard box that the television had arrived in doubled as my dining table. Two borrowed, collapsible, canvas garden chairs were all there was to sit on. One was a recliner and more comfortable than its meagre partner. On evenings when Viola stayed over, we took it in turns on them, an hour each!

For the first time in many years I was completely happy again. I was in love with a wonderful, exciting woman, I was settled in my own home, and I owned a successful, flourishing business. A few weeks previously Viola had joined me on a trip to Gloucester where she had met all my family. They all thought that she was terrific as I knew they would. Mum even commented to me that she was certainly 'top drawer'! I could easily imagine spending the rest of my life with Viola; I wanted to marry her.

It Was The Best Of Times...

One evening in early September, while we were standing at my kitchen sink washing our dishes after dinner, I popped the question! It probably wasn't the most romantic of places or occasions. She turned me down. I was crushed.

She explained that although she was extremely fond of me, she had always hoped that when she was married, she would have children. She knew that I felt differently. Viola was in her mid-30s, I'd had my children and even had two grandchildren. At forty-eight years old, I felt that I was too old to inflict myself on children again.

I so wanted Viola to be happy, and I desperately wanted to share my life with her. After six weeks of heavy soul searching, I came to my senses and realized that my age should not be a barrier to having more children. There were many well-publicized examples of men, a lot older than I was, enjoying a young family. I also knew that Viola would make a fantastic mother.

On Sunday mornings we often liked to stroll along the Thames embankment. Making our way to the Tower of London, crossing the imposing Tower Bridge, and stopping for lunch at one of the restaurants on the renovated Butler's Wharf. Afterwards, we'd walk back along the South Bank, passing the rebuilt Globe Theatre and the Festival Hall complex. That day, having reached the middle of Waterloo Bridge, we stopped to admire the wide London skyline stretching before us.

It was there that I took Viola's hand and told her how much I loved her, and that I was prepared to start another family if she would marry me. This time she accepted but insisted that she wouldn't move in together with me full-time until after we were married. I was elated and happily accepted this proviso, understanding that although she no longer practised her faith, her Catholic upbringing still placed certain restrictions on her. We didn't talk further about when or where we would celebrate the event, but fate was to play its hand and provide an unexpected opportunity.

Chapter 23

A Trousseau in Tucson

It was a cool, autumn Saturday morning not long after our memorable moment on Waterloo Bridge. I'd gone to pick Viola up from the hospital where she was working on a cancer research paper that she was presenting at a conference of the Radiology Society of North America (RSNA), held in Chicago in December. It was the first time that I'd visited her department, and she was happy to show me around.

As a specialist cancer hospital's X-ray unit, it was very well equipped. Apart from the standard sonography, plain X-ray and CT scanners there was an area displaying large signs warning that all metal and magnetic objects were forbidden. Viola explained that this housed the Magnetic Resonance Imaging (MRI) room.

At the time MRI machines were relatively uncommon. Few hospitals could afford them. They cost around half a million pounds and needed a specialist radiologist to interpret the scans. Viola had spent five years at Emory University Hospital in Atlanta, Georgia becoming an expert at reading MRI scans. My interest was piqued.

An MRI machine is basically a seven-ton magnet with a tunnel through the centre; apparently, it's about a thousand times more powerful than a fridge magnet! An MRI image can see *inside* joints, muscles and ligaments, etc. I was captivated by this machine, I thought it was amazing. Plus, there was no potentially harmful radiation used nor unpleasant aftereffects.

I was staggered when Viola told me that patients were charged around £300 for a scan, which only took about half an hour. This set my business thinking into overdrive. Over the years, the colour scanners and ancillary equipment that I had bought had cost similar amounts to these medical scanners, but by comparison I could only charge a fraction for the service.

Later, when I discussed this with Viola, she was equally enthusiastic to explore the possibility of us establishing a medical imaging service. She suggested we do some research into local hospitals as a 'market feasibility study'. I was coming to appreciate that Viola was not only a medical specialist, she also had a very impressive business head on her shoulders.

The government had recently initiated changes to the National Health Service. It was creating statuary bodies, National Health Trusts. They incorporated individual boards of directors, with a CEO, finance director, operations director, etc. These entities introduced the concept of public private partnerships (PPPs). I thought that this might open the door for the installation of an MRI scanning service in collaboration with a local hospital.

Viola and I identified several prospective sites. The most enthusiastic response came from a hospital in Orpington, Kent. I presented our idea to the CEO, a Mr Keith Wood, and several of the board members. Keith even showed me a potential site within the hospital. It was part of the Canada Wing, consisting of three, adjoining four-bed wards on the ground floor. It was perfect for converting into an MRI facility. It had been built in the mid-80s but, shamefully, had stood empty ever since!

Our next problem was to raise the finance. Apart from the cost of the equipment and the essential, expensive lead-lined partition walls, we also needed a sizeable amount of working capital. My regular lenders baulked at my requests. My old friend, the designer, Steve Hicks, introduced me to his accountant, Arvin Shah.

Arvin had an interesting background. His family were from Uganda and they were among the 27,000 Ugandan Asians that came to Britain after they were expelled from their homeland by the murderous dictator, Idi Amin back in the 1970s. These unfortunate refugees lost everything.

Nearly 6,000 businesses, farms and ranches were confiscated and doled out to Amin's sycophants. The Ugandan Asians, who'd been given only ninety days to leave the country had been responsible for most of the country's commerce and administration. Needless to say after the mass expulsion Uganda's economy collapsed into chaos.

It is indeed to their credit that these refugees, who arrived in Britain with just the clothes on their backs, soon established themselves, through their hard work and endeavours, in businesses and positions of responsibility throughout the land.

Arvin's offices overlooked the busy Upper Street in Islington, North London. He had set up a meeting for us with a wealthy client of his, and Viola and I found ourselves facing a kindly looking, elderly Indian gentleman. I always considered myself a salesman, but I welcomed taking a back seat as Viola spoke eloquently and persuasively presenting our business proposition. Mr Patel was evidently sufficiently impressed to agree to fully financing our proposal.

I was in awe of Viola's performance, as throughout the meeting I had found it impossible to concentrate, being distracted by a mesmerising feature around Mr Patel's ears. He had allowed the hair around the rims of each ear to grow to a comical length. Not only were these 'aural bushes' long, they appeared to have been waxed and fastidiously coiffured.

Immediately following the successful outcome of the meeting, Arvin suggested we all celebrate with an early dinner at a small bistro next door to his offices. Granita restaurant had a simple, pared down interior, but the food was exquisite. I was extremely grateful to Arvin for introducing us to Mr Patel, but also for acquainting me with this wonderful restaurant.

Over the following years Pete and I were to make regular use of it as it was just a short distance from our factory. It was always populated by a smattering of well-known actors from the Almeida Theatre around the corner. One lunchtime the young attractive owner, Vicky, told me that the previous evening two young shadow cabinet ministers had dined there. It later transpired that this was the meeting of the two contenders for the disputed leadership of the Labour Party, Tony Blair and Gordon Brown, which famously became known as the Granita Pact!

At the end of November, Viola flew over to Chicago to present her paper at the RSNA. The international conference ran in conjunction with a huge radiology equipment exhibition. I decided to join her there. It would be the perfect opportunity to evaluate the contrasting MRI machines that were on the market.

I flew out before Viola as I wanted to go via New York and spend a few days catching up with my old friend Ken. It was almost a year since I'd left New York and it was just great to be back. The towering buildings, long avenues, crowded sidewalks and the constant honking of the traffic. They say that New York motorists drive with their ears as much as their eyes!

It was early Saturday evening when Ken and I headed straight to our favourite bar, Berry's in SoHo. Ken was full of the excitement of the recent victory of the young Democratic Governor of Arkansas, Bill Clinton, for the 42nd presidency of the United States. The media had labelled him 'The Comeback Kid' after his initial poor polling results. He had beaten the incumbent president, George H. W. Bush, whose popularity had plummeted after he reneged on his promise not to raise taxes. He'd famously said, "Read my lips: no new taxes"; A statement that was to come back and haunt him.

Ken had a night-time photographic assignment so had to leave around midnight. We had been chatting to the personable young English barman, Michael. The bar was closing and he offered to take me to a nightclub nearby on 14th Street in the old meatpacking district.

I thought he had said that it was called the Click Club, and that I would find it 'entertaining'. It had only recently opened and he had a friend there working behind the bar who would ensure that we were allowed in. The club was at the base of a five-storey, red-brick tenement building.

As we walked down the entry steps, I was astounded to see the sign over the door read the Clit Club! I'd hardly led a sheltered life but as my eyes grew accustomed to the dimly lit interior, I have to say that I had never seen such a bizarre assembly of weirdly adorned women in my life. As far as I could tell, apart from Michael's friend, the barman, we were the only males in the place. Judging by the surly looks we were getting from the patrons we weren't that welcome either.

Making our way through the crowded, smoky room to the bar, we ordered our drinks and I took in the alien scene surrounding me. Almost all the revellers were couples. Some were in intimate embraces, some were just standing around talking, and some were dancing together.

There were two energetic, scantily clad go-go dancers performing on a raised dais in one corner, and a soft-porn film playing on small screens around the room. The most striking feature were the couples themselves. In almost all cases, one was an older heavy-set leather-clad woman with short, fiercely cropped hair, many with ugly studs piercing their faces.

These contrasted with their young partners who were predominantly petite and pretty. There must have been over fifty couples in the place. I felt distinctly uncomfortable, not because I found it in any way repugnant; I didn't, I've always thought that a person's sexual preference is their own personal business, I just felt that I was intruding and didn't want to appear as a voyeur. Michael was happily chatting to his friend at the bar so I finished my drink, said my goodbyes and left.

The next day I spent shopping. I treated myself to a full-length, black cashmere overcoat from Barneys on Madison Avenue. I knew that I was going to need it against the bone-chilling December winds in Chicago. Then, after another evening with Ken, visiting all our old haunts in the East Village, I flew on to Chicago to meet up with Viola.

She had booked us into the Mayfair Regent Hotel on East Lake Shore Drive. Built in the 1920s it retained that old-world charm rarely found in hotels these days. We were on a high floor with spectacular views of Lake Michigan. Sadly, it was sold the following year to be converted into expensive condominiums.

Frank Sinatra might have sung "You'll lose the blues in Chicago, Chicago" but the only thing that I managed to lose was one of the fancy front buttons from my new cashmere overcoat. Viola and I were hurrying along the 'Miracle Mile', Chicago's main shopping street, when I noticed it was missing. Snow was beginning to fall, rapidly covering the pavement. Viola insisted we retrace our steps and look for it.

I protested that it would be a waste of time, the snow was deepening by the minute. Viola took off leaving me standing. Her head was moving swiftly from side to side as her eyes scanned the snow-covered sidewalk. About fifty metres ahead of me she let out a whoop of delight, bent down, then turned, holding up the missing button.

She returned triumphant, telling me that that was why she was such a good radiologist; her incredible eyesight for details. I was staggered, this woman just kept amazing me!

Viola had presented her paper to the conference and had already made several appointments for MRI demonstrations at the exhibition. She had also made arrangements for us to visit a specialist MRI clinic in the city.

The Magnetic Resonance facility was in a separate building at the Northwestern Memorial Hospital and just a few blocks from our hotel. On arrival we were shown straight to the director's office.

Dr Gregory Shelk was middle-aged and rather portly. He made no attempt to move from where he was seated behind his desk. In front of him were several open plastic containers. The smell of Asian food filled the room. He asked us to excuse him while he finished his lunch. Lunch! It was barely ten-thirty in the morning!

He had the happy disposition often associated with overweight people. Dr Shelk not only gave us a tour around his clinic, he listened to our business plan and volunteered that he could be interested in investing as a partner as he wanted to "expand into Europe".

A Trousseau in Tucson

After this encouraging meeting we spent the following two days at the exhibition, evaluating and comparing MRI scanners. We narrowed our choice down to the manufacturer Philips Medical Systems. Our selection was assisted by a jolly, bespectacled Anglophile salesman, Dan Mezzano.

After an exhausting but fun end to the week, Viola and I had planned a short holiday. She was flying down to Atlanta to meet up with an old friend for a couple of days. Then she would travel on to meet up with me where I'd booked my old favoured hotel, El Conquistador, in Tucson, Arizona. We both flew our separate ways out of Chicago on the Saturday morning.

****

The hotel was certainly an oasis in that region of the Sonoran Desert. The fairways and greens of the on-site golf course were kept in magnificent condition, a stark contrast to the surrounding arid landscape. I didn't play golf, but it was a pleasure to stroll round this apparently little used amenity.

The gardens had grown magnificently, appearing even more lush against the backdrop of the desolate mountain ranges. Among the tall palm trees and cacti were weeping willow trees bounding a small stream that bordered the property. It was a wonderful escape from the hurly-burly of the big cities. After a weekend of chilling out on my own, Viola arrived to join me at my desert retreat. She too fell in love with it.

There were two local attractions that I wanted to visit during the week ahead, I hadn't had the time to check them out on my previous stay seven years before. When I described them to Viola she was as enthusiastic as I was. The first was 'Old Tucson', then afterwards, the Arizona-Sonoran Desert Museum.

Even though it was early December, it was hot and sunny enough to enjoy the hired, open-topped car as we drove out of the hotel grounds early the following morning. Old Tucson lay about twenty-five kilometres away in the desert. It was a film set that had been built in 1940 and added to over the years. It had been used for hundreds of western cowboy movies including the acclaimed *Gunfight at the O.K. Corral* and John Wayne's *Rio Bravo*. We arrived early and found the place deserted.

Wandering around the hot dusty streets, passing the bank, the saloon and horse stables, it was fascinating to see these weathered, wooden structures still standing some fifty years after being erected. As a bit of a film buff, it was easy to imagine the famous scenes being shot here. Viola and I even staged our own 'shoot-out' in front of the Wells Fargo bullion office!

About three years after our visit, half of it was destroyed in a fire. It was rebuilt as a theme park for children. Among its attractions it now has live-action stunt shows, a haunted mine, and even a narrow-gauge railway encircling the town for kids' rides! I can't help feeling that it will have lost some of its allure for me.

It was a further five-kilometre drive into the desert to reach the Arizona-Sonoran Desert Museum. One always imagines museums to be austere places housed in historic buildings. This museum proclaimed itself to be different. Spread over a hundred acres of desert, it advertised that it was solely dedicated to its locale, the Sonoran Desert. It was said to showcase all the surrounding flora and fauna. From coyotes and cougars, to rattlesnakes, spiders and scorpions. Viola and I were both looking forward to exploring it.

Ominously, on the way, Viola said that she was beginning to feel unwell and quite nauseous. She had forgotten to bring her hat and we had been exposed to the hot desert sun since early morning. She was concerned that she had sunstroke.

As I pulled into the museum's car park, Viola had turned very pale, was in some distress, and obviously close to a bilious attack. She ran from the car, through the entry gates searching frantically for a ladies toilet. Inside the entrance there was a building which looked promising. She didn't make it! Ducking behind a hedge in front of the building she started to retch. I came alongside her and offered to stand with her and hold her hair back away from her face but, doubled over, she waved me away.

She was bent over next to a low retaining wall which bordered the building above which was a terrace to the museum's café. Around the corner there were steps leading up to the terrace. Feeling completely helpless I left Viola and went in search of a glass of water for her. I climbed the half dozen steps and could now take in our surroundings.

The café's kitchen, servery and main seating area were inside the building. French windows allowed patrons to bring their food out onto the terrace. There were about a dozen round tables under shade umbrellas. Most of these tables were occupied with diners enjoying the warm winter sun.

From below the retaining wall at the edge of the terrace came the audible sounds of Viola's sufferings. Even though she was unaware of the proximity of so many people, she was helpless to have done anything about it.

Before long I could see that her prolonged heaving and disgorging was having a disturbing effect on the diners. As each new violent retch rent the air, a palpable shudder passed through the tables.

Finally, after an enormous gut-churning heave, followed by another protracted splattering, two of the diners lifted their plates and walked hurriedly through the French windows and back inside the café. They were followed by an adjacent table of four, all carrying their half-eaten lunches. One more ferocious heave followed by an explosive ejection cleared the rest of the terrace.

I was returning with a glass of water when Viola's ashen face appeared above the retaining wall. Her long, rich, lustrous hair hung in rat's tails, sticking to the side of her face. In an embarrassed, quavering voice she asked, "Did anyone hear me?"

I didn't like to tell her that she'd emptied the entire restaurant, I was more concerned with getting her back to our hotel so she could rest and recover. She wasn't sure whether it was something she'd eaten or a bug, or too much sun but either way, it had left her quite shattered.

Forgoing our tour of the museum, I drove us straight back to the hotel. Against all her opposition I insisted on calling the hotel's doctor. An elderly GP arrived at our room and after much protesting from the patient, I persuaded her to accept a nausea-relieving injection by telling her, "C'mon sweetheart, show the doctor your lovely bottom!"

The old doctor administered the injection and left. I sat with Viola until she fell asleep. She remained in bed the next day, slowly recovering.

I had popped down to the lobby to find a newspaper when I was temporarily distracted watching a small wedding party file into one of the anterooms from the gardens. It dawned on me what a perfect venue the hotel's gardens were for a wedding ceremony.

Seizing the moment, I went straight away and asked the two young women at the reception desk how difficult it was to arrange a marriage in Tucson. They were most helpful. They told me that it was very easy in Arizona, you didn't even need a blood test as in some other states. All you needed was a licence from the Justice Department in town, then a registered celebrant to perform the ceremony. Leaving Viola sleeping, I took our passports for proof of identity and drove into town.

It was as simple as the hotel staff had said. I found the sheriff's office at the Department of Justice, swore the necessary legal forms and was given the licence. Back at the hotel, the young women at the front desk were getting as excited as me. They helped me search through the Yellow Pages to find a celebrant. I went back to our room and found Viola awake and feeling a little better. I told her what I'd been up to. I went on to enthuse how exciting and romantic it would be to get married spontaneously in this beautiful location.

Whether or not I'd caught Viola at a weak moment I don't know. She did say that I must still love her having seen and helped her in her most indisposed state recently. I reiterated that "Of course I still love you and I want us to be married and always be together".

We went on to accept that if we were to marry in England, it would be difficult, if not impossible, for all of Viola's family to join us and some would inevitably be upset. And vice versa for my family if we got married in Australia. It seemed only fair to upset *everybody* equally! With all of this acknowledged, Viola then made me the happiest of men by agreeing to my impulsive proposal.

It was mid-week and we were leaving for London on the Saturday. Friday would be the perfect day for our wedding. Looking through the list of celebrants, we chose one and phoned her. Luckily, she was available to perform the ceremony on Friday afternoon.

We told her that we were both atheists so wouldn't require any religious mumbo-jumbo. This suited her as she claimed some native Indian heritage and offered an Indian love poem instead. With this ideal arrangement in place, all we needed was for Viola to feel fully well again.

She was still very weak and shaky the following morning, but was adamant that she went alone, and drove herself on a shopping trip to find a trousseau for the wedding. After she left, I sought out 'Pappy'.

Roger Key, or 'Pappy' as he preferred to be called, was a local character. Grey-bearded and always wearing a ten-gallon hat, he was the resident cowboy. He had a wagon and a wigwam on the outskirts of the hotel's grounds. He ran it as a small business taking photos of guests dressed in various cowboy and Indian costumes.

I wanted Pappy to take some professional photos of our wedding, and to be one of the two witnesses that we required. I'd spoken to Pappy several times during my stay, so when I told him of our impending nuptials, he was delighted for us and happily agreed.

For our second witness I asked a friendly young waitress, Angela, who had served Viola and I a couple of times. She was also excited for us and agreed. By now word of our impromptu event had spread around the hotel.

It Was The Best Of Times...

The young women at the hotel's front desk told me that they had spoken to management who wished to offer us one of the hotel's luxury chalets, free of charge, for our wedding night. I thought that this was a wonderfully generous gesture, making the day extra special, particularly as it would be our last night at the hotel.

It was early evening and Viola still hadn't returned from her shopping expedition. I went down to the bar to while away some time. I was sitting on a barstool, listening to the live music, courtesy of three Mexican guitarists. They reminded me of the Three Amigos from John Landis's 1986 cult classic comedy of the same name, when the bar entrance door flew open revealing Viola, heavily laden with designer shopping carriers, and singing out, "I'm better"!

She then proceeded to shimmy up to 'the three amigos' joining them in a raucous finale to their song, before running to me with big kisses. She wouldn't let me see what she'd bought. I was to wait until just before we got married the following day.

****

At two o'clock Friday afternoon I was standing in the grateful shade of a mature weeping willow next to a small wooden bridge that crossed the mountain stream that ran through the hotel grounds. With me was Angela, our waitress witness, and Karen, our celebrant. I was wearing my best Lanvin suit that I'd luckily brought with me for the Chicago exhibition. I'd topped it off with a pink carnation.

All our attention was suddenly taken with seeing Viola. She was escorted on Pappy's arm, walking slowly towards us along the winding pathway that led from the hotel. She looked sensational.

From her shopping trip the day before, she'd obviously found an exquisite outfit. A double-breasted, draped, white jacket over a matching, pleated, knee-length white skirt. She wore this over a plain, white, silk crew-neck blouse. Carrying a small bouquet of ribboned white roses, she looked absolutely amazing. She stood next to me and we held hands.

Karen, looking very official in her Justice of the Peace regalia, took us through the legal part of the ceremony. She then delighted us by reciting her Indian love poem, after which I could "now kiss the bride"! We then performed the legal signing of the marriage certificate with our two witnesses.

Afterwards, the hotel had gifted us a magnum of Veuve Clicquot champagne and plates of canapes were set out in the garden for our small wedding party. They also provided us with one of their buggies and a driver to take us to our wedding night mountain chalet that evening.

Finally, relaxing laying on the bed in our new accommodation, I reflected on what had come to pass. How fortunate I was to marry a girl with whom I was so in love and who I respected so much. With my arm around her and pulling her closer to me, I told her how much I loved her and how lucky I felt we both were to have found each other. Viola readily agreed with me, adding, "Mind you, I think you're a bit luckier than I am!"

And now, after twenty-seven years of happy marriage together, I must agree with her!

Postscript

Sadly, we were never to have children of our own. Though we tried, it never happened. Viola has always been a loving and supportive friend to my children, so I feel it's a great shame as she would have been a wonderful mother.

The medical scanning practice didn't quite develop as planned. Due to the sudden death of our major investor, Mr Patel, and the frustrating delays we encountered with the National Health Trust with whom we'd been negotiating, we decided to abandon it. I heard that it was a full six years later before the first public private partnership was signed with a health trust. I guess we were just ahead of our time on that.

My main business continued to prosper and expand, moving to premises in London's Soho and incorporating a design and printing operation. In 1994 together with a fifty per cent partner we launched a virtual reality conference and exhibition in Central London. Then, with the advent of computer-generated imagery (CGI), our show developed into Digital Media World, becoming the largest trade show at Wembley occupying all three exhibition halls, before expanding it into Singapore and Australia.

It was also in 1994 that the Rt Hon Virginia Bottomley, the health minister in John Major's Conservative government, announced closures to many London hospitals. The Royal Marsden, where Viola was working was on her hit list. Even though it transpired that this was just a political manoeuvre to gain acceptance of just *one* hospital closure, the Royal Marsden was reluctant to renew Viola's 'alien' contract. She had not been back home to Australia for eight years so that November she took a break from work to visit her family.

Viola had only been back in Australia a few weeks when she was offered a fabulous job with one of the largest X-ray services in the Southern Hemisphere. Queensland X-ray had clinics in most of the major hospitals throughout Queensland, plus dozens of subsidiary practices around the country. I suggested that she should accept the offer and perhaps work with them for six months or so and I would journey over as often as I could. Next month I flew over to join her for Christmas; this was the start of my love affair with Australia.

The original plan of six months working with Queensland X-ray became extended. Intimations of a future partnership in the practice enticed her to remain with the company. I continued to fly backwards and forwards making the arduous journey over seventy times until tragedy struck.

As we entered the new millennium, Pete, my right-hand man and closest friend, suffered a catastrophic blunder at the hands of a careless ENT surgeon. While undergoing a routine sinus operation, a drill the surgeon was using entered his brain leaving him alive but so severely disabled that he could never work again.

It affected me dramatically; my heart went out of the business. Having Pete as group managing director had allowed me to regularly travel back and forth to Oz, this was now no longer possible. After a short period, I sold off what I could, closed down what I couldn't, then flew off to join Viola permanently.

Australia is an incredibly diverse continent. From mountain ranges to limitless deserts; vast rain forests to green patchwork pastures; overcrowded high-rise capital cities to tiny isolated settlements, all within a coastline of spotless, golden beaches. The downside to now living here is what the author and historian Geoffrey Blainey coined in his 1966 book – the '*Tyranny of Distance*'.

****

Postscript

In my fifties and sixties, I coped with the travel. The joys of visiting my family overcame the discomfort suffered in journeying to them. It saddens me deeply that these days I find the thought of a gruelling 24-hour flight very daunting. All three of my daughters have visited us in Australia, but now, with their own family commitments, none of them have been able to seriously consider migrating here.

In 2018 my granddaughter Hayley and her partner Matt came to stay with us. In her mid-20s she had been a successful model and is now in hotel management. They have expressed an interest in returning to stay more permanently as they too have fallen in love with Australia. It would be wonderful if this comes about.

Luckily, I have found many new opportunities to explore. I have been fortunate enough to work in a remote aboriginal community and to have launched a small television production company. So there are still more stories to tell. I am living the cliché that 'you are never so busy as when you are retired'! But, whether I'll be able to find the time to write more, we'll have to wait and see.

If any of my young descendants are reading this account and wish to explore or further their capitalist ambitions, I urge them to take note of the many mistakes that I made along the way, but I would also encourage them to follow their dream, pushing everything aside to achieve it, because looking back now, it was a whole lot of fun!

www.ingramcontent.com/pod-product-compliance
Lightning Source LLC
Chambersburg PA
CBHW022051160426
43198CB00008B/199